U.S. History

Volume 1
1450-1865

Other Titles in This Series

Economics: A Resource Book for Secondary Schools, James E. Davis and Regina McCormick

Geography: A Resource Book for Secondary Schools, A. David Hill and Regina McCormick

U.S. Government: A Resource Book for Secondary Schools, Mary Jane Turner and Sara Lake

U.S. History, Volume 2—1865 to the Present: A Resource Book for Secondary Schools, James R. Giese and Laurel R. Singleton

Global/International Issues and Problems: A Resource Book for Secondary Schools, Lynn S. Parisi and Robert D. LaRue, Jr.

U.S. History

Volume 1
1450-1865

A Resource Book for Secondary Schools

James R. Giese and Laurel R. Singleton

Social Studies Resources for
Secondary School Librarians, Teachers, and Students
James E. Davis, Series Editor

ABC-CLIO

Santa Barbara, California
Oxford, England

© 1989 by ABC-CLIO, Inc.

Library of Congress Cataloging-in-Publication Data

Giese, James R.
   U.S. history : a resource book for secondary schools / James R.
Giese, Laurel R. Singleton.
     p. cm. — (Secondary school librarians, teachers, and
students)
   Bibliography: p.
   Includes index.
   Contents: v. 1, 1450–1865.
   1. United States—History—Study and teaching (Secondary)
I. Singleton, Laurel R., 1950– . II. Title. III. Series.
   E175.8.G54   1989   973'.07'1273—dc19   88-38952

ISBN 0-87436-505-8 (v. 1) : $32.95

10 9 8 7 6 5 4 3 2 1

ABC-CLIO, Inc.
Santa Barbara, California

Clio Press Ltd.
55 St. Thomas' Street
Oxford, OX1 1JG, England

This book is Smyth-sewn and printed on acid-free paper ∞ .
Manufactured in the United States of America

Contents

How To Use
This Reference Work

This resource book has been written for the secondary school librarian, social studies teacher, and student. The narrative information is presented in a nontechnical manner and is intended to provide introductory information helpful to the study of U.S. history to the end of the Civil War. The resources cited, although not exhaustive, encompass many useful current materials available for teaching and researching history at the secondary school level. The annotated bibliographic information regarding reference and classroom materials can assist teachers in selecting course content and can be used by students to gather information for class assignments or special projects. In addition, this work can serve as a supplementary text in the classroom.

The following are descriptions of how each section of this work might be used:

Chapter 1, "Introduction to the Study of History," provides an overview of the subject for secondary school social studies teachers and students. It highlights the value of thinking historically, examines how historians approach the past, and summarizes some of the recent changes in historians' views of U.S. history. For the student who has not been exposed to history as a disciplined way of thinking, this chapter is a good introduction to the subject matter.

Chapter 2 presents "Chronology of U.S. History to 1865." This chapter includes not only some of the significant events in U.S. history that are often highlighted in traditional history courses, it also presents important developments in art, music, literature, science, technology, and sports—events not often covered in traditional textbooks. Students and teachers of U.S. history will find the chronology a useful reference. The events highlighted are selective. The user is therefore invited and encouraged to examine other events and add them to this chronology. Of course, the mere chronicling of events in this fashion is not enough; the reader should further investigate the events.

Chapter 3, "Historians of the United States," is arranged in alphabetical order by the last name of each historian. Thus, the reader needs to keep in mind the time period in which each historian lived. Each biography provides an introduction to the historian as a person, followed by a discussion of the area of his or her intellectual interest and an assessment of the impact each historian had on history as a discipline. The biographies provide the reader some insight into how the discipline of history has changed during the twentieth century.

Chapter 4, "Historical Data," presents fifteen different types of primary sources that have been extensively used by historians. In this chapter, we have avoided the "great documents approach" on the assumption that the Declaration of Independence, the U.S. Constitution, and similar great documents are included in textbooks or are readily available elsewhere. Furthermore, we believe that students usually do not grapple with primary sources—an essential ingredient in understanding the nature of history. The introduction to each source provides an understanding of how to use and interpret that kind of source. The user is encouraged to go beyond the introduction for a more sophisticated understanding of each document.

Many organizations and groups provide information, resources, and services in history education. Chapter 5, "Directory of Organizations, Associations, and Government Agencies," describes such organizations. These organizations are categorized into three groups: those with general interests in U.S. history (i.e., covering the entire span of U.S. history), state associations, and organizations or agencies with an interest in U.S. history in the time period before 1865. Students and teachers can use the directory to find the following information for each group: address, telephone number, name of president or director, and descriptions of the organization's activities and publications.

Chapter 6, "Reference Works," is an annotated bibliography of reference materials that can be used by students and teachers as they conduct historical research and participate in class and library projects. Complete bibliographic information and costs are provided for each entry. The reference materials are categorized according to type; they include:

Atlases. Atlases can be excellent sources of historical information. Some of the atlases cited include modern maps showing information about the past; others present maps drawn in earlier periods of history. Both students and teachers will find the atlases cited very helpful.

Bibliographies and Printed Indexes. Teachers and students looking for information on various topics for research projects or lectures will find a starting point for their research in these bibliographies and indexes. Only a few printed indexes are listed. Teachers and librarians should note that students may need assistance in learning to use these indexes.

Biographical Dictionaries. Dictionaries listed in this section contain biographical information about historians and prominent Americans throughout history. Students and teachers can use these sources to locate information about individuals they are researching.

Dictionaries. Only those dictionaries dealing specifically with history or the study of history are listed in this section. Excluded are popular general dictionaries to which students can refer for definitions of many historical terms.

Encyclopedias, Almanacs, and Chronologies. This section lists a potpourri of general reference materials on U.S. history. All of these reference materials are suitable for gathering basic information as students begin library research projects. None are likely to provide adequate material to complete such a project.

Handbooks for Conducting Historical Research. The items listed in this section provide guidance on how to go about conducting historical research. As such, they contain extensive bibliographic listings—much more extensive than we could include in this book— and are excellent starting places for research projects. These handbooks also discuss how the results of historical research can be presented.

Online Databases. In this section, we describe online databases that provide information about early U.S. history. The databases cited are available through one or all of the following vendors:

Bibliographic Retrieval Services (BRS) Information
  Technologies
1200 Route 7
Latham, NY 12110
(800) 345-4BRS

DIALOG Information Services, Inc.
3460 Hillview Avenue
Palo Alto, CA 94304
(800) 3-DIALOG

Unisys Corporation
2400 Colorado Avenue
Santa Monica, CA 90406
(213) 829-7511

For each database, we include computer connect hour costs (this
does not include telecommunication costs, usually around $9.00
per connect hour using UNINET, TELENET, or TYMNET) and
citation costs. Citation costs given are for the full record. Citation
costs for BRS, which has various pricing options, are for maximum
citation charges.

Periodicals. The listing of periodicals is a very selective one. Cited
are outstanding historical periodicals that might be of interest to
students doing fairly sophisticated research projects (e.g., projects
for the National History Day competition) or teachers pursuing
an advanced degree, as well as periodicals specifically addressing
history education. Additional information regarding journals and
newsletters can be found in the "Publications" section of listings
in Chapter 5.

Resources on Teaching History. Included in this section are materials that provide teaching models, background readings, curriculum plans, rationales, or analyses of history education.

Chapter 7 contains annotated listings of classroom materials.
Again, complete bibliographic information, plus grade levels, prices,
and a brief description, are provided for every item. Entries are
organized according to the type of material. Sections include:

Computer Software. In this section are microcomputer software
packages in history. The types of software programs are indicated

in the heading for each entry. These include drill and practice, tutorials (lessons conducted in the form of a dialog), games, simulations, and databases. The systems on which the software programs can be used are also indicated in the heading.

Filmstrips, Slide Programs, and Media Kits. This section lists an array of audiovisual materials from which teachers can select appropriate supplements. Programs on various events in the early period of U.S. history are included.

Games, Simulations, and Dramatizations. Another excellent way to supplement a history course is through the use of games and simulations. A great variety, including role plays, simulations, card games, and board games, are described in this section.

Posters, Study Prints, and Other Visual Aids. Described in this section are posters, study prints of various kinds (including historical photographs), wall maps, transparencies, and other visuals. Teachers and librarians can use these materials for instructional purposes or to motivate student interest in historical topics.

Supplementary Print Materials. This section contains a range of materials on various topics and groups in U.S. history, arranged alphabetically by author. Many of the products included here are priced so modestly that they are within the budget of virtually every school. This section is a must for teachers.

Textbooks. Teachers looking for new basal U.S. history texts will find this section helpful. Both texts covering only the early period of U.S. history and survey texts covering the entire span of our nation's development are included. They are arranged alphabetically by author.

Videocassettes and Films. Teachers looking for videocassettes and 16mm films to supplement history units will find this section of interest. These two media are excellent ways to enliven a classroom and stimulate discussion. Video formats are indicated, as are both rental and purchase prices.

Note: Given the volatility of our economy, prices rarely remain the same for more than a year. Thus, despite efforts to have price information as current as possible, one may find in speaking with the publisher of a particular item that the price is not exactly as listed here. Despite the fact that prices will be dated quickly, we have included this information to give teachers and librarians a general, comparative notion of the costs of various resources.

The Glossary provides definitions for terms selected to cover important ideas and events in U.S. history to 1865, as well as terms related to the study of history and historical research.

An index has been provided to further enhance the reader's use of this work. Teachers and students can consult the index for specific subjects or items of particular interest, as well as refer to it as a source of potential research topics or project ideas. By using the index in conjunction with the Contents, readers will have easy access to the information in this volume that is most pertinent to their needs.

Introduction to
the Study of History

1

THE PROBLEM WITH HISTORY

If you were born in the United States and attended schools here, you have studied history at several grade levels. If your experience was typical, you likely experienced at least three courses in United States history and probably an additional course or two in world history and world geography. In these courses, you were probably buffeted by hundreds of "objective" historical facts—about colonial America, the Revolutionary War, the Founding Fathers and the writing of the Constitution, the frontier, the industrial revolution, the progressive movement, the New Deal, and World Wars I and II. Again, if your experience was typical, these facts and thousands like them probably had little significance to you; it is likely you forgot them at least as fast as you memorized them for the test.

According to recent survey data, high school students see the typical history classroom as "one in which they listen to the teacher explain the day's lesson, use the textbook, and take tests. Occasionally they watch a movie. Sometimes they memorize information or read stories about events and people. They seldom work with other students, use original documents, write term papers, or discuss the significance of what they are studying" (Ravitch and Finn, 1987, p. 194). If this description is true (or even partly so), it may explain why high school students dislike their history courses to the extent they do. Students rate their history courses lower than virtually any other course. They do not see the relevance of history, they say those classes are boring, and consequently, they do not enjoy this formal study of history. You may share this attitude, or you may be among the fortunate few who have had teachers who make history come alive for their students.

If you are one of these critics of history, you are certainly not alone. Many people besides students have questioned the value of history. Industrialist Henry Ford said, for example, that "history is more or less bunk." Others have said that history is "a pack of lies agreed upon," and that history is "simply one darned thing after another." Andrew Jackson, seventh president of the United States, saw no connection between history and the present; he said, "the past we cannot recall . . . but the future we can provide for" (in Commager, 1942, p. 260).

It is one thing to see history as irrelevant, but quite another to view it as horribly misleading. "Be it remembered," wrote novelist John Barth (1964, p. 793), "that we all invent our pasts, more or less, as we go along, at the dictates of Whim and Interest." "History is the most dangerous product which the chemistry of the mind has concocted. . . . It produces dreams and drunkenness," Paul Valery (in Fischer, 1970, pp. 307–308) accused, "it fills people with false memories, exaggerates their reactions, exacerbates old grievances, torments them in their repose" (among other evils). Such commentaries on the dangers and inadequacies of history are legion. So if history is really dead or even misleading, why are we writing this book?

EVERYONE HIS OR HER OWN HISTORIAN

It is our belief that the study of history is a characteristically human and humane enterprise for all people, regardless of who they are, what their occupations are, or what their special interests may be. We agree with Carl Becker (1935), who argued that "everyman [is] his own historian," although we would update the language and say that "every person is his or her own historian." This phrase means simply that every person engages in some form of historical inquiry some of the time.

Some of the common forms of historical inquiry consist of specific investigations into small events. They take hundreds, even thousands, of humble forms:

a renter tries to remember if she paid the rent

a student wants to know if a teacher is "easy" or "tough"

a doctor develops a patient's case history

a jury weighs a fact in dispute in a trial

a dress designer studies market trends

a coach analyzes a team's tendencies

a judge seeks a legal precedent

a businessman wants to know whether to increase his inventory

a homeowner seeks to build an addition onto her house

a child wants to know when his grandfather came to the United States

a voter compares a political candidate's speeches with her voting record in Congress

a citizen wants to clarify his views about United States intervention in Central American affairs

Each of these inquiries is in some respects historical. Some are little more than exercises of personal memory. Others are attempts to discover a story in collective memory. Yet others seek a more organized sequence of events; several pursue some explanation of a series of "facts." Each of the items on the list calls for some exercise of memory, whether individual, collective, or systematic collective memory. As one moves down the list, the inquiries call for increasingly sophisticated procedures and the manipulation of larger bodies of information.

Most of these operations do not involve inquiry on the scale conducted by professional historians. Few are concerned with the kinds of issues with which professional historians are commonly engaged. The history of World War II, the Spanish-American War, the industrial revolution in the United States, New Deal programs, or the feminist movement, for example, have little apparent relevance to the more or less historical questions in the list above. On the other hand, if the individuals seeking answers to the questions on the list are to achieve the best possible answers, their method of inquiry, of explanation, and of argument, should be much like that of working professional historians.

The point of all this is that seeking answers to historical questions seems to be a characteristic of human beings, at least some of the time. And if everyone is already involved in historical inquiry (to a greater or lesser degree) and uses the product, history, then it follows that they should become better practitioners of that craft. Untrained and left to one's own devices, the individual may produce rather poor history. If such history had no effect on anyone, one could ignore the problem and chalk it all up to "human frailty." History has great influence in our daily affairs, just as the past does. Now you may ask what this last sentence means; aren't history and the past the same thing?

THE PAST, THE HISTORICAL RECORD, AND HISTORY

It is conventional to distinguish among the concepts of "the past," "the historical record," and "history." For our purposes, the past is everything that has occurred at all places at all times up to the present moment. This conception makes the past rather imposing. Historians consequently limit their study of the past by inquiring into those things in which human beings were in some way involved. So conceived, geological formations have a past, as do many organisms (found in the fossil record). But these pasts (and areas of inquiry) have little relevance for the historian unless human beings are a part of the story. Historians leave nonhuman pasts to geologists and vertebrate paleontologists, among other scientists.

If the past that interests historians deals with all human activity in all places at all times up to the present (the meeting of past and future), then what is "the historical record"? Simply put, the historical record is the evidence of human activity in the past. The record is therefore composed of the traces of actual human activity—the evidence, artifacts, books, papers, other documents, sometimes oral accounts, etc., that occurred as a result of humans' actions at some point (or points) in the past. The evidence contained in the historical record is, on the one hand, intimidating in its volume. Archives containing huge collections of documents, museums full of artifacts, libraries housing millions of books, papers, and other evidence can be found all over the world. Indeed, the number of accumulated facts about the human past is staggering. On the other hand, the historical record is never complete. Although the historical record is essential, it is not sufficient for producing history.

History, then, is the reconstruction of the past, as best it can be done, based on the historical record—the evidence of past activities that is left to us. We have asserted that the past can never be reconstructed in its entirety and that the historical record is never complete. Working in the context of these constraints, historians attempt to produce the best possible representation of the past, based on the available evidence. History is, however, not just a chronological arrangement of the record. History can be produced only when a person brings some questions and some reasonable order to the record of the past.

An example may serve to clarify these distinctions. While poking around in your storage closet at home, say, you discover a trunk full of family memorabilia, including photographs, letters, newspaper clippings, and assorted artifacts. You find literally hundreds of items, including your report cards from elementary school, papers you wrote, letters from your grandmothers and grandfathers and aunts and uncles, newspaper snippets concerning your sister's volleyball team, your Little League team, your parents' marriage announcement, and much more. At first glance it looks as though you have uncovered your family's entire past. But a moment's reflection will tell you that what you have discovered is only a portion of your family's historical record—some of the evidence of your family's past.

Think, for example, about any memorable occasion in your life. Say you find a photograph taken at your ninth birthday party. It shows your brother and sister, mother and father, Aunt Tilly, and six friends eating birthday cake and ice cream. The photo does not show Uncle Fred—he was taking the picture. As you look more closely at the photo, you see some of the presents you received on the table. You got several of the things that you really wanted. Aunt Tilly (because you were her favorite) gave you a new watch. Your brother gave you a basketball and your sister gave you four back issues of a comic book series you still collect. Your parents gave you a nifty AM/FM radio-cassette player as well as several pairs of jeans and three shirts (items not high on your wish list). But you just can't recall what your friends gave you, and no other gifts can be seen in the photo.

You dig deeper in the trunk of stuff and discover that twelve birthday cards have also been preserved. Three of the cards contain one-page letters; short notes were written in the others. Several of the cards indicate that some of your relatives sent you money instead of other gifts. One showed that Uncle Gary sent you two dollars—"just like him; he's always pinched a dime," or so your father always said. You also remember the generosity of your mother's cousin Lucille, who always sends birthday presents to everyone in your family.

Because the event was memorable—basically because it was the first "real" birthday party your parents let you have—you have some fairly solid evidence about that occasion even if much of it derives from your own memory of it. (But you also know that your memory has failed you in that you can't remember what presents your friends gave you.) In addition, you shared this experience with others who may also vividly recall the occasion. On the other hand, because it was your birthday, not theirs, they may not remember it well, or at all! You recall that every now and then, you and your family chuckle about your friend Jimmy getting sick after eating five pieces of cake and what seemed like a gallon of ice cream. Jimmy was always doing stuff like that. You recall in passing that Jimmy moved away when you were eleven. You wonder where he is now.

Even though the trunk provides some very good evidence about your ninth birthday party and your memory brings back many warm and enjoyable thoughts about this occasion, a moment of reflection tells you that the entire experience—even as you experienced it and remembered it—cannot be recaptured or reconstructed entirely. You were nine years old only once (even if for a whole year). What's more, you can truly experience that specific day only one time—the combination of people, weather, atmosphere, mood, and all the other things (and their specific interaction at that time) that may have influenced that occasion can never be completely recaptured.

All of this is simply to say that while there is often a pile of evidence, and sometimes vivid memories, about any given historical event, the past can never be relived and its evidence is never complete. What is true with respect to this hypothetical example is equally (and maybe more) true of all historical inquiries.

Think about the difficulty someone who was not at your birthday party might have in reconstructing this episode in your life. Because this person would have no memory of the events of that day, the primary evidence would be your artifact trunk. But without the contents of your memory, or the memories of others who were there that day, this evidence is pretty slim pickings. Many of the things you recalled to put flesh on the evidence in the trunk would have to be discovered or uncovered in some different way. For example, knowing that Uncle Fred took the photograph (which may or may not be important to the story of your ninth birthday party) or that you were Aunt Tilly's favorite nephew and that the watch she gave you was on your wrist as shown in the photograph would not necessarily be known by any persons other than those there that day. Now, our hypothetical investigator may be able to turn this information up. If anyone who was present at your birthday party is still alive, then they could be interviewed about that day. And the more information from these people, the better. If virtually everyone who was there is still alive and accessible, then all could be interviewed and their memories of that event could be cross-checked. In this manner, our hypothetical historian might be able to reconstruct the day of your ninth birthday party and perhaps do it more completely and objectively than you could do it yourself.

So far, you have sorted through the evidence at hand and have laid it all out, as best you can, in chronological order. Would you have thereby produced a history of this episode? No, not yet. You have pieced together some random memories and some stories about your past, and although, both memory and stories are important for producing history, they are not by themselves sufficient. Why not? Don't genealogists and others who dig around in family history do this kind of thing?

Certainly, and this kind of activity can be both interesting and rewarding. But these folks aren't really doing history. What distinguishes history from such encounters with the past as genealogy and antiquarianism is that history must be an *integrative* narrative, description, or analysis of past events or facts *written in a spirit of critical inquiry for the whole truth.*

Stringing together some, or even all, of the available evidence from your family's past does not constitute history, although doing so may be the beginning of producing such a history. The evidence you have discovered in your attic must be processed by an inquiring mind, which gives order and meaning to the data. In our example, piecing together the shards of your family's past would serve little useful purpose because it does not attempt to explain the meaning of the evidence. Historians tell not only what happened, but how, when, and to what end.

History is a special mode of inquiry—it is the study of the past, and study implies a method—a set of procedures, a way of searching for the truth, no matter how tentative the truth may be when you have finished. The historian (whether professional or "everyperson") must eschew common beliefs and standard assumptions and must cultivate a healthy attitude of uncertainty about the nature of accepted truth. Historians must also cultivate disciplined thought about the past and the evidence of that past. History may be seen as a mental construct of the past based on evidence that has been carefully scrutinized, put to tests of validity, and then systematically ordered and interpreted to present a story about mankind's past.

Continuing with the example we used above may also shed some light on this aspect of our problem. So far, you have rummaged around in an old trunk of memorabilia and in your own memory of a historical event. You have found some interesting things there. Most of the documents you have found in the trunk seem to confirm your own recollection about what occurred that day. But you have also discovered several things that lack confirmation or corroboration.

Your brother Frank, as you recall, was being a jerk at your birthday party. As you recall that day, several things had happened to Frank which you thought caused his sour mood. He was having continuous spats with his girl friend (what was her name?—you can't recall). Your parents complained to him about his grades. He was thinking about quitting the basketball team. Frank's behavior at your party wasn't out of line, but it was also clear he didn't want to be there. You wonder if his mood affected your mother, father, or friends in some way. This part of the occasion was noteworthy because Frank was generally a great brother who was hardly ever moody or out of sorts.

You decide to talk with Frank and the rest of your family about that day. You discover his recollection was almost entirely different from yours. He barely remembered your ninth birthday party, and didn't recall being moody. He had already broken up with that girl friend, and had just begun dating someone else. If he was out of sorts at all, it was probably because he couldn't stand your friend Jimmy—it certainly had nothing to do with any of the things you thought.

HOW HISTORIANS WORK

Just like everyone else, historians are fascinated by the complexity of the world around them. But perhaps more than most folks they seek to put their study and training to work in exploring what they take to be significant problems or questions about the past. Historians, just like other people, are quite different in their experiences, interests, and values. As a consequence, the number of questions that historians (and others) think are significant are almost infinite. However, not all questions have equal significance (or potential significance). Historians must therefore choose wisely among the available questions. How do they choose?

First, there are some questions that cannot be resolved empirically. "Is there a God?" "What is the nature of the universe?" "Why does evil lurk in the world?" These are examples of metaphysical questions—questions that cannot be resolved by historical (or other empirical) inquiry. Questions of this type are better attended to by philosophers and theologians.

Second, some questions can be resolved by historical inquiry, but one must ask "so what?" The history of your ninth birthday party in our example above would be one of those. The first person to wear a shirt with a button-down collar might be another such example. The lack of utility of these types of questions should be obvious. The problem for historians is usually not in choosing among trivial questions, but choosing wisely among the important questions that can be answered through empirical research.

In the real professional world of historians, a variety of influences help determine the questions on which they will focus their attention for several years. A historian's choice is influenced—perhaps only semiconsciously—by such things as the time in which he or she is living, background and training, funding sources, personal values, or what is most likely to be published by the best journal or the best academic press.

When the historian has chosen a question to research, another set of questions immediately appears. First, the historian must ask what evidence is essential for resolving his/her research question. Does such evidence exist? If it exists, where can it be found? Is it accessible? Are the sources in a language that can be read by the historian? Are they deposited in a country that allows access to them? Are they in a library (or other archive) that has cataloged the sources? These and other questions must be resolved before the historian sets out on the research.

Once these questions have been resolved, yet another set of questions arises. Is the evidence authentic, genuine? Does it relate to the subject as the historian defined the topic? Is the evidence reliable (who produced the evidence, and in what manner)? How accurate does the evidence seem to be; how does it check out against other sources of known reliability? What biases do the records contain? Do these sources conflict with others? How are the conflicts resolved? Finally, is this body of evidence the most relevant for the question at hand?

Determining the reliability of evidence is a very difficult problem. For a variety of reasons, evidence may be inaccurate, biased, or even fraudulent. As E. H. Carr put it in his book *What Is History?* "no document can tell us more than what the author of the document thought—what he thought had happened, what he thought ought to happen or would happen, or perhaps only what he wanted others to think he thought, or even only what he himself thought he thought" (1961, p. 16). Eyewitness accounts, although they may be very close to the event, are notoriously unreliable. Conflicting courtroom testimony about traffic accidents and other mishaps attests to the fact that although persons may have no intention of misinforming, their accounts are often inaccurate.

Historians tend to seek the best evidence available about a specific question and usually assume the doctrine of immediacy (i.e., the closer in time and place to the event, the better the evidence). Often, however, the historical actors closest to the event are the most embroiled in its net—and therefore their testimony can be the least accurate. This principle is really quite commonsensical: the closer you are to an event, the more you are involved in it, the less likely you will be an objective, impartial observer of the event. Consequently, historians can never rely on a single participant to tell "the truth, the whole truth, and nothing but the truth." What they must do in such cases is to collect all the evidence possible— all the available accounts produced by all the witnesses—and very carefully compare the accounts.

Yet the weight of evidence is not necessarily the best guide to "truth." There are certainly situations in which ten observers witnessed an event and nine of them were less accurate than the one. The historian is able to sort this out only after intimate familiarity with all the available sources and a good deal of critical thinking about what is read or otherwise assimilated.

As we all should know, even official statements about events can often be misleading. Sometimes such statements are made in the interests of pure propaganda. At times official statements are made to conceal more than they reveal. Occasionally government, interest groups, and individuals make "official" statements they wish other people to believe; sometimes they hope people will act on such "information." The sad truth is that often their intent becomes actuality.

Sometimes misleading statements are made by the government or other groups inadvertently. For example, occasionally the federal government is required to publish statistical information about the economy (for example, unemployment statistics or figures concerning general economic activity) before the best available information can be collected. Occasionally, reports sponsored by foundations or other nongovernment groups become public in draft form, before all the results are verified. Such information can be quite misleading.

Bias in sources is yet another matter that vitiates their "pureness." In general, people's attitudes toward the world influence the way they perceive and report their experiences. Certainly young people and their parents do not see eye to eye on all things. While the parents may have grown up listening to the Supremes, the Rolling Stones, or the Shirelles, their children's tastes may run more toward Los Lobos, Dokken, Ziggy Marley, or Lisa Lisa. And obviously, there are many other parents whose tastes run more toward Marvin Gaye, Julio Iglesias, and Carly Simon. Indeed, some folks greatly appreciate Beethoven, Leonard Bernstein, and Leontyne Price. There is no accounting for such tastes—in music, or in other areas of interest as well. The point is that people differ as to their values, their attitudes, and their tastes, and these differences influence the way they interpret and report the world they experience.

Once the evidence is amassed, the historian is ready to organize it into some meaningful whole. This is certainly not to say that the sources speak for themselves. Quite the contrary. The ultimate task of the historian is to organize the collected material toward a particular end or conclusion. After all, the historian became engaged with this material to answer a specific and meaningful question. Little wonder, then, that the historian adduces an answer to the question. If the question is meaningful and the evidence accumulated in legitimate ways, the answer to the question must be meaningful and important.

Once the historian is satisified that the evidence supports some conclusion, he/she is obliged to report the evidence and how the evidence points to the conclusion. Quite often, however, the evidence found through exhaustive research will point to hypotheses (and possible conclusions) different from those with which the historian began. In addition, the historian is responsible for reporting all contrary data—those items that do not support his/her conclusion—as well as all the evidence that does support it. In doing so, the historian must persuasively demonstrate that the evidence supporting his/her conclusion is stronger than the contrary information.

All of the foregoing may indicate that the work of historians is somewhat more interesting than you had previously thought; that their work consists of more problem solving and question answering than you might have imagined (did you think they simply memorized a bunch of facts and then played "twenty questions" with everyone else?). In actuality, history is not even close to a bunch of facts that everyone must memorize. Not only is history about change through time, but history and the manner in which its practitioners pursue their tasks also change through time. In short, historians do not typically ask the same questions from one generation to the next. What is important for one generation of humans is not necessarily of equal importance for subsequent generations. Public issues change. The conventional wisdom changes. The collective body of knowledge changes. As a consequence, one generation's questions of the present and of the past are not the same as that of preceding or subsequent generations.

This situation has led some commentators to believe that history is totally subjective or relative, and therefore meaningless. If history can be written by every generation in its own way, these people argue, then it is not (and cannot be) objectively true. If history cannot be objectively true, then what's the point? Although a case may be made for that position, we think it is essentially a false concern, a distraction. There are historical facts that are true for all time, as, for example, the fact that George Washington was the first president of the United States. There are millions of such facts of history. However, when the historian gets to the most important question of "so what?" the meaning of that fact and all others tends to be different from time to time, generation to generation, historian to historian.

This situation should not concern us greatly. Even in the "hard sciences"—physics, chemistry, and biology, for example— the facts of research deemed to be important depend to a very great extent on the questions the researcher brings to the experiment. Indeed, one of the most profound findings of quantum physics in the twentieth century is the "uncertainty principle" (so called by German physicist Werner Heisenberg), which essentially means that if you ask certain questions you are likely to get certain (predictable) answers.

In *What Is History?* E. H. Carr (1961) deals with this issue as it relates to history. The commonsense view, Carr argues, holds that "history consists of a corpus of ascertained facts. The facts are available to the historian in documents, inscriptions, and so on, like fish on a fishmonger's slab. The historian collects them, takes them home, and cooks and serves them in whatever style appeals to him." Such a conceptualization, he argues, "presupposes a complete separation between subject and object. Facts, like sense impressions, impinge on the observer from outside. . . . The process of reception is passive: having received data, he then acts on them" (p. 6).

Carr, however, does not subscribe to this view. The facts are not at all like fish on a fishmonger's slab. "They [the facts of history] are like fish swimming about in a vast and sometimes inaccessible ocean; and what the historian catches will depend partly on chance, but mainly on what part of the ocean he chooses to fish in and what tackle he chooses to use . . . depending on the kind of fish he wants to catch" (p. 26). To write history is in some sense to create it. "The facts of history never come to us 'pure,' since they do not and cannot exist in a pure form: they are always refracted through the mind of the recorder" (p. 24).

HISTORIOGRAPHY: THE HISTORY OF HISTORY IN THE UNITED STATES

Students often have difficulty understanding that history is not only about change through time, but that history—as produced by historians through what they write—is also ever-changing. First, students are most often exposed to history as a body of agreed-upon facts that have to be mastered, if not for "cultural literacy" and "good citizenship," then for good grades on the weekly tests in their history classes. Second, students are not often exposed to historiography, which we may define as the history of history. When students study historiography, however, they can see at a glance that history has changed markedly since it first became a self-conscious, professional discipline in the nineteenth century. Indeeed, history is vastly different today than it was even twenty years ago.

"History," writes Michael Kammen (1980, p. 19), "has been written in what is now the United States ever since the early seventeenth century, when Captain John Smith and Governor William Bradford first began to record the circumstances of exploration and colonization in North America." When the American Historical Association was founded in 1884, however, history came of age as a professional discipline. Since that time, following the general growth of higher education in the United States, the historical profession has expanded greatly. Not only has the profession grown in the sense of numbers of practitioners, but the discipline itself has changed from time to time. Although the changes have not been systematic or even predictable, the characteristic style of historians—in terms of both substance and methods—has changed periodically through the twentieth century.

When history as a discipline came of age in the late nineteenth century, historians emphasized what they called "scientific history." By that they meant the accumulation and cataloging of the sources or the facts from which history was derived. However, changes were soon in the wind, and this school of historians soon gave way to a new "progressive" generation, which emphasized looking at history in new ways.

The progressives were concerned about making history relevant, creating an instrumental knowledge that could serve mankind's need for useful, practical knowledge. It was not enough for such historians as James Harvey Robinson and Charles Beard to collect facts as though for a museum. They wanted to know about the processes that pushed "history" forward. Accordingly, the progressives emphasized conflict in the American past. They saw "good guys" and "bad guys" lined up on either side of the major issues that comprised American history. Writing during a time of great social and political ferment, they saw conflict between social and political groups as the primary dynamic in American history. Conflict, for them, was not a problem, for they were certain that the "good guys" would win in the end.

The progressive view of the past in turn gave way to yet another school of historical thought—what historians call the "consensus" approach to American history. The optimism of the progressives and their characteristic reform-mindedness soured during the 1930s and 1940s. The rise of totalitarian dictatorships, the barbarity of World War II, and a seemingly intractable "cold war" between the United States and the Soviet Union pricked the bubble of optimism that was so much a part of the progressives' mindset. Also seeking a usable past, the consensus historians looked to the past not for the history of conflict but for the things upon which, they argued, Americans had by and large agreed throughout the nation's history. Americans, they argued, had reached a consensus on certain fundamentals—free-enterprise capitalism, liberal democracy, and equal opportunity, among others—that set them apart from the rest of the world. In an environment torn by war, racism, death camps, and the like, the American consensus could continue to guide the nation in times of peril.

During the past two decades, the consensus school of historians has been succeeded by yet another period of ferment. At no time since the beginning of the twentieth century has the change of historical style and approach been more apparent than in the 1970s. This shift encompassed many things, some of which are described next.

The "New Social History"

Social history has involved the reorientation of historians from the public sector and politics to social structure, social mobility, and such social institutions as hospitals, asylums, prisons, and churches. In addition, historians have rediscovered the history of women, children, families, blacks and other minority groups, ethnic groups, and the laboring and "dangerous" classes. "The outpouring of new work in the history of women and of the family," Carl Degler (1980, p. 308) has said about two topics of social history, "has been the most recent example of the way in which the content of the remembered past is constantly being reshaped. . . . As new concerns arise in the present, we ask fresh questions of the past, thereby bringing novel subjects into the purview of the historian." The social concerns of the 1960s and 1970s produced a new set of relevant questions about the past.

"Social history," according to Peter Stearns (1983, pp. 4–5), "involves two broad subject areas that conventional history has largely ignored. First, it deals with ordinary people, rather than the elite . . . [and second] the history of ordinary activities, institutions, and modes of thought." The early slogan of these practitioners, "doing history from the bottom up," suggested that common folk had a vibrant past and contributed greatly to larger historical processes. The perception is that traditional historians had largely ignored such people in the past.

More Explicit Historical Methods

Related to the expansion in the number of topics with which historians now deal was the near revolution in historical methods. With respect to social history, "the people studied were relatively inarticulate, in that few of them spoke or wrote as a matter of public record, but social historians working imaginatively with new sources have found that few if any groups are really inarticulate" (Stearns, 1983, pp. 4–5). Stearns continues:

> Related to topical expansion is the explosion of source materials, as inarticulate people and private activities literally speak volumes. Census data, police records, wills, a surprising array of heretofore neglected worker autobiographies,

> diaries of unheralded middle-class women, and some limited
> re-entry into the evidence provided by material artifacts,
> these records as well as some re-use of more conventional
> sources have easily supported the range of socio-historical
> interests. (p. 11)

One consequence of trying to use new types of sources was the
increasing use of computers to manipulate large quantities of data
gleaned from such sources as the manuscript census pages, wills
and other legal documents, town records, and business records, to
name a few.

A second result has been that more traditional literary (written) sources are being handled much more self-consciously and
circumspectly. "Although it might be exaggerating the case to
speak of a methodological revolution in the 1970s," argues Michael
Kammen (1980, p. 31), "a revolution in methodological *awareness*
surely has occurred" (emphasis in original). Historians now feel
an obligation to explain their frames of references, their choices
of method, and their borrowings from other social science
disciplines.

The Complexity of History

"If there is a single way of characterizing what happened in our
historical writing since the 1950s, it must be," according to Richard
Hofstadter (1968, p. 442), "the rediscovery of complexity in American history: an engaging and moving simplicity, accessible to the
casual reader of history, has given way to a new awareness of the
multiplicity of forces." "If those words seemed true more than a
decade ago," writes Michael Kammen (1980, p. 20), "how much
more compelling they are today!" "Social historians undeniably
complicate our sense of what the past was," says Peter Stearns
(1983, p. 6).

This complexity may be more the concern of historians than
any other users of history. Despite the great accomplishments in
women's and family history, Carl Degler (1980, p. 324) has said,
"we must still admit that neither women's nor family history has
made much headway in being integrated into general history, or,
to put the matter more precisely if more mundanely, into college
or high school history survey courses or general textbooks." The
same thing may be said of other social history topics. Part of the

problem is still the absence of apparent linkages among the materials of the social historian and those of other historians and general readers. Bernard Bailyn (1980, p. 38) may have put it best when he wrote:

> The amount of quantitative information available has become so great that *latent* events—events of which contemporaries were largely unaware and which became discernible only in quantitative terms (shifts in birth rate, changes in family size or structure)—have become centers of attention; and they have become important independent of any framework of interpretation that can bring them together with the course of *manifest* events—that is, events that were matters of conscious concern. [Emphasis in original.]

Linking these two types of historical "events" is the central concern of historians in the 1980s, "for the essence and drama of history," Bailyn (1980, p. 38) argues, "lie precisely in the relationship between latent conditions, which set the boundaries of human existence, and the manifest problems with which people consciously struggle" (see also Bailyn, 1982).

The People of History

History "from the bottom up" was motivated by a concern for the common folk of history. Ironically, social historians have tended to drop people out of their writing. "Compared to conventional historians," argues Peter Stearns (1983, p. 6), "social historians are uncomfortable with events. They deal instead with processes, with distinctive trends within the period they mark out. Single events like battles or individual cases of epidemic diseases rarely cause major or durable changes in the way ordinary people behave or in the ordinary activities of life." "An emphasis on events tends to put people into the foreground," observes Kammen (1980, p. 39), "whereas an emphasis on structures and series calls our attention to large socio-economic forces." As real people have fallen out of history, nonhistorians have fallen away from history as well.

A Reorientation of Historians' Values

Traditionally, historians in the United States have strongly held two values in their work: nationalism and detachment. According to Michael Kammen (1980, p. 22), "there has been a stunning inversion with respect to these two traditional values." Nationalism and chauvinism have given way to national self-criticism. The liberal tradition has been severely challenged. National self-congratulation in foreign affairs has been challenged by those who see U.S. foreign policy to be less motivated by altruism than cynical self-interest. National leaders have been shown to have warts as well as virtues. Social reformers have been shown to be motivated by fear of the masses as well as by humane concern about the insane, the infirm, and the diseased.

At the same time, historians have taken a different approach with respect to moral criticism of the society in which they live and have studied. "One thing that has been forced on university teachers by their students in recent years," wrote Henry F. May (1976, p. xvii), "is that they abandon the comforting pose of academic impartiality and declare their allegiances, even—contrary to all their training—admit their emotions." In his presidential address to the American Historical Association in 1976, Gordon Wright (1976, pp. 1–11) asserted that "our search for truth ought to be quite consciously suffused by a commitment to some deeply held humane values." It is in part due to such commitment that historians rediscovered the inarticulate masses who have peopled U.S. history.

THE VALUE OF HISTORY

In *Historians' Fallacies,* David Hackett Fischer (1970) summarized five of the common justifications for historical study professed by historians themselves. According to Fischer, at least some historians have justified history by saying

"It is such fun!"

"It is there."

"Every educated person needs to know certain facts."

"It is an outlet for the creative impulse."

"It promises future usefulness."

Fischer finds each of these justifications for doing history wanting.

First, he argues, to say that history is fun is "scarcely sufficient to satisfy a student who is struggling to master strange masses of facts and interpretations which are suddenly dumped on him in History I" (p. 309).

Second, if historical study can be justified only "because it is there" (to paraphrase Sir Edmund Hillary's reason for climbing Mount Everest), then there is little reason for requiring masses of students to study history. If history can be justified only in this manner, then historical study, just like climbing high mountains, should be left to those strange few who are fulfilled by doing it.

Third, although there is good evidence to show that the more a person knows the better that person is able to read a newspaper or book or to decipher the arguments of a political candidate, "there are," according to Fischer (1970, p. 311), "*no* facts which *everyone* needs to know—not even facts of the first historiographical magnitude" (emphasis in original). There are simply too many facts—even professional historians don't know all the facts—and how do you decide which facts everyone needs to know? Furthermore, the danger of this rationale for history study is that such factual knowledge is often merely an empty emblem of learnedness.

Fourth, although history may be a creative outlet, there are many outlets to the creative urge of human beings, and such a rationale presents no unique reason for studying history instead of, for example, tombstone rubbing.

Finally, historians cannot, willy-nilly, proceed to investigate just any historical problem in the hopes that someday, someone else will come along and find something worth doing with the results of such study. If historical research is to be relevant, the historian must seek to ask and answer relevant questions from the very beginning.

We believe, with Fischer, that history is a valuable form of inquiry and knowledge, a fact sometimes unappreciated even by historians themselves. Over the years, there have been many definitions of history put forth by its practitioners, but June Goodfield (1980, p. 38) penned one as good as any:

History is the study of the human past as a form of collective self-understanding of human beings and their world. It is the story of human activities, what men did, what they thought, what they suffered, what they aimed at, what they accepted, what they rejected or conceived or imagined. It tells us about their motives, their purpose, their ambitions, their ways of acting and their ways of creating.

Some people allegedly have argued that history is too important to be left to historians. Yet we would make a counterclaim: History is too important—too much is at stake—to leave history in the hands of ahistorical, present-minded investigators. As William A. Dunning wrote in 1913 (in Kammen, 1982, p. 19), "influence on the sequence of human affairs has been exercised, not by what really happened, but by what men erroneously believed to have happened."

Michael Kammen (1982, p. 19) said it best: "I am utterly persuaded by E. P. Thompson's argument that 'the discipline of history is, above all, the discipline of context; each fact can be given meaning only within an ensemble of other meanings.'" Furthermore, he continues, "to fulfill these imperatives with absolute respect for the particularity of people and the specific integrity of varied social institutions and modes of thought requires the patience of a plodding historian."

REFERENCES

Bailyn, Bernard. 1980. "The Peopling of British North America: Thoughts on a Central Theme in Early American History," in Michael Kammen, ed., *The Past Before Us: Contemporary Historical Writing in the United States.* Ithaca, N.Y.: Cornell University Press.

––––––. 1982. "The Challenge of Modern Historiography," *American Historical Review,* 87, pp. 1–24.

Barth, John. 1964. *The Sot-Weed Factor.* New York: Grossett and Dunlap.

Becker, Carl. 1935. "Everyman His Own Historian," in Carl Becker, *Everyman His Own Historian.* New York, pp. 233–255.

Carr, E. H. 1961. *What Is History?* New York: Vintage.

Commager, Henry Steele, ed. 1942. *Documents of American History.* New York: F. S. Crofts.

Degler, Carl N. 1980. "Women and the Family," in Michael Kammen, ed., *The Past Before Us.* Ithaca, N.Y.: Cornell University Press, pp. 308–326.

Fischer, David Hackett. 1970. *Historians' Fallacies: Toward a Logic of Historical Thought.* New York: Harper.

Goodfield, June. 1980. "Humanity in Science: A Perspective and a Plea," in Michael Kammen, ed., *The Past Before Us.* Ithaca, N.Y.: Cornell University Press.

Hofstadter, Richard. 1968. *The Progressive Historians: Turner, Beard, Parrington.* New York: Vintage.

Kammen, Michael. 1980. "The Historian's Vocation and the State of the Discipline in the United States," in Michael Kammen, ed., *The Past Before Us: Contemporary Historical Writing in the United States.* Ithaca, N.Y.: Cornell University Press.

———. 1982. "Vanitas and the Historian's Vocation," *Reviews in American History: The Promise of American History,* 10, pp. 1–27.

May, Henry F. 1976. *The Enlightenment in America.* New York: Oxford University Press.

Ravitch, Diane, and Chester E. Finn, Jr. 1987. *What Do Our 17-Year-Olds Know? A Report of the First National Assessment of History and Literature.* New York: Harper.

Stearns, Peter N. 1983. "The New Social History: An Overview," in James B. Gardner and George Rollie Adams, eds., *Ordinary People and Everyday Life.* Nashville: American Association for State and Local History.

Wright, Gordon. 1976. "History as a Moral Science," *American Historical Review,* 81, pp. 1–11.

Chronology of
U.S. History to 1865

A N IMPORTANT ASSUMPTION guided the construction of the timeline that follows. We have assumed that the textbooks you use contain substantial amounts of political history, including accounts of wars, treaties, elections, and the like. Therefore, we have decided to include only some of these things in the timeline. We have instead emphasized items your textbook may not contain—social and economic history, information concerning sports and games, the history of artworks and buildings, and some of the great books written throughout the course of U.S. history. In addition, we have included as much of the history of science and technology as possible in the space available.

In all of these categories, we have barely scratched the surface of the items that could be listed. We hope our work will inspire you to dig more deeply into the study of our past.

Date	Event
c. 10,000 BC	Asian peoples cross the land bridge between the Asian and North American continents.
c. 1000	Norseman Leif Eriksson lands on the North American coast at "Vinland" (now Nova Scotia).
1492	Christopher Columbus searches for a western route to Asia, first landing on a small island he calls San Salvador and then "discovering" Cuba and Haiti; he discovers native "Indians" using tobacco in religious ceremonies and as a medicine.
1493	On his second voyage, Columbus lands on Puerto Rico, Jamaica, and other West Indian islands; he brings cattle, sugar cane, wheat, and other European plants and animals to the Caribbean islands.
1494	The Treaty of Tordesillas, in which Pope Alexander VI divides the non-Christian world between Portugal and Spain, is signed.
1497–1498	John Cabot, an Italian sailing for England, reaches the coast of North America; on a second voyage in 1498, he sails as far south as Maryland.
1502	Columbus makes his fourth and final voyage seeking a passage to Asia—this time landing at Honduras and Panama.
1507	Martin Waldseemuller, a German cartographer, is the first to call the new world "America," after Amerigo Vespucci.
1508	First New World sugar mill is established in the West Indies.
1513	Juan Ponce de Leon lands on the Florida peninsula in search of a Fountain of Youth; he claims the area for Spain.
	Vasco Nunez de Balboa explores the isthmus of Panama; he and his party are the first Europeans to see the Pacific Ocean from the New World.
1519	Hernando Cortes, Spanish conquistador, captures Tenochtitlan (now Mexico City) and imprisons Montezuma, Aztec emperor.
1524	Giovanni da Verrazano, Italian sailor serving France, explores the east coast from Maine to North Carolina; he finds the Hudson River.
1525	Esteban Gomez explores the east coast from Nova Scotia to Florida for Spain.

Date	Event
1526	Spanish explorer Gonzalo Valdes publishes *Natural History of the West Indies,* which details plants and animals of the New World.
1531	Tobacco cultivation is begun in the West Indies.
1534	Jacques Cartier makes the first of his three voyages of exploration for France. He lands on the Gaspé peninsula and claims it for France.
1539	Spanish explorer Hernando de Soto searches for gold in parts of Georgia, Alabama, and Arkansas.
	Antonio de Mendoza establishes the first printing press in the New World in Mexico City.
1540	Francisco Coronado leads a Spanish expedition through the American southwest in search of gold; his party discovers the Grand Canyon and the Pueblos of New Mexico.
	Priests traveling with de Soto make the first recorded baptism in the New World (of their Indian guide).
1542	Spanish conquistador Juan Rodriguez Cabrillo explores the California coast and claims it for Spain.
	Alvar Cabeza de Vaca publishes *Relacion,* an account of his walk across Texas, New Mexico, and Arizona after surviving a shipwreck in the Gulf of Mexico.
1562	Jean Ribaut lands in Florida and claims the region for France; the colony he establishes on Parris Island (now South Carolina) is soon abandoned.
1563	Construction of the great cathedral in Mexico City is begun.
	John Hawkins, English slave trader, brings sweet potatoes and tobacco to England from the Americas.
1564	French Huguenots establish Fort Caroline, a colony near the mouth of the St. Johns River in Florida.
1565	The Spanish destroy Fort Caroline and establish the colony of San Mateo (in turn destroyed by French in 1568).
	St. Augustine, which became the oldest permanent city in what is now the United States, is founded.
1566	Jesuit priests establish a mission in Florida.
1569	Nicolas Monardes, Spanish physician, describes the medicinal uses of New World plants.

Date	Event
1576	English begin their first expeditions to North America in search of a northwest passage to the Orient; Martin Frobisher makes first voyage to Arctic regions.
	There are already approximately 40,000 slaves of African ancestry in South America.
1578	Sir Francis Drake lands on the coast of California and claims the region for England; Drake's crew holds the first Protestant religious services in the New World.
1580	Tobacco cultivation begins on Cuba.
1582	Richard Hakluyt publishes *Divers Voyages,* which makes known American discoveries to English-speaking peoples.
1583	Friar Bernardino de Sahagun publishes *Psalmodia Christiana* in Mexico City; it contained psalms in the Aztec language, which were also set to native melodies.
1584	Sir Walter Raleigh sends an expedition to the New World; it lands in what is now Virginia (named for the virgin queen, Elizabeth I).
1585	Roanoke Island, North Carolina, is settled by English.
	Iron is discovered in North Carolina.
1586	Sir Francis Drake plunders Spanish settlements in West Indies and Florida; he also rescues the Roanoke settlers.
	The potato is introduced into Europe from New World.
1587	Second Roanoke settlement is established by Raleigh; the settlers disappear in 1588.
	Virginia Dare is first white child born of English parents in the New World.
1588	English scientist Thomas Harriot publishes *A Briefe and True Report of the New Found Land of Virginia,* which described some natural resources.
1590	Spanish missionary José d'Acosta publishes a natural history of the New World.
1595	Raleigh leads an expedition up the Orinoco River in Venezuela in search of El Dorado.
1598	Juan de Onate leads an expedition into New Mexico, claims the region for Spain and establishes a settlement.

Date	Event
1605	French found their first permanent settlement in North America at Port Royal, Nova Scotia.
1607	First permanent English colony in North America is established at Jamestown in Virginia.
1608	Champlain establishes French colony at Quebec.
	Captain John Smith's account of Jamestown is considered the first American book although it is published in London.
1610	Spanish found Santa Fe on the site of ancient Indian ruins.
	Jamestown colony experiences its "starving times."
1612	John Rolfe discovers a method for curing tobacco that allows large-scale trade in the crop.
1616	John Smith writes *Description of New England,* telling of excellent farming and fishing conditions and containing the first accurate map of the region.
1617	Tobacco becomes the major industry of the New World; nearly 50,000 pounds are exported to England.
1619	House of Burgesses meets for first time in Jamestown.
	Dutch ship carries first blacks to Jamestown to be sold as indentured servants.
	Population of Virginia estimated to be 2,000.
	Virginia law requires all persons to attend church on the Sabbath.
1620	Pilgrims, chartered to settle in Virginia, land on Cape Cod after a difficult three-month voyage; they sign the Mayflower Compact, giving them a basis of local government.
	Congregational Church is established in Massachusetts by Pilgrim separatists who rejected the Church of England.
1621	Plymouth colony makes a treaty with the Wampanoag Indians, ensuring a peace that lasted 20 years.
	First iron processing blast furnace is erected at Falling Creek, Virginia.
1622	George Morton compiles a book called *Mourt's Relation* (from writings of Plymouth governor William Bradford), which gives firsthand account of voyage and landing of the *Mayflower* and life in Plymouth colony.

Date	Event
1623	Dutch West India Company founded.
1624	Dutch establish New Amsterdam (now New York City) on the tip of Manhattan Island.
	John Smith publishes *A General History of New England,* in which he tells the story of Pocahontas.
	Cattle are introduced into New England.
1626	Plymouth colony limits the cutting and sale of timber (the first conservation law in the colonies).
1627	English establish a colony on Barbados, and Dutch and French establish colonies on other West Indies islands; this leads to fighting to control the islands.
1628	Puritans settle at Salem in Massachusetts.
	Dutch Reform Church is established in New Amsterdam.
1629	Dutch West India Company grants special rights to persons willing to transport colonists to New Netherlands (now New York and New Jersey).
1630	John Winthrop and members of the Massachusetts Bay Company establish a Puritan settlement at Boston, thus beginning the "great migration" of English Puritans to New England; Winthrop begins a journal, which he keeps until his death in 1649—a prime source of information about life in early New England.
	Colonial population estimated to be 5,700.
	First criminal execution in the colonies (for murder).
1631	Tobacco cultivation is begun in Maryland.
	First American-built ship is launched.
	Boston has its first serious fire; wooden chimneys and thatched roofs are subsequently prohibited.
1633	Dutch build a trading post on the Connecticut River near what is now Hartford.
	Puritans enact laws against strong liquor, games, and dancing, and soon forbid wearing clothes with gold, silver, lace, or silk.
1634	A Roman Catholic colony is founded in Maryland by Cecilius Calvert, Second Lord Baltimore.

Date	Event
1635	English build Fort Saybrook at the mouth of the Connecticut River and begin competing with the Dutch for control of the region.
1636	Puritan minister Roger Williams establishes Providence, Rhode Island, after being banished from Salem for heretical religious views; Rhode Island becomes the first colony to grant complete religious freedom.
	Adam Thoroughgood house built in Norfolk, Virginia (is the oldest house from English-speaking colonies).
1637	Pequot Indians are nearly wiped out by colonial armed forces, ending almost four years of war—the first Indian war in New England.
	Thomas Norton provides a view of the more festive side of New England life in *New English Canaan.*
	Taunton, Massachusetts, is founded by a woman (a 48-year-old "ancient maid")—remarkable because of the many restrictions (and ridicule) heaped on unmarried women.
1638	Anne Hutchinson, banished from Massachusetts Bay colony for heretical religious views, founds Pocasset (now Portsmouth), Rhode Island.
	Log cabins are introduced by Swedes in settlements along the Delaware River.
	First Lutheran congregation in the New World is established by Swedes.
	First almanac is published in English-speaking colonies.
1639	The Fundamental Orders, one of the first legal documents in the New World, are adopted in Connecticut colony.
	First English colonial printing press is established at Harvard College.
1642	French establish settlement at Montreal.
	Compulsory education is enacted in Massachusetts.
1643	Roger Williams compiles a dictionary of New England Native American languages.
	The New England Confederation is established for common defense against Native Americans and against intrusion by Dutch and French.
	First American wool mill is established in Rowley, Massachusetts.

Date	Event
1647	Peter Stuyvesant arrives in New Amsterdam to begin his rule as governor of that colony.
	Rhode Island General Assembly drafts a code of civil law that separates church and state affairs.
	Nathaniel Ward publishes *The Simple Cobbler of Agawam in America*, which describes current fashions and customs.
	Massachusetts requires all towns of 50 families to provide a teacher to teach reading and writing; towns of 100 families must establish a Latin grammar school.
1649	Edward Winslow writes *Glorious Progress of the Gospel Amongst the Indians in New England*.
1650	Population of the English colonies is estimated to be 52,000.
	Anne Bradstreet publishes *The Tenth Muse*.
1653	Puritan missionary John Eliot publishes *Catechism in the Indian Language*, assumed to be the first book in a native language in the colonies.
1656	First Quakers arrive in Boston, where they are imprisoned for 15 weeks, then deported; thereafter Quakers are prohibited from entering the colony. (Three years later two of the Quakers return and are hanged on Boston Common.)
1662	*The Day of Doom*, written by Michael Wigglesworth, describes the day of judgment and is a best-seller of the times.
	Printed material is censored in Massachusetts.
1663	John Eliot completes his translation of the New Testament into the Algonkian language—the first Bible printed in the New World.
1664	Maryland law provides for lifelong servitude of Negro slaves; similar laws are passed in other colonies.
	English forces capture New Amsterdam (New York) and Fort Orange (Albany), breaking Dutch power in the region.
	Richard Baxter's *A Call to the Unconverted* is a popular book of sermons.
1665	First Native American graduates from Harvard College.
1666	George Alsop, an indentured servant in the colonies, returns to England and publishes *A Character of the Province of Maryland*, a lively account of life in that colony.

Date	Event
1667	Smallpox epidemic spreads through Virginia.
1669	*New England's Memorial,* by Nathaniel Morton, describes life in Plymouth colony.
1670	First permanent colony in South Carolina is established near present-day Charleston.
	Virginia enacts law making non-Christian servants slaves for life (repealed in 1682).
1673	Frenchmen Jacques Marquette and Louis Joliet explore the Mississippi River as far south as Arkansas.
1676	King Philip's War (the bloodiest in New England) ends with the killing of Philip.
	Nathaniel Bacon leads a rebellion against the government of Virginia, seeking protection against Indian attacks in outlying regions of the colony.
	Peter Folger writes *A Looking-Glass for the Times,* a satirical look at life in New England.
	Connecticut forbids anyone to wear garments that do not match their place in society.
1679	Fire destroys docks, warehouses, and 150 houses in Boston; after this all houses are required to be made of brick and tile.
1681	Quaker William Penn receives charter for the lands that become Pennsylvania; he then founds Philadelphia.
	Frenchman Sieur de La Salle explores the Mississippi River to its mouth, claiming all for France.
	Penn writes *Frame of Government,* which sets forth his ideas on religious liberty.
1687	John Clayton writes of medical practices among the Indians, the first of many scientific papers he would write about the New World.
1688	Francis Bacon's *Essays* published in the colonies; it becomes one of most widely read books in colonies.
1689	King William's war begins; the French, aided by Indian allies from Maine and Canada, attack English settlements.
	First public school is founded in Philadelphia—tuition is charged only to those who can afford it.

Date	Event
1690	Benjamin Harris publishes *New England Primer,* an elementary textbook of rhymed sayings designed to teach reading and Christian virtues at same time.
1692	Witchcraft trials begin in Salem, Massachusetts.
1693	Postal service is established between New York and Philadelphia.
1697	Treaty of Ryswick officially ends King William's war between the English and French. By terms of the treaty, neither side gained anything.
1699	The New Haven Ironworks are exempted by Connecticut government from having to pay taxes. Such inducements to private businesses greatly stimulate industrial activity.
	Yellow fever epidemic strikes several colonial cities—up to 20 percent of the people in these cities die.
1700	Samuel Sewell writes *The Selling of Joseph,* an antislavery tract.
	English-speaking colonies now boast a population of 275,000; Boston, the largest city, has a population of 7,000.
1701	Fort Pontchartrain (now Detroit) and other forts in Michigan and Illinois are established by the French.
1702	Queen Anne's war begins between the English and the French and Spanish.
1705	Virginia's slave law dictates that all imported Negroes are lifelong slaves unless they are Christians.
1707	*The Redeemed Captive,* written by John Williams, plays on a favorite colonial theme of capture and release from Indians.
1708	*The Sot-Weed Factor,* believed to be written by Ebenezer Cook, satirizes life in Maryland, especially with respect to tobacco.
1711	Parliament prohibits colonists from cutting trees; henceforth all lumber is reserved for the Royal Navy.
1712	Negro slave uprising in New York City results in the execution of over 100 Negroes.
1713	Tuscarora Indian war, which had been raging in the southern colonies for several years, comes to an end.
	Treaty of Utrecht ends Queen Anne's war; the English make substantial gains in the eastern regions of Canada.

Date	Event
1714	Tea is introduced into the colonies.
1718	New Orleans is founded by French settlers from Canada.
	San Antonio is founded by Spanish as a mission and fort (presidio).
	Governor of Virginia offers rewards for pirates—dead or alive; soon thereafter, Blackbeard is captured and his severed head brought back on a pole.
1721	Smallpox breaks out in Boston. Boylston is first American to inoculate patients against smallpox, causing an outrage among many people; he soon offers statistics suggesting the effectiveness of such inoculations.
1732	A Royal charter is granted James Oglethorpe for an English colony in Georgia; in 1733, he founds Savannah in Georgia, the last of the 13 colonies to be settled.
	Ben Franklin begins *Poor Richard's Almanac.*
1733	Molasses Act places severe duties (taxes) on sugar, rum, and molasses brought into the English colonies from other nations' colonies.
	The sermons of Jonathan Edwards and others, which stress man's sinful nature and salvation by faith alone, begin the "first Great Awakening," an important religious revival.
1736	Regular stagecoach service is established between Boston and Newport.
1744	Franklin invents his famous stove, which provides more heat with less fuel.
1747	Ohio Company is formed to extend colonial settlement west of Virginia; penetration of the Ohio valley increases the conflict between France and England.
1750	Parliament passes the Iron Act, prohibiting the colonists from manufacturing finished iron.
1755	English General Braddock is ambushed and defeated by French and Indians near Fort Duquesne (Pittsburgh).
1761	James Otis opposes English writs of assistance (essentially search warrants) as violations of natural rights of British citizens.

Date	Event
1763	Treaty of Paris ends the French and Indian War (Seven Years' War); British receive virtually all French territory east of Mississippi River as well as Florida from Spain (a French ally).
1764	Parliament passes the Sugar Act to raise funds in the colonies to pay the British war debt; Currency Act prohibits colonies from issuing money. Both are protested by colonists.
1765	Parliament enacts the Stamp Act, requiring the purchase of tax stamps for all documents, newspapers, and other goods. The Stamp Act creates a storm of protest in the colonies.
1766	Because of protests, Parliament repeals the Stamp Act, but then passes the Declaratory Act, which asserts Parliament's right to make laws for the colonies.
	Stageline between New York City and Philadelphia takes two days in good weather.
1767	Townsend Acts are passed requiring colonies to pay duties on a number of items including tea, glass, and lead. Merchants in many cities make nonimportation agreements, essentially a boycott of British goods.
1770	Boston Massacre occurs when British soldiers kill several persons in Boston.
1773	Parliament passes the Tea Act in order to bail out the British East India Company from financial difficulty as well as to reassert its power to tax the colonies. The Boston Tea Party follows closely.
1774	Parliament enacts the "Intolerable Acts" to punish Massachusetts for the Tea Party; Boston port is closed until the tea is paid for.
	First Continental Congress, representing all colonies except Georgia, convenes in Philadelphia.
1775	Patrick Henry delivers his famous speech against tyrannical British rule, ending with "Give me liberty or give me death."
	Paul Revere warns residents of Concord and Lexington, Massachusetts, about impending British action against them, a military action that begins the American Revolution.
	Second Continental Congress meets and appoints George Washington as commander-in-chief of the Continental Army.

Date	Event
1776	Congress adopts the Declaration of Independence.
	Thomas Paine publishes *Common Sense,* which urges the end of union with England; more than 100,000 copies are sold in less than three months.
1777	American forces defeat British General John Burgoyne at the Battle of Saratoga, a turning point in the war.
	Congress adopts the Articles of Confederation and Perpetual Union.
1778	Congress ratifies treaty of alliance with France while rejecting a British peace offer.
	Jonathan Carver publishes *Travels Through the Interior of North America,* which contains information about Indian culture and natural features of the Great Lakes region.
1781	French fleet defeats British naval force at Hampton Roads and blockades Chesapeake Bay. At same time Continental troops surround British at Yorktown and force General Cornwallis to surrender.
1782	Ben Franklin, John Adams, and John Jay negotiate peace treaty with British in Paris.
	J. Hector St. John Crevecoeur publishes *Letters from an American Farmer,* a set of essays about life in America.
1783	Treaty of Paris ends the Revolutionary War.
	U.S. independence recognized by a number of nations.
	Noah Webster publishes *The American Spelling Book,* known as the "blue-backed speller," part of his attempt to create an "American national language."
1784	Thomas Jefferson publishes *Notes on Virginia.*
	Oliver Evans creates an automatic production line in a flour mill.
1785	By this year, Ralph Earl is quite active as an itinerant portrait painter in New England.
	U.S. and Spain begin arguing over navigation of the Mississippi River.
1786	Daniel Shays leads a rebellion of debt-ridden farmers in western Massachusetts against high taxes.
	Charles W. Peale opens the first art gallery in the United States.

Date	Event
1787	Congress enacts the Northwest Ordinance, one of the more important accomplishments of first U.S. government.
	Congress calls for constitutional convention to consider modification of the Articles of Confederation—instead it drafts an entirely new frame of government.
	Royall Tyler's *The Contrast,* considered the first American comedy, is performed.
	John Fitch launches the first American steamboat.
1788	Constitution is ratified after great struggle and debate—not all Americans are convinced the new frame of government is better than the old.
	The Federalist Papers, among the most important U.S. political documents, are written anonymously by Hamilton, Jay, and Madison and published serially to support the ratification of the newly written Constitution.
1789	New government is fleshed out in a series of acts of Congress.
	Federalist party is formed.
1790	Secretary of Treasury Alexander Hamilton proposes such far-reaching financial programs as a national bank, assumption of state war debts, taxes, and manufactures.
	First national census estimates U.S. population at 4 million; Philadelphia is largest city at 42,000 people.
	Sam Slater builds first steampower-driven textile machinery in Rhode Island, an event some date as beginning of industrial revolution in the United States.
1791	U.S. settlements in Northwest Territory are attacked by British-armed Indians.
	Congress passes first internal revenue law, an excise tax on whiskey; causes rebellion in western parts of the new nation.
	First ten amendments of the Constitution (Bill of Rights) are ratified.
	Ben Franklin's *Autobiography* is published in Paris.
1792	Republican party is formed (by such luminaries as Jefferson and Madison) to oppose Federalist policies.
	The Farmer's Almanac is first published.

Date	Event
1793	Congress passes the Fugitive Slave Act, which makes it illegal to aid runaway slaves or prevent their arrest.
	Invention of cotton gin, a simple machine that will greatly stimulate cotton production.
	Yellow fever epidemic in Philadelphia kills 5,000 (of 42,000) people—the worst epidemic in United States to that time.
	Architect James Hobans designs the White House.
1794	Whiskey rebellion breaks out in western Pennsylvania in response to excise tax on spirits; it is put down by the new government.
	Jay's Treaty is concluded with Great Britain; it provides for British evacuation of Great Lakes posts.
1795	Treaty of San Lorenzo, which sets Florida boundary and gives U.S. navigation rights on Mississippi River, is signed with Spain.
	Treaty of Grenville is signed between Indian tribes in Northwest Territory; they cede their lands to white settlers.
1796	Washington's farewell address warns of U.S. involvement in foreign affairs.
	Shakespeare's complete works are first published in the United States.
1797	Charles Newbold patents the first cast-iron plow; detractors claim the iron will poison the soil.
1798	Alien and Sedition Acts, which limit political opposition to Federalist policies and restrict the civil rights of foreign citizens, are enacted.
	Jefferson and Madison frame the Kentucky and Virginia Resolutions, which declare the Alien and Sedition Acts to be unconstitutional and claim that states can nullify such enactments.
1800	Charles B. Brown publishes *Arthur Mervyn,* a realistic fictional treatment of yellow fever epidemic in Philadelphia.
	Benjamin Waterhouse gives first U.S. smallpox vaccination to his son.
	Shoemaker William Young is first to make different shoes for right and left feet.
	Second national census shows U.S. population to be 5.3 million, including 800,000 slaves.

Date	Event
1801	John Marshall becomes chief justice of Supreme Court.
	Architect Ben Latrobe uses Greek architectural style in United States in Bank of Pennsylvania building.
1803	United States buys Louisiana Territory from France.
	Marbury v. *Madison* case establishes the principle of judicial review of acts of Congress.
	Lewis and Clark begin their exploration of the Louisiana Territory.
1805	First large shipment of ice from New England to the West Indies begins profitable commerce in this product.
	Rappites, a German pietist group, establish Harmony, a settlement in Pennsylvania.
1806	Gas street lighting is introduced in Newport, Rhode Island.
	Zebulon Pike explores the Southwest Territory (in what later became part of the United States).
1807	Robert Fulton launches the steamboat *Clermont* and navigates the Hudson River from New York City to Albany in 32 hours.
	Eli Terry and Seth Thomas begin the manufacture of clocks in large quantity by using interchangeable parts.
	Tensions between the United States and Britain and France increase; an Embargo Act is passed to stop British and French interference with U.S. trade.
1808	Congress prohibits importation of African slaves, the earliest it could under provisions of U.S. Constitution.
	John J. Astor forms the American Fur Company for trade in the western territories.
1809	*Phoenix* is the first seagoing steamboat traveling from New York City to Philadelphia.
	United States continues trade restrictions with France and England.
1810	Third U.S. census shows its population to be 7.2 million people, including 60,000 immigrants and 1.2 million slaves.
	United States annexes Florida.
1811	William Henry Harrison defeats Indians at the Battle of Tippecanoe.

Date	Event
1812	First steamboat to sail down the Mississippi reaches New Orleans in January.
	Congress declares war on Great Britain.
1814	Francis Lowell opens first fully mechanized factory for processing cloth.
	First institution for higher education for women is established in Middlebury, Vermont.
	Hartford Convention, called by Federalists opposed to War of 1812, urges revision of Constitution.
	Francis Scott Key writes the verses to "The Star Spangled Banner."
1816	Supreme Court affirms its right to review state court decisions in *Martin* v. *Hunter's Lessee.*
	First *protective* tariff act is passed.
	U.S. cotton textile production has increased by nearly 200 percent since 1800.
1818	The *Savannah* is first steam-powered ship to cross Atlantic Ocean (it used its sails through most of voyage).
	Regular transatlantic shipping lines (sail) established between New York City and Liverpool, England.
	The tin can is introduced in United States by Englishman Peter Durand.
1819	*McCulloch* v. *Maryland* establishes the right of Congress (through the doctrine of implied powers) to establish the Bank of the U.S.
	William Ellery Channing leads the formation of the Unitarian Church in Boston.
1820	Fourth national census shows that U.S. population is 9.6 million; New York City is largest urban area (124,000).
	First football games are played at U.S. colleges—seen as a form of hazing at some schools.
	Washington Irving publishes *The Sketch Book,* a volume of short stories including "Rip Van Winkle" and "The Legend of Sleepy Hollow."
	First canning factory is opened in Boston.

Date	Event
1821	New York and Massachusetts follow Connecticut in abolishing property qualifications for voting.
	James Fenimore Cooper establishes himself as a writer with *The Spy,* a novel set during the Revolutionary War.
	First copper-zinc battery is invented.
	First public high school is established in Boston.
1822	Rebellion of Negro slaves is suppressed in Charleston, South Carolina; rebellion leader Denmark Vesey and 34 others are hanged.
	Timothy Dwight publishes *Travels in New England and New York.*
	Water-powered machinery begins producing cotton textiles.
1823	Monroe Doctrine is promulgated.
	Cooper publishes *The Pioneer,* a splendid portrait of frontier life.
1824	In *Gibbons* v. *Ogden,* the Supreme Court defines very broadly the term commerce and gives the federal government vast (although as yet unused) powers to regulate commerce.
1825	Texas (still Mexican territory) is opened to settlement by U.S. citizens.
	Creek Indians reject treaty that would cede their lands in Georgia to the United States.
	Thomas Cole establishes what eventually is called the Hudson River School of landscape painting.
	Erie Canal is opened, greatly affecting the commercial development of New York City and the Mississippi valley.
1826	First railroads, all short lines, begin to be built; the Baltimore and Ohio is the first passenger line.
1827	Massachusetts requires a high school to be established in every town with at least 500 families.
	Freedom's Journal, first Negro newspaper, is printed in New York City.
1828	*Cherokee Phoenix,* first Indian newspaper, is begun.

Date	Event
1829	Jacob Bigelow coins the term "technology" when he publishes *The Elements of Technology.*
	Encyclopedia Americana, first in the United States, is published by Francis Lieber.
1830	Mexico forbids further immigration of U.S. citizens into Texas.
	Oliver Wendell Holmes writes poem "Old Ironsides."
	Peter Cooper builds *Tom Thumb,* first commercially successful steam locomotive.
	Lady's Book (later *Godey's Lady's Book*) begins publication.
1831	Nat Turner leads unsuccessful slave revolt in Virginia; Turner is captured and hanged.
	William Lloyd Garrison begins printing *The Liberator,* an influential abolitionist journal.
	Supreme Court upholds Georgia order for removal of Cherokee Indians beyond the Mississippi.
1832	Samuel F.B. Morse designs an improved electromagnetic telegraph.
	Horse-drawn streetcars begin to be used in New York City.
	A South Carolina convention declares federal tariffs of 1828 and 1832 null and void.
1833	American Antislavery Society is founded.
	Early form of baseball is played in Philadelphia.
	Oberlin College is founded in Ohio—first to admit both men and women (two years later it admits Negroes).
	Legend of Davy Crockett is begun with his publication of *Sketches and Eccentricities.*
1834	William Dunlap publishes *History of the Rise and Progress of the Arts of Design in the United States.*
	Cyrus McCormick patents a successful reaper machine.
	Antiabolition riots occur in New York and Philadelphia.
	Americans begin eating tomatoes, formerly considered to be poisonous.
1835	Samuel Colt designs a pistol with a revolving cylinder.

Date	Event
1836	U.S. citizens in Texas declare independence from Mexico.
	Ralph Waldo Emerson publishes *Nature,* in which he explains transcendentalist philosophy.
	First two booklets of *McGuffey's Readers* are published—become standard elementary textbooks.
	Thomas Cole paints "The Course of Empire," a series of five very large paintings.
	Massachusetts enacts a child labor law.
1837	Nathaniel Hawthorne's *Twice-Told Tales,* his first signed work, brings him recognition.
	Painter George Catlin exhibits "Gallery of Indians" (more than 500 paintings and sketches).
	Emerson publishes *The American Scholar,* which asserts American literary independence from England.
	John Deere invents the first plow with a steel mold board—revolutionizes prairie farming.
1838	U.S. troops forcibly remove Cherokee Indians from Georgia to eastern Oklahoma (the "trail of tears").
	Many northern states enact "personal liberty laws," which obstruct enforcement of the Fugitive Slave Act.
	Steamboat *Moselle* explodes on Ohio River, killing 100 persons.
1839	Abner Doubleday lays out first baseball diamond in Cooperstown, New York.
	Charles Goodyear discovers vulcanized rubber by accident.
1840	Edgar Allan Poe publishes *Tales of the Grotesque and Arabesque.*
	Samuel Cunard establishes first regularly scheduled transatlantic steamship line.
	Sixth national census reveals a U.S. population of over 17 million and the fact that over 600,000 immigrants had arrived since 1830.
1843	Great migration begins over the Oregon Trail.
	The word "millionaire" is first used in the obituary of Pierre Lorillard, a wealthy banker and tobacco grower.

Date	Event
1845	Margaret Fuller publishes *Women in the Nineteenth Century,* a feminist work.
	Alfred Beach begins publication of *Scientific American.*
1846	Michigan becomes first state to abolish capital punishment.
	Architect James Renwick designs the Smithsonian Institution castle in the Gothic Revival style.
	Howe patents the lock-stitch sewing machine.
1847	Irish immigration is 105,000 for the year, three times more than the year before, because of the potato famine.
1848	American Academy for the Advancement of Science (AAAS) is established; Maria Mitchell is first woman elected to membership.
	James Bogardus erects a five-story factory building using cast iron for structure.
	Seneca Falls (New York) convention begins modern feminist movement.
1849	U.S. Department of Interior is created to meet the needs of Western settlers.
	George Corliss patents a new type of steam engine.
	Elizabeth Blackwell is first woman in the world to receive a medical degree.
1850	Hawthorne publishes *The Scarlet Letter.*
	Herman Melville publishes *White-Jacket,* which creates a furor over abusive treatment of sailors in U.S. Navy.
	Cholera epidemic sweeps Midwest after ravaging South.
	Stephen Foster writes song "De Camptown Races."
1851	Melville publishes *Moby Dick.*
	Maine enacts law prohibiting alcohol.
	Isaac Singer invents a continuous-stitch sewing machine.
	First U.S. Young Men's Christian Association is founded in Boston.
	Foster writes song "Swanee River."

Date	Event
1852	Harriet Beecher Stowe publishes *Uncle Tom's Cabin,* a novel that profoundly influenced the debate over slavery.
	Otis designs a passenger elevator.
	Boston Public Library is founded.
	American Society of Civil Engineers is formed in New York City.
1853	Commodore Matthew Perry arrives in Edo Bay (now Tokyo Bay), seeking to open Japan to U.S. trade.
	Congress authorizes surveys for a transcontinental route to the Pacific.
	Yellow fever epidemic hits New Orleans; 5,000 people die in two years.
	Baltimore and Ohio Railroad is completed to Ohio River, linking Chicago to East coast by rail.
1854	Republican party is founded, calls for abolition of slavery, high protective tariffs, and internal improvements.
	Henry David Thoreau publishes *Walden: or, Life in the Woods.*
	Immigration of 13,000 Chinese marks vast increase in their numbers in U.S. (highest number in any previous year had been 42).
	Foster writes song "Jeannie with the Light Brown Hair."
1855	U.S. citizen William Walker overthrows government in Nicaragua and makes himself dictator (he is overthrown two years later).
	Walt Whitman anonymously publishes *Leaves of Grass.*
	First U.S. oil refinery established in Pittsburgh.
1856	Gail Borden receives patent for condensing milk.
	Western Union Company is founded.
	Printing telegraph is invented.
1857	*Dred Scott* decision holds that Congress cannot prohibit slavery in the territories.
	William Kelly, Pennsylvania inventor, patents method for making steel similar to that of English inventor Henry Bessemer.

Date	Event
1858	Cyrus Field lays first successful transatlantic telegraph cable.
	Hamilton Smith invents mechanical washing machine.
1859	Daniel Emmett composes "Dixie" and "Turkey in the Straw."
	Edwin Drake drills first U.S. oil well.
1860	South Carolina secedes from the Union, condemning North's attack on slavery.
	Pony Express begins overland mail service between St. Joseph, Missouri, and Sacramento, California.
	First kindergarten in English founded in Boston.
	U.S. scientists react both positively (Gray) and negatively (Agassiz) to Charles Darwin's evolutionary theory propounded in *The Origin of Species*.
1861	Ten more southern states secede from the Union and create the Confederate States of America.
	Civil War between North and South begins.
	Telegraph wires are strung between New York and San Francisco, greatly facilitating communications and ending Pony Express.
1862	Gail Borden patents a process for concentrating fruit juice.
	Pacific Railway Act authorizes construction of a transcontinental railroad.
	Congress authorizes printing of first paper bank notes, known as "greenbacks."
1863	President Lincoln issues Emancipation Proclamation, thus changing war aims of North in Civil War.
	The battles of Gettysburg (in Pennsylvania) and Vicksburg (in Mississippi) mark turning point of war in favor of North, although victory is surely still in doubt.
	Samuel L. Clemens adopts pen name "Mark Twain."
	George Plimpton invents four-wheel roller skate and introduces that sport.
1864	Ulysses S. Grant becomes commander of the Union armies and begins his vicious assault on Confederate armies in Northern Virginia; he pursues them until end of war.

Date	Event
1864 *(cont.)*	Colorado militia forces slaughter Cheyenne and Arapahoe Indians (including women and children) at Sand Creek.
	Two-train collision in Pennsylvania kills 65 persons.
1865	Slavery is abolished by 13th Amendment to the Constitution.
	Walt Whitman publishes *Drum Taps,* a collection of poems about the Civil War.
	Massachusetts Institute of Technology is founded.
	Union stockyards open in Chicago, which soon becomes meat-packing center of the country.
	Tremendous increase of interest in baseball after the war—soon 91 clubs belong to national association.

Historians of
the United States

3

THIS CHAPTER PRESENTS brief biographies of 15 historians of the United States. We have included only a select few, choosing historians who have had great influence on how we think about the past or how we go about researching and writing about the past. Some have exerted this influence through their own scholarship and writing. Others have not only written widely, but have trained and guided younger scholars who, in turn, have exerted substantial influence on the profession. Some have even had great social influence by force of their personalities, their personal courage in taking unpopular stands on current issues of the day, and their work in or around government, the military, or the diplomatic corps.

We have tried to include representatives from the major fields of historical scholarship (economic, social, intellectual, and political history) as well as subfields within those broad areas of scholarly interest (e.g., such topics as the family, slavery, diplomacy, technology, and women). To a certain extent, the intellectual biography of each historian may serve to gauge the state of the art of United States history when that individual was doing his or her major scholarly work. The most significant aspects of these historians' lives for our purposes here are their ideas and influence on how we think about history, but these biographies also sketch a personal dimension.

You will probably notice several things about the historians we have included. First, there are few young people. Even though a young historian may have influenced the way we think about history or practice historical research, judging the significance of a young scholar's work is difficult because so much of that work, presumably, is yet to be done. Second, biographical information about younger historians is much more difficult to gather.

One consequence of the foregoing is that the historians included here tend to be (1) older—many were even born in the nineteenth century; (2) male—women in prior generations had great difficulty becoming professional historians; and (3) white—blacks and other minorities also faced difficulties in securing professional training and employment opportunities in the historical profession. To say this is to say that the history of the historical profession in this country reflects many of the characteristics of the larger society. Until fairly recently the historical profession was dominated by white males trained mainly at northeastern universities. The historical profession now reflects much greater pluralism within its ranks than was once the case, and the discipline's creativity and substance reflect this change.

Bernard Bailyn (1922–   )

Bernard Bailyn was born in Hartford, Connecticut. While attending Williams College, he discovered his interest in history. World War II interrupted his college studies; he served in the Army Security Agency and Army Signal Corps. He received his B.A. in 1945. In 1947, Bailyn received his M.A. from Harvard University, and he continued with his doctoral studies there under the tutelage of Oscar Handlin and Samuel Eliot Morison.

Bailyn's work has profoundly influenced the study of early American history. His scholarly work has set much of the research agenda in social and economic history, as well as in political and intellectual history. In addition, Bailyn pioneered in the application of new research and analytic techniques, particularly quantitative data and methods (using large bodies of data that can be counted and manipulated by statistical procedures), and collective biography. His students Gordon S. Wood and Michael Kammen, among others, have been among the most influential and prolific in the recent historiography of colonial and early national history.

Bailyn has written several seminal books, beginning with the publication of his doctoral dissertation *New England Merchants in the Seventeenth Century* (1955), which explored the tension between commercial interests and Puritan culture and ideas. His book *Massachusetts Shipping, 1697–1714: A Statistical Study* (1959) was less a narrative history than a statistical compendium. It was nevertheless an important contribution to colonial economic history. The next year Bailyn published *Education in the Forming of American Society: Needs and Opportunities for Study* (1960), which hypothesized that the family had been the most important educational institution in early America. The church, the community, and apprenticeship practices assisted the family in educating young people. Before long, however, their effectiveness was undermined by the abundance of land, shortage of labor, and religious pluralism common in the American colonies.

Pamphlets of the American Revolution, 1750–1776 (1965) was an edited collection of primary source documents. In addition to providing editorial notes and background on the context and author of each document, Bailyn wrote a provocative introductory essay that attached new meaning to a set of beliefs known variously in England as Radical Whig, the Country, or Opposition ideology. Bailyn argued that this set of radical ideas (actually an ideology or set of ideas) had a much greater influence in the American colonies than anyone had ever suspected. In 1967, Bailyn expanded this essay in *The Ideological Origins of the American Revolution,* in which he described more fully this ideology, its exaggerated fear of governmental authority, and its use of such language as "slavery," "corruption," and "conspiracy"—words their users meant literally, not solely metaphorically.

Bailyn's later works include *Law in American History* (1972), *The Ordeal of Thomas Hutchinson* (1974), and the first section of *The Great Republic* (1977), perhaps the best textbook on U.S. history ever written. *The Peopling of British North America* (1987), concerned with early demographic history, is Bailyn's most recent effort. Through his writing and students, Bailyn has almost single-handedly set the agenda for early American history.

Charles A. Beard (1874–1948)

Few scholars have been as influential in the intellectual and cultural life of the United States as Charles Beard. Beard was an expert on municipal government, a proponent of public administration as a field of academic study, an educational reformer who believed that school should be more relevant to current problems and needs, and a political scientist who helped orient that discipline toward realistic analysis of current problems and issues. In addition, Beard was a towering figure as a historian. As such, Beard is most commonly associated with (1) the economic interpretation of American history, particularly *An Economic Interpretation of the Constitution of the United States* (1913); (2) "the new history," which urged that historical study encompass the full range of human experience as well as politics; and (3) the idea that history should be an instrument for improving the present and reshaping the future.

In the period between World War I and World War II, as historian John Higham (1970, p. 131) wrote, Beard "came close to dominating the study of American history." But Beard was not simply an ivory tower scholar. Indeed, after he resigned from Columbia University in 1917 to protest the dismissal of several other faculty members who were opposed to American entry into World War I, he did not hold a full-time university post until 1940. Although he himself firmly supported American entry, he resigned to defend its opponents. Historian Richard Hofstadter (1968, p. 287) says of this: "It is on such courageous moments of self-assertion that the American tradition of academic freedom has been built."

During much of his life, Beard was a controversial figure, often taking unpopular stands on the issues of the day as well as staking out innovative and sometimes unpopular scholarly positions. "When I come to an end," Beard wrote, "my mind will still be beating its wings against the bars of thought's prison." His passion was "new facts . . . [which were] constantly challenging old mental patterns and imagery" (Braeman, 1983). The words *skeptical, pragmatic, realistic, hard-bitten, irreverent,* and *iconoclastic* were often used by both devotees and critics to characterize the man. In addition to dispelling myths, challenging conventional wisdom (even his own), and provoking his audiences, Beard was concerned with social uplift, with helping society's disadvantaged persons—with generally "doing good."

Beard's background helps, in part, to explain his behavior and beliefs. He was born in Indiana in 1874 to a well-to-do family. His father, William, was a successful farmer, contractor, and land speculator, as well as a loyal Republican who strongly believed in

America as the land of opportunity. His parents encouraged Charles to expand his horizons through extensive reading and other intellectual pursuits. Perhaps most important was his exposure to local Quakers (several of his family members had been Quakers, too), whose beliefs had a deep and lasting impact on him.

After Beard graduated from high school, his father bought the local weekly newspaper, *The Knightstown Sun,* for him and his brother Clarence. They successfully operated the paper for four years, but then Charles was persuaded to go to college. He enrolled at DePauw University, where he was very active in campus social and political affairs. Beard graduated in only three years, but his experience there was formative. In one social science course, for example, Beard and his fellow students were required to supplement their academic reading with actual field experiences. Beard spent part of the summer of 1896 in Chicago where he was shocked by the slums and poverty he saw. That same summer, he visited Jane Addams' Hull House, a settlement house for immigrants, and was exposed to reform ferment (intellectual and political) at work there.

From DePauw, Beard went on to Oxford and Columbia Universities for graduate studies. He received his Ph.D. in 1904 and stayed at Columbia until resigning in 1917. He was a prolific writer, producing at least 35 books not counting those he edited. In addition, he wrote hundreds of articles for academic journals and other periodicals and hundreds of book reviews. It is impossible to summarize this volume of work, but Richard Hofstadter (1968) may help us judge this prolific scholar: "He had never been content with the role of the historian or academic alone: he always hoped to be politically relevant, had always aspired to become a public force . . . he relished the part of the public moralist, the gadfly, the pamphleteer. . . . He had made himself foremost among the American historians . . . in the search for a usable past" (pp. 343–345).

Carl Becker (1873–1945)

Becker was born on a farm near Waterloo, Iowa. His father, a Civil War veteran, had moved west from New York to seek a better life for his family. Succeeding in that quest as farmers, the Becker family moved from farm to town by the time Carl was eleven years old. He did quite well in school. After he graduated from high school he enrolled at Cornell College, a Methodist school in Mt. Vernon, Iowa. Finding the atmosphere there to be stifling, even repressive, Becker threw over his religious affiliation and training and moved on to the University of Wisconsin.

After receiving his B.A. from Wisconsin in 1896, Becker went to Columbia University, where he studied for one year with such scholars as James Harvey Robinson (another of the progressive historians) and Herbert Osgood. In 1899, Becker began to teach before completing his graduate studies, and in 1902 he began a fourteen-year association with the University of Kansas while earning his Ph.D. from the University of Wisconsin in 1907. In 1917, Becker joined the faculty of Cornell University (not to be confused with Cornell College), where he stayed until he retired in 1941.

During his career, Becker was prolific. He produced 16 books, around 75 articles in scholarly journals, and roughly 200 book reviews. He was as much interested in European history as the history of the United States. His book *The Heavenly City of the Eighteenth-Century Philosophers* (1932) was probably his best work in European history; *The Declaration of Independence: A Study in the History of Political Ideas* (1922) may have been the best example of his work in United States intellectual history.

While studying at the University of Wisconsin, Becker was greatly influenced by Frederick Jackson Turner, prominent progressive historian of the American frontier. Becker was not so much interested in Turner's subject as the way he taught it. Turner had speculated that all history was relative; that is, people in every age rewrote history to suit their own needs, to answer their own questions. Becker came to share that belief. In addition, Becker argued that all historical studies were functional or instrumental— that was the measure of their worth. As he wrote in 1913 in the *American Journal of Sociology* (Becker, 1913, p. 641),

> the historians of any age are likely to find those aspects of the past interesting or important which are in some way connected with the intellectual or social conditions of the age in which they live; so that the historical work that is

most characteristic of any time may be regarded as em-
bodying an interpretation of the past in terms of present
social interests. . . . Historical thinking is . . . a social
instrument, helpful in getting the world's work more effectively done.

Part of Becker's relativism was the view that the truth or falsity
of ideas or beliefs in the past could be judged only in reference
to the practical uses to which those ideas and beliefs were put.
In short, how effective were ideas as instruments? Relativism,
including the idea that everyman is his own historian, became
central to Becker's view of history.

It is interesting to note how Becker's own ideas changed in
response to external events. In the years immediately before and
during World War II, his relativistic views changed. As Robert
Allen Skotheim (1966, pp. 121–122) said, "In the face of totali-
tarianism [Nazi Germany, Fascist Italy, and Soviet Russia], Becker
modified his emphasis upon a theoretical relativism in favor of an
emphasis upon virtually 'absolute,' 'universal' ideas or values in
man's history." It is not without irony that environmental factors
led to a revision of Becker's (and Charles Beard's) environmental
interpretations of history.

Bruce Catton (1899–1978)

Bruce Catton did not train to be a professional historian.
Nevertheless, he wrote 14 books on the Civil War, some of
which are magnificent pieces of work. As an "amateur" historian
who wrote for a wide popular audience, Catton was sometimes
shunned by professionally trained historians who criticized his
work for being too popular or for not being scholarly enough.
Although Catton wrote on several other historical topics, his reputation as a popular historian stems from his vast body of writing
on the Civil War.

Catton was born in a northern Michigan lumber town. In
1916 he left to attend Oberlin College in Ohio, but service in the
U.S. Navy during World War I cut short his college career. Rather
than finishing college when the war ended, Catton started working

for a newspaper, first as a reporter, then as an editor and columnist. In the period between the two world wars, Catton worked for a variety of newspapers from Cleveland, Ohio, to Boston, Massachusetts.

In 1943, Catton quit the newspaper business and became director of information for the War Production Board. His firsthand observations led him to write his first book, *The War Lords of Washington* (1948), in which he recounted his observations of wartime (especially bureaucratic) Washington. Writing *The War Lords* was an experience that redirected his life. That year he decided to quit government work and began writing history fulltime.

Catton's first project, a three-volume history of the Union Army of the Potomac during the Civil War, marked the beginning of his lifelong infatuation with that era. These three books—*Mr. Lincoln's Army* (1951), *Glory Road* (1952), and *A Stillness at Appomattox* (1953)—launched his reputation as a Civil War historian. The last-mentioned book earned Catton a Pulitzer Prize. What was notable about Catton's work was that he avoided narrow scholarly topics and the trappings of scholarly research, especially numerous and lengthy footnotes. Virtually all his books were criticized for not using more primary sources and for not drawing on the vast range of available secondary sources. But by using the types of primary historical sources he did—diaries, newspaper accounts, and regimental histories, among others—Catton was able to make the war an exciting human and personal experience. Catton told of common soldiers as well as generals; he wrote of their warts as well as their heroics.

Catton produced another trilogy, *The Centennial History of the Civil War.* These three books—*The Coming Fury* (1961), *Terrible Swift Sword* (1963), and *Never Call Retreat* (1965)—are among Catton's best. These books are characterized by increased attention to primary historical sources and a broader look at the war than Catton had taken before. But his focus was still on individual participants—what they saw, felt, feared.

In addition to his voluminous work on the Civil War, Catton was a driving force on *American Heritage,* a magazine of popular history, from 1954 until his death in 1978. He served as editor, wrote articles on a wide range of topics, and encouraged prominent historians to become involved in the magazine. At his direction, such special projects as *The American Heritage History of the Civil War* and *The American Heritage History of the American Revolution,* both wonderful pictorial histories, were undertaken.

To the end, Catton was dedicated to the idea that historians should write for those beyond the profession. If historians spoke only among themselves, of what possible worth were they? To be sure, Catton believed, the historian should search for truth and be true to the facts. Within those constraints, however, the historian should entertain readers, should take them into worlds beyond their own, and should enhance their sensibilities about the lives of other persons in other times. For Catton, this formula seems to have worked well. At the time of his death, all his major books were still in print—surely a testimonial to the popularity of this historical writer's work.

Merle Curti (1897–   )

Merle Curti was born and raised in Nebraska but received all his academic degrees from Harvard University. In 1942, he was appointed to the history faculty at the University of Wisconsin, where he remained for the rest of his professional career. Curti became an elder statesman (and sometimes an embattled defender) of United States intellectual history. He received the Pulitzer Prize for his book *The Growth of American Thought* (1943), which was selected in a poll of historians as the "most preferred" book written between 1936 and 1950. For many years this book served as a major synthesis of the history of ideas in the United States. Its standing declined in the 1970s, when intellectual history as a subfield of U.S. history fell into disfavor among professional historians.

Curti's social views were very close to the "progressive" views of Beard, Becker, and Robinson. The nature of his specific social views can be seen in the scholarship he pursued. His earliest works, in the 1920s and 1930s, were concerned with pacifist ideas and peace movements in American history. *The American Peace Crusade, 1815–1860* (1929) and *Peace or War: The American Struggle, 1636–1936* (1936), to name two, were sympathetic to pacifist ideas. Moreover, these ideas were presented as possible instruments to change the world. Arguments against war, Curti contended, had failed in the past, not as a result of defeat by other "rational" ideas but because of turbulence in the social, economic, and political environment. Curti believed that this "body of brilliant arguments against war" might serve as a reservoir of resources that could influence people's future behavior. Indeed, Curti wrote in another context that "the historian should select and emphasize those memories of the past that will impel men consciously to seek and build a more desirable future" (Curti, 1935a, p. 117), thus agreeing with both Beard and Becker.

In *The Social Ideas of American Educators* (1935), Curti stressed the connection between ideas and the social and economic system. This book championed those educators whose ideas promoted democratization of the schools and criticized those whose ideas retarded educational reform. Curti reproached those in both camps who failed to understand the connection between the schools and their environment. As he said, "education cannot rise above the existent social system and the virtues sponsored by that system" (Curti, 1935b, p. 424).

In *The Growth of American Thought,* Curti extended his earlier views to all of American intellectual history. The book was organized around the conflict between reform ideas (which, not surprisingly, looked forward) and antireform ideas (which tended to look backward). Like other "progressive" historians, Curti was more likely to emphasize the environmental origins of ideas for which he had little sympathy than those ideas he admired. Despite Curti's basic historical relativism, however, his book seemed to celebrate the achievements of American ideas and institutions.

In a review of *The Growth of American Thought,* Richard Shryock (1944) noted that, "Most striking is the catholicity of interests, the broad conception of what constitutes the cultural life of a people" (p. 732). What Shryock referred to was Curti's treatment of science and education, the arts and architecture, popular culture and minority thought as well as that of the elite. It is little wonder that many considered Curti's work encyclopedic.

In *The Making of an American Community: Democracy in a Frontier County* (1959), Curti applied social science methods and concepts to the study of history to a much greater extent than had his mentors Beard and Robinson. This book was his attempt to write scientific history, in the sense of discovering the connection between environmental factors and the beliefs that sprang from them. His investigation not only showed what Americans in this Wisconsin county believed and thought, it also suggested a good deal about the nature of the community in which those ideas came to life.

John Hope Franklin (1915–   )

John Hope Franklin is one of the most celebrated current historians in the United States. In part, at least, his professional career mirrors an important aspect of twentieth-century American social history—the struggle for equal social, economic, and political rights for black Americans.

In 1832, Franklin's great-grandfather, a slave, was taken from Alabama to Oklahoma by his Chickasaw Indian masters. His son David Burney escaped slavery to join the Union Army during the Civil War. David eventually changed his surname to Franklin, married a half-Indian woman, and settled on a ranch deeded to him by the federal government. Buck Franklin, John Hope's father, attended college in Tennessee, became an attorney, and moved to Rentiesville, Oklahoma (an all-black town of about 2,000 people) to practice law and double as the town's postmaster.

Growing up, Franklin intended to follow his father in the practice of law. After graduating from high school, he enrolled at Fisk University in Nashville, Tennessee (his parents had studied in Nashville; his brother had attended Fisk). But his plans for becoming a lawyer changed abruptly when he met Theodore S. Currier, a young white professor of history. About the American history course Franklin had taken from Currier, Franklin said, "I had never had such an intellectual experience."

Franklin graduated from Fisk with honors when he was twenty years old, even though he had worked the entire time to put himself through school. He applied to and was accepted by Harvard University for graduate work. But in 1935, the United States was in the depths of the Great Depression. As Franklin put it, "My father's law business had been crushed by the Depression, so the family could not finance my graduate study." He went home for the summer wondering how he could pay for graduate school. When Professor Currier discovered Franklin's problem, he said, "Money will not keep you from going to Harvard," and proceeded to take out a personal bank loan to pay for Franklin's first year at Harvard. Thereafter, Franklin taught and received several fellowships, which defrayed the costs of his education. He was awarded his Ph.D. in 1941.

Between 1943 and 1981, Franklin authored or edited 17 books (an average of nearly one book every two years) and numerous scholarly articles. Considering this volume of work, it may not be surprising that he calls his office "the slave quarters." Franklin's primary scholarly concern was this history of black Americans and of the South. His first book, *The Free Negro in North Carolina, 1790–1860* (1943), looked closely at the social and economic dimensions of black degradation in antebellum North Carolina. In *From Slavery to Freedom: A History of American Negroes* (first edition, 1947), Franklin surveyed the black experience in America from colonial times to World War II. Since its publication, this book has been revised several times and has sold over a half million copies. In *The Militant South, 1800–1860* (1956), Franklin moved beyond the history of blacks to a description of the emergence of a unique military spirit in the South before the Civil War. More recently, Franklin published *Southern Odyssey* (1975).

In addition to teaching and substantial scholarly work, Franklin is notable for the many "firsts" he has experienced. He was, for example, the first black president of the American Historical Association, of the Organization of American Historians, and of the Southern History Association. Of these and other firsts, Franklin says, "What business did I have being on the front page of the *New York Times* for becoming a history department chairman, except that it told you something about where we were, or where we were not [in making racial progress in the United States]?" He believes that scholars should have an impact on society as well as pursue academic interests. As one example of his social activism, in 1954 Franklin supplied a historical brief for the lawsuit *Brown* v. *Topeka Board of Education,* which led to the Supreme Court's declaring school segregation unconstitutional. An unpretentious man despite celebrity, Franklin's scholarly and personal lives have served similar ends.

Eugene D. Genovese (1930–   )

Genovese was born and raised in a mainly working class neighborhood in Brooklyn, New York. He attended Brooklyn College, receiving his B.A. in 1953. He earned his M.A. (1955) and Ph.D. (1959) from Columbia University, where he studied United States and Latin American history. It is interesting to note that Genovese has never lived in the South, the region that has occupied most of his scholarly attention. The lack of firsthand knowledge of the region and its institutions has made him vulnerable to the charge that his knowledge is only "out of books." He has taught history at the Brooklyn Polytechnic Institute, Rutgers University, Sir George Williams University (in Montreal), and the University of Rochester.

Genovese is a professed Marxist and holds a set of beliefs that has shaped not only his scholarship but his personal/public life as well. While at Rutgers University in the mid-1960s, for example, he loudly and frequently expressed his opposition to the war in Vietnam and frankly proclaimed he would welcome a Vietcong victory against the American troops. The New Jersey public was outraged by such a position, at least in 1965, and his removal from the Rutgers faculty became an issue in the campaign for governor of the state. Even future President Richard Nixon called for his firing. Genovese voluntarily left Rutgers in 1967, as he said, "to the great relief of all concerned."

This episode (there were others as well) is relevant because it attests to the strength of his Marxist convictions as well as the strength of opposition to Marxism in the United States. Yet Genovese is no conventional Marxist. Indeed, he finds the idea of "economic determinism" (an idea associated with Marxian analysis) repugnant. In addition, his emphasis on cultural influences and the subtlety of his scholarship often allow one to forget his basic philosophical orientation. His later work is a good example of the potential of Marxism's analytical side, without the baggage of propaganda and dogmatism.

What is really important is how Genovese's beliefs undergird (and enrich) his scholarly work. His scholarship has centered on three distinct but related areas: (1) comparative slave systems in the Western Hemisphere; (2) the nature of the slave system in the American South; and (3) contemporary black and New Left radicalism in the 1960s. This sketch focuses on the first two.

Genovese has done fine scholarly work in the comparative history of slave systems. He argued in *The World the Slaveholders Made* (1969) that the development of various slave systems (for example, in the South, in Brazil, and in the French and British West Indies) cannot be understood apart from one another or apart from the parent European cultures that spawned them.

However, Genovese's primary work has not been comparative history, but rather the imaginative and rich study of slavery in the American South. In his *The Political Economy of Slavery* (1965), Genovese applied Marxist principles to the study of life in the South, including slave labor, soil exhaustion, and the expansion of slavery into the western territories of the United States, among other topics. His analysis indicated that the slave system was economically harmful to the South, but the institution was maintained despite these economic disincentives.

In 1974, Genovese published a masterpiece of historical scholarship titled *Roll, Jordan, Roll: The World the Slaves Made*. As he said about its subject, "I started studying the masters and decided I could not understand much about them unless I studied the slaves closely. Once I started, they became an obsession." The book received wide acclaim and became quite popular, despite its 800-plus pages. The book exhaustively re-created the world the slaves made, covering food and clothing, religious practices, sexual and marital habits, entertainment, and naming practices—every facet of slave life. Although Genovese finds slavery to be an abhorrent system, his portrait of slaves and of slavery gives them a face at once less victimized (their victimization is never questioned—slavery is not made over into "happy days") but more dignified and human because of the resiliency of their adaptation to a horrible system and the cleverness of their strategies for dealing with that system on a day-to-day basis. "The result is a work of uncommon insight," according to Michael Bordelon (1983). "In Genovese's hands Marxism is a tool for analysis, not polemic or propaganda." The nature of *Roll, Jordan, Roll* gives a reader "confidence that the book has been written by an author in relentless search of the truth" (Bordelon, 1983).

Oscar Handlin (1915–   )

O scar Handlin ranks as one of the most prolific and influential historians of the modern era. Handlin was born in New York City to recently arrived Jewish immigrants. Although he was expelled from school on several occasions, Handlin excelled at academics and by age eight had decided to become a historian. Not surprisingly, Handlin became a voracious reader. After graduating from high school in 1931, Handlin attended Brooklyn College, where he earned his bachelor's degree in three years. He was then admitted to the graduate program at Harvard University.

Handlin had wanted to study medieval history, but Charles Haskins, the Harvard professor with whom he wanted to study, had retired. He therefore decided to study with Arthur M. Schlesinger, Sr., because he was reputed to be the next best person on the Harvard faculty. It was Schlesinger who suggested that Handlin write his doctoral dissertation on Boston's Irish immigrants. In 1940, he received his doctoral degree; the next year his dissertation was published as *Boston's Immigrants, 1790–1865: A Study in Acculturation.* The book was a model study of the manner in which poor Irish immigrants adapted to Boston, a rather unpromising city both culturally and economically. For this effort, Handlin received immediate and widespread acclaim. The author was praised for his use of primary historical sources, including census materials and the immigrant press, and his use of social science concepts to explain Irish adaptation.

Handlin soon showed that he would not be a one-book wonder. Since the publication of *Boston's Immigrants,* Handlin has written or edited more than 30 books. These include *This Was America: True Accounts of People, Places, Manners and Customs, As Recorded by European Travelers . . .* (1949); *The Uprooted* (1952), one of the most beautifully written books ever produced about European immigrants to the United States; *The American People in the Twentieth Century* (1954), a history of ethnic groups in the United States; *Race and Nationality in American Life* (1957), a collection of essays on immigration and ethnic history; *Al Smith and His America* (1958), a lively sketch of the governor of New York and 1928 presidential candidate; *Fire Bell in the Night: The Crisis in Civil Rights* (1964), in which Handlin argued against busing, quotas, and other preferential treatment for blacks while emphasizing vastly expanded educational opportunities; and *Facing Life: Youth and the Family in American History* (1971), a history of adolescence.

In these books and through his influence with his students, Handlin has made pioneering and profound contributions to U.S. history, especially in the fields of social, ethnic, and urban history. The list of his former graduate students is like a *Who's Who of American History*—Bernard Bailyn, Anne Firor Scott, Moses Rischin, David Rothman, Neil Harris, Nathan Huggins, Stephan Thernstrom, Sam Bass Warner, to name just a few. These scholars have been among the most influential in their respective chosen specialties. In 1979, Handlin's former students published *Uprooted Americans: Essays to Honor Oscar Handlin,* a collection of essays written and published in his honor. Although Handlin has made substantial contributions to many areas of American history, he will probably be best remembered for his contributions to social history, the history of immigration, and the history of American cities.

Richard Hofstadter (1916–1970)

Hofstadter was one of the most influential historians in the United States in the period after World War II. The subjects of his work ranged from the Puritans to the 1960s, but despite such breadth, his work was always penetrating and suggestive. For much of his professional life, he sought to counter the often single-cause explanations of such "progressive" historians as Charles Beard, whose economic explanations of the American past Hofstadter found wanting. Because he often criticized Beard and other progressive historians, Hofstadter is commonly associated with the so-called "consensus" school of American historiography (as are Daniel Boorstin and Louis Hartz), which emerged in the 1950s. Consensus historians minimized the degree of conflict in the American past, asserting that there was little disagreement on fundamental social and political values. Because of the subtlety and complexity of Hofstadter's work, however, it is difficult to categorize him so simply.

Born in 1916 in Buffalo, New York, Hofstadter attended the university there and moved on for graduate work at Columbia University in New York City. From 1937 to his death in 1970, Hofstadter was affiliated with Columbia for all but four years. He received his Ph.D. in 1942 after completing the manuscript of what would become his first book, *Social Darwinism in American Thought, 1860–1915*.

This book had less to do with the active role of evolutionary ideas in the late nineteenth century than about contemporary social thinkers whose ideas rationalized the status quo—the existing political, social, and moral order. As Hofstadter said, "there is nothing in Darwinism that inevitably made it an apology for competition or force." This book showed Hofstadter's interest in ideas as powerful historical forces, a central theme in most of his subsequent scholarship.

His next project was *The American Political Tradition and the Men Who Made It* (1948), a book that earned him fame. It consisted of 12 essays about key political figures in American history including the Founding Fathers, Thomas Jefferson, Andrew Jackson, John C. Calhoun, and Abraham Lincoln. According to Hofstadter, the American political tradition "overwhelmingly supported exploitative individualism and a rapacious entrepreneurial capitalism." In this, Hofstadter's work ran counter to progressive historians' views that the American past could be explained by the battles between the forces of good and evil, liberal democracy versus conservative interests.

Hofstadter suggested that all Americans (not just conservatives) were in some measure influenced by material forces and perceived self-interest. In addition, the story became even more complicated as political traditions, ideas, and ideologies themselves became forces in history. Indeed, over time, these ideas became so powerful as to impede adjustments in thinking necessitated by changes in the material environment. His point was that ideologies could be dysfunctional as well as functional, but were powerful historical forces in either case. As the United States was transformed by such material forces as industrialization, immigration, and urbanization, the American political tradition of Jeffersonian democracy and equality of opportunity (and the assumptions on which this tradition was based) became outdated. Material conditions had changed faster than Americans' ideas, resulting in inappropriate responses to new problems. Only Franklin D. Roosevelt was able to discard such outmoded thinking during the tremendous economic crisis that characterized the 1930s. Yet Hofstadter was no great fan of Roosevelt, whom he saw as unable to provide the nation with what it needed most—a revitalized democratic philosophy appropriate to an industrial age.

The Age of Reform: From Bryan to FDR (1955) was perhaps Hofstadter's best book. It combined his twin interests in political and intellectual history, describing the impulse to reform as the dynamic political force in the period from 1890 to the New Deal. The book also described the tenacity of traditional values and ideas and how these influence people's actions and self-perceptions. According to Hofstadter, emerging reform strategies were defined and constrained by such American values as equality of opportunity, free enterprise, and rugged individualism even after these ideas were no longer appropriate or effective. Therefore the liberal ideology of which these ideas and values were a part was also a conservative tradition, and reform strategies were steeped in nostalgia for the certainties and superiority of bygone eras. The Populists (farmer-reformers) were inspired by a pre-industrial, Jeffersonian worldview, which cast farmers as exemplars of virtue; Progressives were inspired by small-town America, a place where God-fearing, Protestant people were respected leaders of the community. The problem was that no one perceived that all this was only nostalgia, not instrumental knowledge for solving current problems.

Hofstadter always worked hard, often with a discipline that astonished his colleagues. Historian C. Vann Woodward commented that "he was not always an easy man to vacation with . . . langorous tropical mornings tended to be disturbed by the clatter of a typewriter. He gave us all an inferiority complex" (Fass, 1983).

In the last two years of his life, Hofstadter published two books: *The Progressive Historians: Turner, Beard, Parrington* (1968) and *The Idea of a Party System: The Rise of Legitimate Opposition in the United States* (1969). In addition, he completed several chapters of what was to have been a massive project; after his death, it was published, in part, as *America at 1750: A Social Portrait* (1971).

Forrest McDonald (1927–   )

Forrest McDonald was born in Orange, Texas. He had athletic ambitions but was too small to play football. He decided instead to take up baseball; it was that interest that led him to enroll at the University of Texas. World War II interrupted his studies. He joined the U.S. Navy, but the war ended just after he completed his training, so he saw no combat. Returning to his studies at Texas, McDonald had to pay his own way and support a wife and family by working at odd jobs around Austin. Nevertheless, he jumped from freshman to master's degree graduate in just three years! An English major as an undergraduate, McDonald switched to history as a graduate student and received his Ph.D. in 1955.

Just as his background is different from that of most professional historians, so too are his political views and loyalties. Unlike so many historians, who seem to be either liberal or radical with respect to their politics, McDonald has been assertively—even aggressively—conservative. In 1964, for example, he served as chairman of the Rhode Island state Goldwater for President Committee. Since 1978, his name has appeared on the masthead of the conservative journal *National Review.* McDonald's scholarly work cuts in a similar direction. His work in economic and business history has been critical of progressive reformers and regulation; his scholarly work on the Confederation, Constitution, and ratification periods has debunked the views and interpretations of the progressive historians, especially those of Charles Beard.

Few contemporary historians have been as prolific as McDonald. Although he has written extensively in economic and business history, much of this work falls outside the time period covered in this volume. His scholarship on the Constitution and ratification periods, however, is important and quite germane.

In 1958, McDonald published *We the People: The Economic Origins of the Constitution.* This book attacked Charles Beard's

An Economic Interpretation of the Constitution on virtually every possible ground. Beard had argued that the Constitution was more than anything else a document designed to protect the economic interests of its framers. The power to tax, the commerce power, and power to dispose of western lands were all given to the national government, according to Beard, to protect powerful commercial and financial interests. The struggle for ratification saw this consolidated group "putting one over" on the small farmers and debtors in the new nation.

Other scholars, such as Richard E. Brown in *Charles A. Beard and the Constitution* (1956), have attacked Beard's interpretations, but none has done so as completely as McDonald. David Potter, for example, judged *We the People* "one of the most smashing analyses every mounted in the literature of historical criticism." McDonald found that economic interests had, indeed, played a role in the writing and ratification of the Constitution, but he concluded those interests had been far more pluralistic than Beard had allowed and too diverse to suggest any systematic patterns of economic self-interest. McDonald's scholarship, in turn, was criticized, although even the most severe critics conceded that he had "substantially increased our knowledge."

McDonald has also looked closely at the so-called critical period in *E Pluribus Unum: The Formation of the American Republic, 1776–1790* (1965) and the early national period in *The Presidency of George Washington* (1974). Interestingly, Alexander Hamilton, rather than Washington, was the focus of the latter book because, McDonald argued, it was Hamilton's financial system that kept the new nation together. In *The Presidency of Thomas Jefferson* (1976), McDonald judged Jefferson to have been successful in some ways (reducing the nation's debt, abolishing most internal taxes), but quite destructive in others (enforcing an embargo against European goods, trying to weaken the judiciary). McDonald judged that "He and his followers set out to deflect the course of History, and History ended up devouring them and turning even their memory to its own purposes." In *Alexander Hamilton: A Biography* (1979), McDonald reasserted his view that this man was most responsible for launching a powerful nation.

McDonald's scholarly production has been immense and his influence has been great. Even those who disagree strongly with his interpretations and conclusions must come to terms with what his research has uncovered.

Perry Miller (1905–1963)

Perry Miller, born in Chicago and educated at the University of Chicago, taught English at Harvard University from 1931 to his death in 1963. Although not trained as a historian, Miller is closely identified with the intellectual history of the Puritans in colonial New England. A self-proclaimed atheist, Miller almost single-handedly revitalized historians' scholarly interest in the Puritans. Miller never wanted to be their apologist, commenting "respect for them is not the same thing as believing in them." Miller was simply starting his scholarly work at the beginning of the American experience and that experience happened to be intellectual and theological. "This was not a fact of my choosing," he wrote.

In Miller's many books on the history of Puritan ideas, he expressed admiration for "the majesty and coherence of Puritan thinking." What was more, Miller seemed to believe that their thought was in some senses true. As Miller put it, "Puritanism failed to hold later generations largely because the children were unable to face reality as unflinchingly as their forefathers." One of the reasons Miller respected the Puritans so much was that he thought ideas were crucial in all periods of history and, moreover, the Puritans took ideas seriously. Miller argued that many contemporary historians, much to their discredit, did not treat ideas in similar fashion: "I have difficulty imagining that anyone can be a historian without realizing that history itself is part of the life of the mind; hence I have been compelled to insist that the mind of man is the basic factor in human history."

As you might guess, Miller's thinking ran in a direction opposite that of many contemporary historians. He assailed the "new history" of Beard, Becker, and Robinson because "'new history,' written in terms of economic factors, or of class warfare, or of sectionalism and the frontier, has a way of becoming as quickly dated as has [Jonathan] Edwards' history in terms of the Old Testament." Miller was not enamored of the "relativistic" view of history either, nor did he share Beard's enthusiasm for the social sciences.

Furthermore, Miller emphasized the power and importance of ideas themselves, rather than their connections with the environment that produced them (although in his own work he did not entirely ignore the social and economic environment of ideas). Again disagreeing with his "progressive" contemporaries, Miller was uninterested in the pragmatic worldly consequences of ideas, although he believed that ideas had decisive historical importance.

These themes were expressed throughout the many volumes Miller devoted to the colonial New England experience, especially *Orthodoxy in Massachusetts, 1630–1650* (1933), *The New England Mind: The Seventeenth Century* (1939), *The New England Mind: From Colony to Province* (1953), and his biographies of Jonathan Edwards (1949) and Roger Williams (1953). In addition, Miller edited a number of collections of documents—letters and sermons—which made (and still make) the Puritan historical record accessible to students and scholars alike.

Edmund S. Morgan (1916–   )

Edmund Morgan was born in Minneapolis, Minnesota, but he spent much of his youth in Cambridge, Massachusetts. He graduated from Harvard with his A.B. degree in 1937, eventually receiving his Ph.D. there in 1942. The outbreak of World War II presented Morgan with a dilemma. Although he objected to war in principle, Morgan had few illusions concerning the dangers of Fascism or Nazism. As war engulfed Europe in 1940 and U.S. intervention in the conflict increasingly seemed necessary, he withdrew his petition for conscientious objector status from the local draft board. In 1942, Morgan enrolled in an intensive course to learn to become a machinist, a trade he plied in the radiation laboratory at MIT for the duration of the war.

Morgan has written over 15 books, edited many more, and produced scores of important scholarly articles. His research and writing deal with topics that span two centuries of American history. Characterizing Morgan's work briefly is difficult because of its great breadth and depth. Nevertheless, his primary scholarly contributions fall in three areas: the Puritans, early colonial Virginia, and the American Revolution.

Morgan has done much to resuscitate interest in the Puritans. Following the lead of his mentor Perry Miller, Morgan has made the Puritans accessible to modern readers through his work. His first book, *The Puritan Family: Religion and Domestic Relations in Seventeenth-Century New England* (1944), was concerned with how people actually related to each other. His topics included marriage, love, child-rearing, and education, among others. He portrayed the Puritans as "a much earthier lot than their modern critics have imagined." In *The Puritan Dilemma: The Story of John Winthrop* (1958), Morgan treated "the central Puritan dilemma, the problem of doing right in a world that does wrong." Focusing on John Winthrop, Morgan again made the Puritans understandable, human, even sympathetic historical figures. These books are not Morgan's most important from a scholarly point of view, but they have done as much as any to revive popular interest in and understanding of the Puritans.

Morgan was also interested in researching the history of colonial Virginia. *Virginians at Home: Family Life in the Eighteenth Century* (1952) resembled *The Puritan Family* and is still useful on such topics as the home, childhood, marriage, and slavery. Of far greater importance, however, is *American Slavery, American Freedom: The Ordeal of Colonial Virginia* (1975), a controversial book that made a major contribution to colonial historiography.

Morgan set out to explain how African slavery came to dominate Virginia's labor system. He also wanted to know how poor whites who were former indentured servants became the large planters' political and social allies. Morgan found that Afro-American slavery did not come easily to colonial Virginia. For many years white indentured servants were preferred to black slaves, in part because of blacks' high death rates in early Virginia. Only when these conditions changed did planters begin to purchase slaves. Slavery was seen as a preferable method of labor (as well as broader social) control. In time, the planter elite consciously began to promote racial hatred of blacks among the "dangerous free whites" in an effort to control the latter.

What was more, Morgan posited an important connection between the development of the ideas of "equality and liberty" on the one hand and "the rise of slavery" on the other. He asked,

"Was the vision of a nation of equals flawed at the source by contempt for both the poor and the black? Is America still colonial Virginia writ large?"

Morgan also has contributed greatly to our understanding of the American Revolution. In *The Stamp Act Crisis: Prologue to Revolution* (1953), he argued that the most important aspect of this crisis was the emergence of "well-defined constitutional principles" about which the war was finally fought. In *The Birth of the American Republic, 1763–1789* (1956), Morgan provided a historical synthesis of the era that is still useful. In these and other books, Morgan questioned progressive historians' emphasis on the conflict of social classes as an explanation for the American Revolution. Instead, Morgan emphasized the importance of ideas as primary motivating forces in the coming of that conflict. In so doing, Morgan helped chart the path to a better understanding of this important era of American history.

Samuel Eliot Morison (1887–1976)

Samuel Eliot Morison believed strongly in the literary basis of the historians' craft. Following in the footsteps of such narrative historians as George Bancroft and Francis Parkman, Morison felt that history should not only be accurate and exhaustively researched, but should be fine literature as well. In practicing that belief, he wrote over 40 books and well over 200 articles for scholarly periodicals, all of which were quite understandable and enjoyable to the popular reader.

Morison was born in his grandfather's house in Boston in 1887. He would eventually acquire that dwelling and live there for most of his 88 years. He was consequently surrounded with reminders of history—his own, his family's, his nation's. Educated in a Boston preparatory school, Morison went on to attend Harvard University as both an undergraduate and graduate student. After receiving his Ph.D. in 1912 and undertaking a short teaching assignment in California, Morison returned to Harvard as a faculty member. He stayed at Harvard until his retirement in 1955.

Morison's scholarly work was fashioned around several themes or, to be more accurate, passions. First was his captivation by the history of his own family, which for years (even centuries) had been prominent in the affairs of Massachusetts and the nation. His passionate love of family history led him, second, to his interest in the history of the New England region, particularly during its colonial period. Third, his childhood interest in sailing led to a lifelong passion for the sea. Much of his best historical scholarship has to do with sailors, navigation, exploration, and war on the high seas. Fourth, Morison was captivated by the role of "great men" in history—explorers, political leaders, war heroes. Again, this interest was manifested in much of his historical writing. He combined many of these interests in the projects he undertook and in the history he wrote.

Morison's doctoral dissertation was based on a large collection of papers he discovered as a young man in the wine cellar of his grandfather's house. Many of these manuscript sources belonged to Harrison Gray Otis, his great-great-grandfather, who had been a leader in the Massachusetts Federalist party in the period after the ratification of the U.S. Constitution. In 1913, Morison published his first book, based on those papers, *The Life and Letters of Harrison Gray Otis, Federalist, 1765–1848*. Later works that reflected his interest in the history of the New England region included *The Maritime History of Massachusetts, 1783–1860* (1921), *Builders of the Bay Colony* (1930), and *The Intellectual Life of Colonial New England* (1956). As Morison said, "My attitude toward seventeenth-century puritanism has passed through scorn and boredom to a warm interest and respect. The ways of the puritans are not my way, and their faith is not my faith . . . nevertheless they appear to me a courageous, humane, brave, and significant people."

Morison may be best known and appreciated for combining his love of the sea and his belief in great men. His *Admiral of the Ocean Sea: A Life of Christopher Columbus* (1942) is one example. This work has appeared in three forms: a two-volume scholarly book complete with extensive footnotes, a single-volume edition designed for the popular reader, and a shortened paperback version titled *Christopher Columbus, Mariner* (1955).

In the work, Morison also made a contribution to historical method. He was always a great believer in visiting the scene of historical events, to become steeped in the scene, the smells, the weather, etc. Because Columbus spent much of his time exploring at sea, Morison organzied the Harvard Columbus Expedition in 1939. He used a sailing vessel of about the same size as Columbus's flagship *Santa Maria* and, using historical charts and Columbus's journal, sailed Columbus's path from the Canary Islands to the West Indies. To further embellish his sense of Columbus's experience, Morison made many shorter trips to the Caribbean Sea, exploring the islands from the air, land, and sea.

Mary Beth Norton (1943–   )

Mary Beth Norton was born in Ann Arbor, Michigan, in 1943. Her father was an employee of the Library of Congress and her mother was a professor. Norton received her A.B. from the University of Michigan and her A.M. and Ph.D. from Harvard University. She has written a history of Americans who remained loyal to the British during the revolutionary period, titled *The British-Americans: The Loyalist Exiles in England, 1774–1789* (1972). Norton has also coauthored a splendid textbook titled *A People and a Nation,* which is widely used in college history courses and occasionally in high school advanced placement U.S. history courses. What is most notable about this textbook is its very strong thread of social history.

Norton is best known, however, for her research and writing on the history of women in America. In the past decade or two, much of the most exciting historical scholarship has occurred in the area of social history. Within that rather broad catchall has been extraordinary work on the history of women and the history of the family. As Lawrence Stone commented in reviewing Norton's *Liberty's Daughters: The Revolutionary Experience of American Women, 1750–1800* (1980), "Until now, the two have proceeded largely on parallel tracks." Norton's work has greatly contributed to pulling these two "tracks" together.

Norton's primary concern in this book was to trace the decline of patriarchy, the idea of choosing one's own spouse, the increase in marital and educational equality between the sexes, the more intense parental concern for children's education, and the phenomena of increasingly permissive child-rearing and increasing cooperation of husbands in such wifely burdens as home-making and child-rearing. According to Norton, these changes occurred within the context of the traditional "two spheres"—that is men's roles were defined largely by work outside the home whereas women's roles were defined in terms of domestic duties and child-rearing.

Norton suggests that the changes described above were the result of two factors. First, women had gained a good deal of practical experience during the Revolutionary War era in such traditionally masculine concerns as family finances, taxes, and other issues of household solvency. Second was the influence of republican ideology, with its emphasis on equality. These ideas thrust women into politics, from which they gained unprecedented concessions with respect to equality for women. In 1790 in New Jersey, for example, free adult women (widows and spinsters, because married women were not considered to be free) were given the right to vote—probably the first time in world history that right was extended to women. The right to vote there was then rescinded in 1806.

The importance of Norton's work (and that of other scholars as well) lies in the fact that she rather conclusively demonstrates that the emergence of the modern family was not the result of the industrial revolution in the United States. The second feature of importance is that Norton demonstrates that women did not experience high status when they were engaged in productive economic work on the farm, which status declined as women's roles came to be more confined to domestic management and child-rearing. Norton argues that the contrary order was true, that both men and women in the eighteenth century believed in the inferiority of women, and that women possessed rather low self-esteem and a very limited conception of their social and familial roles. The American Revolution, Norton argues, "had an indelible effect upon American women," especially "in changes in women's private lives—familial organization, personal aspirations, self-assessment."

Mary Beth Norton and many of her young colleagues have begun to have an extraordinary impact on historical scholarship and the way we think about the past.

David M. Potter (1910–1971)

David M. Potter was an extremely gifted writer as well as a clear thinker. Despite these virtues (ones that only some professional historians possess), his work remains largely unknown to the broad reading public. Known in the profession as an "idea man," "conceptual," or as a "historian's historian," Potter wrote synthetic and interpretive, rather than narrative, works. As one commentator wrote, "As a writer and interpreter of history, Potter, in a figurative sense, was much more the Haydn or Beethoven of his profession than its Cole Porter or John Lennon" (Carlton, 1983). Because most of his work appeared in scholarly journals, in books published by university presses, or in presentations at scholarly meetings, Potter never developed a popular following. Yet his impact on the history profession was immense.

Potter was born in Augusta, Georgia. Over the years he revealed little of his personal life. In the preface to a collection of his essays, *The South and the Sectional Conflict* (1968), Potter did reveal a part of himself that explains much of his interest in the history of the South and the Civil War era, his lifework:

> In one of her incomparable sketches, Frances Gray Patton once observed that no one born in the South later than World War I could remember the Civil War personally. I found this statement most arresting, because though I was born in Georgia in 1910, I have always had a feeling that in an indirect, nonsensory way I could remember what was still called "The War"—as if there had been no other. If I did not see the men in gray march off to battle, I saw great numbers of them march in parades on a Memorial Day which did not fall on the same day that was observed in the North. If I did not experience the rigors of life "behind the lines in the Southern Confederacy," I lived in the long backwash of the war in a land that remembered the past very vividly and somewhat inaccurately, because the present had nothing exciting to offer, and accuracy about either the past or the present was psychologically not very rewarding. . . . Certainly no longer a Southerner, I am not yet completely denatured.

Potter did as much as any other historian to help us understand the South and the causes of the Civil War, but his scholarly work was certainly not confined to those areas of historiography.

Potter's first major published work was *Lincoln and His Party in the Secession Crisis* (1942), which still is regarded as one of the better books on American political history. Potter set out to reevaluate the problems contemporaries encountered in the period from Lincoln's election to the southern attack on Fort Sumter. He found that most Republicans, including the newly elected Abraham Lincoln, no longer took Southern threats of secession very seriously. Southerners had threatened to secede many times before and had not done so. Why should the renewed threats in 1860 be any different? Even when several Southern states did secede, Lincoln believed the secessionists to be a minority. When it became clear their demands for the admission of slavery in the territories would not be met (and therefore he would not compromise or make concessions to them), Lincoln believed they would be discredited in the eyes of the majority of Southerners. What Potter showed was fallible human beings on all sides of the issues who, as they made the choices that appeared available to them, blundered into situations that had certainly not been clear at the beginning.

Potter's most comprehensive scholarly work appeared in print after his death. *The Impending Crisis, 1848–1861* (1976), completed and edited by his friend and colleague Don Fehrenbacher, was a sequel, of sorts, to the Lincoln book. Potter focused on the roots of the Civil War from the Mexican War in the late 1840s through the 1850s. As reviewer Thomas H. O'Connor (1976) wrote, the book was "a fascinating and sophisticated analysis of a wide range of alternatives that might have led the nation onto different paths. . . . Potter takes no outcome for granted and sees nothing as absolutely inevitable" (p. 211).

Some of Potter's best work appeared in collections of his essays. In a review of one of those collections, Martin Duberman (1971, pp. 75, 79) wrote:

> David Potter may be the greatest living historian of the United States . . . to read him is to become aware of a truth that only the greatest historians have been able to show us: that the chief lesson to be derived from a study of the past is that it holds no simple lesson, and that the historian's

main responsibility is to prevent anyone from claiming that is does.

As an epitaph for a historian, one could scarcely have better.

REFERENCES

Becker, Carl. 1913. "Some Aspects of the Influence of Social Problems upon the Study and Writing of History," *American Journal of Sociology,* 18, pp. 641–675.

Bordelon, Michael. 1983. "Eugene Genovese," in Clyde N. Wilson, ed. *Twentieth-Century American Historians,* Volume 17 of *Dictionary of Literary Biography.* Detroit: Gale Research Company.

Braeman, John. 1983. "Charles A. Beard," in Clyde N. Wilson, ed. *Twentieth-Century American Historians,* Volume 17 of *Dictionary of Literary Biography.* Detroit: Gale Research Company.

Carlton, Mark T. 1983. "David M. Potter," in Clyde N. Wilson, ed. *Twentieth-Century American Historians,* Volume 17 of *Dictionary of Literary Biography.* Detroit: Gale Research Company.

Curti, Merle. 1935a. "Review of Carl Becker, *Everyman His Own Historian: Essays on History and Politics,*" *American Historical Review,* 41, p. 117.

_____. 1935b. *The Social Ideas of American Educators: Report of the American Historical Association Commission on the Social Studies, Part 10.* New York: Charles Scribner's Sons.

Duberman, Martin. 1971. *The Uncompleted Past.* New York: E. P. Dutton.

Fass, Paula. 1983. "Richard Hofstadter," in Clyde N. Wilson, ed. *Twentieth-Century American Historians,* Volume 17 of *Dictionary of Literary Biography.* Detroit: Gale Research Company.

Higham, John. 1970. *Writing American History: Essays on Modern Scholarship.* Bloomington: University of Indiana Press.

Hofstadter, Richard. 1968. *The Progressive Historians: Turner, Beard, Parrington.* New York: Knopf.

O'Connor, Thomas P. 1976. "Review of David M. Potter, *The Impending Crisis,*" *America,* 134, p. 211.

Shryock, Richard. 1944. "Review of Merle Curti, *The Growth of American Thought,*" *American Historical Review,* 49, p. 732.

Skotheim, Robert Allen. 1966. *American Intellectual Histories and Historians.* Princeton, N.J.: Princeton University Press.

Historical Data

4

THIS CHAPTER CONTAINS examples of many different kinds of primary sources. Historians use these and other kinds of primary (and secondary) sources to reconstruct the past. The intent of the chapter is fourfold. First, we want you to be aware of the great variety of materials that comprise the historical record of human activity. Second, we want to introduce you to the uses and limitations of specific kinds of primary sources. Not all sources are equally reliable; each type of source has its strengths and weaknesses; each type of source must be handled by the historian in different ways.

Third, we think that you should know that any one source (or even many of the same types of source) is usually not adequate evidence upon which to base reliable history. Historians use multiple sources in order to achieve as complete an image of the past as possible, to cross-check one source against others, and to verify the truthfulness and possible bias of specific sources, among other things. Fourth, we want you to be aware that primary sources are not simply inert objects, truth just lying around to be discovered. In other words, not only does the historian need his or her facts to produce history, but the facts need their historian before they are of any value to anyone. The historian must closely question each source, much like a trial lawyer questions a witness. Only through such open dialog with the sources is the historian able to discover their usefulness and validity.

Each of the following primary sources is prefaced by a description of the source and some of the questions that a historian should ask about such sources. The sources are quite varied; the topics about which the sources deal are also quite different. Yet we have obviously only scratched the surface. There are many other types of primary historical sources that, because of limitations of space, have not been included in this chapter. For example, we have not included excerpts of sermons, literature, business account books, or foreign policy pronouncements. In addition, we have not been able to include sources that relate to many of the important topics in U.S. history. There are literally thousands of worthy historical topics, and we can obviously mention only a few. Despite these limitations, we hope this excursion into the historical record is both interesting and enjoyable.

One final word is in order. In the following sources, we have retained the original language, punctuation, capitalization, and so forth. This may make the sources somewhat more difficult to read than if we had modernized the language, but it allows you to experience the sources as historians do. Don't be dismayed as you enter the working world of the historian.

Promotional Tract

Advertising and promotion have been a part of U.S. history from the beginning of European settlement. The primary question you should consider when reading the following source is to what extent can such tracts be used as accurate evidence by historians. To what extent do those who write promotional tracts accurately represent the situation they describe? To what extent can the historian control for bias and exaggeration in such sources? Does the historian discount such evidence because of its obvious bias or are there ways to read between the lines to get clues about the actual situation?

In the following excerpt, John Hammond, a resident and enthusiastic promoter of the Chesapeake region (Virginia and Maryland), describes in rather glowing terms the opportunities available to immigrants to the region. Knowing Hammond wanted to promote immigration, how useful do you think this document would be for understanding life in the Chesapeake region in 1660?

Those Servants that will be industrious may in their time of service gain a competent estate before their Freedomes, which is usually done by many, and they gaine esteeme and assistance that appear so industrious: There is no Master almost but will allow his Servant a parcell of clear ground to plant some Tobacco in for himself, which he may husband at those many idle times he hath allowed him and not prejudice, but rejoyce his Master to see it, which in time of Shipping he may lay out for commodities, and in Summer sell them again with advantage, and get a Sow-Pig or two, which any body almost will give him, and his Master suffer him to keep them with his own, which will be no charge to his Master, and with one years increase of them may purchase a Cow Calf or two, and by that time he is for himself; he may have Cattle, Hogs, and Tobacco of his own, and come to live gallantly; but this must be gained (as I said) by Industry and affability, not by sloth nor churlish behaviour.

And whereas it is rumoured that Servants have no lodging other then on boards, or by the Fire side, it is contrary to reason to believe it: First, as we are Christians; next as people living under a law, which compels as well the Master as the Servant to perform his duty; nor can true labour be either expected or exacted without sufficient cloathing, diet, and lodging; all which both their Indentures (which most inviolably be observed) and the Justice of the Country requires.

But if any go thither, not in a condition of a Servant, but pay his or her passage, which is some six pounds: Let them not doubt but it is money well layed out (yet however, let them not fail) although they carry little else to take a Bed along with them, and then few Houses but will give them entertainment, either out of curtesie, or on reasonable tearms; and I think it better for any that goes over free, and but in a mean condition, to hire himself for reasonable wages of Tobacco and Provision, the first year, provided he happen in an honest house, and where the Mistresse is noted for a good Housewife, of which there are very many (notwithstanding the cry to the contrary) for by that means he will live free of disbursment, have something to help him the next year, and be carefully looked to in his sicknesse (if he chance to fall sick) and let him so covenant that exceptions may be made, that he work not much in the hot weather, a course we alwayes take with our new hands (as they call them) the first year they come in.

If they are women that go after this manner, that is paying their own passages; I advise them to sojourn in a house of honest repute, for by their good carriage, they may advance themselves in marriage, by their ill, overthrow their fortunes; and although loose persons seldome live long unmarried if free; yet they match with as desolate as themselves, and never live handsomly or are ever respected. . . .

The Country is very full of sober, modest persons, both men and women, and many that truly fear God and follow that perfect rule of our blessed Saviour, to do as they would be done by; and of such a happy inclination is the Country, that many who in England have been lewd and idle, there in emulation or imitation (for example moves more then precept) of the industry of those they finde there, not onely grow ashamed of their former courses, but abhor to hear of them, and in small time wipe off those stains they have formerly been tainted with; yet I cannot but confesse, there are people wicked enough (as what Country is free) for we know some natures will never be reformed, but . . . if any be known, either to prophane the Lords day or his Name, be found drunk, commit whoredome, scandalize or disturb his neighbour, or give offence to the world by living suspiciously in any bad courses; there are for each of these, severe and wholsome laws and remedies made. . . .

The profit of the country is either by their labour, their stockes, or their trades.

By their labours is produced corne and Tobacco, and all other growing provisions, and this Tobacco however how low-rated, yet a good maintenance may be had out of it.

Of the increase of cattle and hoggs, much advantage is made, by selling biefe, porke, and bacon, and butter &c. either to shipping, or to send to the Barbadoes, and other Islands, and he is a very poor man that hath not sometimes provision to put off.

By trading with Indians for Skine, Beaver, Furres and other commodities oftentimes good profits are raised; The Indians are in absolute subjection to the English, so that they both pay tribute to them and receive all their severall king from them, and as one dies they repaire to the English for a successor, so that none neede doubt it a place of securitie.

Several ways of advancement there are and imployments both for the learned and laborer, recreation for the gentry, traffique for the adventurer, congregations for the ministrie (and oh that God would stir, up the hearts of more to go over, such as would teach good doctrine, and not paddle in faction, or state matters; they could not want maintenance, they would find an assisting, an imbracing, a conforming people.)

(Source: John Hammond, "Leah and Rachel, or, the Two Fruitful Sisters, Virginia and Mary-land," in Peter Force, comp., *Tracts and Other Papers* [4 vols., 1836–1846], vol. 3, no. 14, pp. 14–16, 19–20.)

Legislative Resolutions

Resolutions of legislative bodies are a kind of government document, and one might therefore assume such documents have some special veracity attached to them. Resolutions, however, often do not carry the force of law. Usually they are intended to declare some sort of principle, often to sway opinion or to warn other persons of possible action. The following two documents show you two forms of the same set of resolutions: one as printed in the official *Journal of the House of Burgesses of Virginia,* the other as printed in the *Newport Mercury.*

In late May 1765, Patrick Henry rose in the Virginia House of Burgesses to introduce a series of resolutions for that body's consideration. The British had only recently enacted the Stamp Act, which would tax all paper goods and legal documents used in the colonies and which would, in the colonists' eyes, severely affect virtually all areas of their lives.

Part of what colonists perceived to be a conspiracy against their liberty, the Stamp Act produced a wave of negative reactions. It appeared that British law would be challenged throughout the North American colonies. Read after two hundred years, Henry's resolves seem tame enough. But in the context of the times, many perceived them to be radical, indeed. In addition, the Virginia legislature passed only the first four of Henry's resolutions, but the newspapers in other colonies printed all seven as though all had been passed. As you read both sets of resolutions, ask yourself what difference did it make that two versions were printed.

The Resolutions as Printed in the
Journal of the House of Burgesses of Virginia

Resolved, that the first Adventurers and Settlers of this his Majesty's Colony and Dominion of Virginia brought with them, and transmitted to their Posterity, and all other his Majesty's Subjects since inhabiting in this his Majesty's said Colony, all the Liberties, Privileges, Franchises, and Immunities, that have at any Time been held, enjoyed, and possessed, by the people of Great Britain.

Resolved, That by two royal Charters, granted by King James the First, the Colonists aforesaid are declared entitled to all Liberties, Privileges, and Immunities of Denizens and natural Subjects, to all Intents and Purposes, as if they had been abiding and born within the Realm of England.

Resolved, That the Taxation of the People by themselves to represent them, who can only know what Taxes the People are able to bear, or the easiest Method of raising them, and must themselves be affected by every Tax laid on the People, is the only Security against a burthensome Taxation, and the distinguishing Characteristick of British Freedom, without which the ancient Constitution cannot exist.

Resolved, That his Majesty's liege People of this his most ancient and loyal Colony have without Interruption enjoyed the inestimable Right of being governed by such Laws, respecting their internal Polity and Taxation, as are derived from their own Consent, with the Approbation of their Sovereign, or his Substitute; and that the same hath never been forfeited or yielded up, but hath been constantly recognized by the Kings and People of Great Britain.

(Source: John Pendleton Kennedy, ed., 1907, *Journals of the House of Burgesses of Virginia, 1761–1765*, Richmond, Va.: The Colonial Press, E. Waddey Company, p. 360.

The Resolutions as Printed in the
Newport Mercury, June 24, 1765

Whereas the Hon. House of Commons, in England, have of late drawn into Question, how far the General Assembly of this Colony hath Power to enact Laws for laying of Taxes and imposing Duties, payable by the People of this his Majesty's most antient Colony: For settling and ascertaining the same to all future Times, the House of Burgesses of this present General Assembly have come to the following Resolves:—

Resolved, That the first Adventurers, Settlers of this his Majesty's Colony and Dominion of Virginia brought with them and transmitted to their Posterity, and all other his Majesty's Subjects since inhabiting in this his Majesty's said Colony, all the Privileges and Immunities that have at any Time been held, enjoyed and possessed by the people of Great-Britain.

Resolved, That by two Royal Charters, granted by King James the First, the Colony aforesaid are declared and entitled to all Privileges and Immunities of natural born Subjects, to all Intents and Purposes, as if they had been abiding and born within the realm of England.

Resolved, That his Majesty's liege People of this his antient Colony have enjoy'd the Right of being thus govern'd, by their own Assembly, in the Article of Taxes and internal Police; and that the same have never been forfeited, or any other Way yielded up, but have been constantly recogniz'd by the King and People of Britain.

Resolved, therefore, That the General Assembly of this Colony, together with his Majesty or his Substitutes, have, in their Representative Capacity, the only exclusive Right and Power to lay Taxes and Imposts upon the Inhabitants of this Colony: And that every Attempt to vest such Power in any other Person or Persons whatever, than the General Assembly aforesaid, is illegal, unconstitutional and unjust, and have a manifest Tendency to destroy British as well as American Liberty.

Resolved, That his Majesty's liege People, the Inhabitants of this Colony, are not bound to yield Obedience to any Law or Ordinance whatever, designed to impose any taxation whatsoever upon them, other than the Laws or Ordinances of the General Assembly aforesaid.

Resolved, That any Person, who shall, by speaking or writing, assert or maintain, that any Person or Persons, other than the General Assembly of this Colony, have any Right or Power to impose or lay any Taxation on the People here, shall be deemed an Enemy to his Majesty's Colony.

(Source: *Newport Mercury,* June 24, 1765.)

Eyewitness Accounts

The following two documents each give an "official" account of the battle that marked the first fighting of the American Revolution. One was written from an American point of view, the other by the British Army officer in charge of the troops who marched on Lexington. As you read the documents, ask yourself how each account of the events of April 18 and April 19, 1775, differs from the other. How do you interpret the differences? Which one (if either) might be seen as more accurate than the other, and why? To what extent are both accounts entirely truthful? To what extent do assumptions (about life, values, the good, the true, the beautiful) account for different truths from the same or similar information or observations?

From the Provincial Congress at Watertown, Massachusetts, April 26, 1775

Friends and fellow subjects—Hostilities are a length commenced in this colony by the troops under the command of general Gage, and it being of the greatest importance, that an early, true, and authentic account of this inhuman proceeding should be known to you, the congress of this colony have transmitted the same, and from want of a session of the hon. continental congress, think it proper to address you on the alarming occasion.

By the clearest depositions relative to this transaction, it will appear that on the night preceding the nineteenth of April instant, a body of the king's troops, under the command of colonel Smith, were secretly landed at Cambridge, with an apparent design to take or destroy the military and other stores, provided for the defence of this colony, and deposited at Concord—that some inhabitants of the colony, on the night aforesaid, whilst travelling peaceably on the road, between Boston and Concord, were seized and greatly abused by armed men, who appeared to be officers of general Gage's army; that the town of Lexington, by these means, was alarmed, and a company of the inhabitants mustered on the occasion—that the regular troops on their way to Concord, marched into the said town of Lexington, and the said company, on their approach, began to disperse—that, notwithstanding this, the regulars rushed on with great violence and first began hostilities, by firing on said Lexington company, whereby they killed eight, and wounded several others—that the regulars continued their fire, until those of said company, who were neither killed nor wounded, before the provincials fired on them, and provincials were again fired on by the troops, produced an engagement that lasted through the day, in which many of the provincials and more of the regular troops were killed and wounded.

To give a particular account of the ravages of the troops, as they retreated from Concord to Charlestown, would be very difficult, if not impracticable; let it suffice to say, that a great number of the houses on the road were plundered and rendered unfit for use, several were burnt, women in child-bed were driven by the soldiery naked into the streets, old men peaceably in their houses were shot dead, and such scenes exhibited as would disgrace the annals of the most uncivilized nation.

There, brethren, are marks of ministerial vengeance against this colony, for refusing, with her sister colonies, a submission to slavery; but they have not yet detached us from our royal sovereign. We profess to be his loyal and dutiful subjects, and so hardly dealt with as we have been, are still ready, with our lives and fortunes, to defend his person, family, crown and dignity. Nevertheless, to the persecution and tyranny of his cruel ministry we will not tamely submit—appealing to Heaven for the justice of our cause, we determine to die or be free. . . .

By order,
Joseph Warren, President

(Source: Hez. Niles, ed., 1822, *Principles and Acts of the Revolution,* New York: A. S. Barnes and Company, p. 350.)

Report of Lieutenant-Colonel Smith to Governor Gage, April 22, 1775

SIR,—In obedience to your Excellency's commands, I marched on the evening of the 18th inst. with the corps of grenadiers and light infantry for Concord, to execute your Excellency's orders with respect to destroying all ammunition, artillery, tents, &c, collected there, which was effected, having knocked off the trunnions of three pieces of iron ordnance, some new gun-carriages, a great number of carriage-wheels burnt, a considerable quantity of flour, some gun-powder and musquet-balls, with other small articles thrown into the river. Notwithstanding we marched with the utmost expedition and secrecy, we found the country had intelligence or strong suspicion of our coming, and fired many signal guns, and rung the alarm bells repeatedly; and were informed, when at Concord, that some cannon had been taken out of the town that day, that others, with some stores, had been carried three days before, which prevented our having an opportunity of destroying so much as might have been expected at our first setting off.

I think it proper to observe, that when I had got some miles on the march from Boston, I detached six light infantry companies to march with all expedition to seize the two bridges on different roads beyond Concord. On these companies' arrival at Lexington, I understand, from the report of Major Pitcairn, who was with them, and from many officers, that they found on a green close to the road a body of the country people drawn up in military order, with arms and accoutrements, and, as appeared after, loaded; and that they had posted some men in a dwelling and Meeting-house. Our troops advanced towards them, without any intention of injuring them, further than to inquire the reason of their being thus assembled, and, if not satisfactory, to have secured their arms; but they in confusion went off, principally to the left, only one of them fired before he went off, and three or four more jumped over a wall and fired from behind it among the soldiers; on which the troops returned it, and killed several of them. They likewise fired on the soldiers from the Meeting and dwelling-houses. . . . Rather earlier than this, on the road, a countryman from behind a wall had snapped his piece at Lieutenants Adair and Sutherland, but it flashed and did not go off. After this we saw some in the woods, but marched on to Concord without anything further happening. While at Concord we saw vast numbers assembling in many parts; at one of the bridges they marched down, with a very considerable body, on the light infantry posted there. On their coming pretty near, one of our men fired on them, which they returned; on which an action ensued, and some few were killed and wounded. In this affair, it appears that, after the bridge was quitted, they scalped and otherwise ill-treated one or two of the men who were either killed or severely wounded. . . . On our leaving Concord to return to Boston, they began to fire on us from behind the walls, ditches, trees, &c., which, as we marched, increased to a very great degree, and continued without intermission of five minutes altogether, for, I believe, upwards of eighteen miles; so that I can't think but it must have been a pre-concerted scheme in them, to attack the King's troops the first favorable opportunity that offered, otherwise, I think they could not, in as short a time from our marching out, have raised such a numerous body, and for so great a space of ground. Notwithstanding the enemy's numbers, they did not make one gallant attempt during so long an action, though our men were so very much fatigued, but kept under cover.

I have the honor, &c.,

F. Smith, Lieutenant-Colonel 10th Foot.

(Source: Massachusetts Historical Society, 1876, *Proceedings,* p. 350.)

Recollections

Samuel Breck (1771–1862) was the son of a wealthy Boston merchant. In 1792, he moved with his family to Philadelphia, which was then still the capital of the United States. He went on to lead a distinguished civic life. The document below is an excerpt from his personal recollections, which were published after his death. With this background in mind, several questions should be asked as you read this and similar sources. Under what circumstances were the recollections (or autobiography) published (who published them and why)? What do the facts of publication suggest about its author (class bias? an able observer? well-connected?)? Do persons of all social classes and ethnic and racial groups publish recollections, memoirs, or autobiographies in similar proportions? What does this suggest about such sources? Is the author equipped and able to make commentary on those topics included? When were the recollections written—contemporary with the events they describe, from notes, journals, letters, or from memory long after the fact?

I had scarcely become settled in Philadelphia when in July, 1793, the yellow fever broke out, and, spreading rapidly in August, obliged all the citizens who could remove to seek safety in the country. My father took his family to Bristol on the Delaware, and in the last of August I followed him. Having engaged in commerce, and having a ship at the wharf loading for Liverpool, I was compelled to return to the city on the 8th of September, and spend the 9th there. My business took me down to the Swedes' church and up Front street to Walnut street wharf, where I had my countinghouse. Everything looked gloomy, and forty-five deaths were reported for the 9th. In the afternoon, when I was about returning to the country, I passed by the lodgings of the Vicomte de Noailles, who had fled from the Revolutionists of France. He was standing at the door, and calling to me, asked me what I was doing in town. "Fly," said he, "as soon as you can, for pestilence is all around us." And yet it was nothing then to what it became three or four weeks later, when from the first to the twelfth of October one thousand persons died. On the twelfth a smart frost came and checked its ravages.

The horrors of this memorable affliction were extensive and heart-rending. Nor were they softened by professional skill. The disorder was in a great measure a stranger to our climate, and was awkwardly treated. Its rapid march, being from ten victims a day in August to one hundred a day in October, terrified the physicians, and led them into contradictory modes of treatment. They, as well as the guardians of the city, were taken by surprise. No hospitals or hospital stores were in readiness to alleviate the sufferings of the poor. For a long time nothing could be done other than to furnish coffins for the dead and men to bury them. At length a large house in the neighborhood was appropriately fitted up for the reception of patients, and a few preeminent philanthropists volunteered to superintend it. At the head of them was Stephen Girard, who has since become the richest man in America.

In private families the parents, the children, the domestics lingered and died, frequently without assistance. The wealthy soon fled; the fearless or indifferent remained from choice, the poor from necessity. The inhabitants were reduced thus to one-half their number, yet the malignant action of the disease increased, so that those who were in health one day were buried the next. The burning fever occasioned paroxysms of rage which drove the patient naked from his bed to the street, and in some instances to the river, where he was drowned. Insanity was often the last stage of its horrors.

The attendants on the dead stood on the pavement in considerable numbers soliciting jobs, and until employed they were occupied in feeding their horses out of the coffins which they had provided in anticipation of the daily wants. There speculators were useful, and, albeit with little show of feeling, contributed greatly to lessen, by competition, the charges of interment. . . . The whole number of deaths in 1793 by yellow fever was more than four thousand. Again it took place in 1797, '98 and '99, when the loss was six thousand, making a total in these four years of ten thousand.

(Source: H. E. Scudder, ed., 1876, *Recollections of Samuel Breck,* Philadelphia: Porter and Coates, pp. 193–196.)

Census Information

The practice of taking censuses is quite old, but the newly formed United States was the first country to begin taking systematic counts of its population every ten years. The Constitution adopted in 1787 called for a census in order to apportion taxes and representation. As a census report noted in 1908:

> The task of making the first enumeration of inhabitants was placed upon the President. Under this law the marshals of the several judicial districts were required to ascertain the number of inhabitants within their respective districts, omitting Indians not taxed, and distinguishing free persons . . . from all others; the sex and color of free persons; and the number of free males 16 years of age and over.
>
> The object of the inquiry last mentioned was, undoubtedly, to obtain definite knowledge as to the military and industrial strength of the country. This fact possesses special interest, because the Constitution directs merely an enumeration of inhabitants.

Two examples of census information follow. Figure 1 is a general summary table of the first census undertaken in 1790. As you look over this document, you should ask yourself what it tells you. How many slaves appear in the table and what was their distribution? How many free white males over 16 years of age? Why are white males separated as to age whereas free white women are not? How many other free persons appear in the table? Who are these persons? Others will no doubt occur to you as well.

The second census document, Figure 2, is a duplication of the manuscript census for one section of Boston in 1790. The manuscript census pages show the population house by house. What information about the population, living conditions, etc., can be gleaned from the manuscript census? If you had a complete set of such manuscript census pages, what could you do with them? What if you had them, not only for 1790, but for the succeeding 50 years—what could you tell about the population, household size, family size, etc.? How do you think historians have been able to use such sources?

Figure 1
1790 Census Summary Page

The Return for SOUTH CAROLINA having been made fince the foregoing Schedule was originally printed, the whole Enumeration is here given complete, except for the N. Weftern Territory, of which no Return has yet been publifhed.

DISTICTS	Free white Males of 16 years and upwards, including heads of families.	Free white Males under sixteen years.	Free white Females, including heads of families.	All other free persons.	Slaves.	Total.
Vermont	22435	22328	40505	255	16	85539
N. Hampſhire	36086	34851	70160	630	158	141885
Maine	24384	24748	46870	538	NONE	96540
Maſſachuſetts	95453	87289	190582	5463	NONE	378787
Rhode Iſland	16019	15799	32652	3407	948	68825
Conneƈicut	60523	54403	117448	2808	2764	237946
New York	83700	78122	152320	4654	21324	340120
New Jerſey	45251	41416	83287	2762	11423	184139
Pennſylvania	110788	106948	206363	6537	3737	434373
Delaware	11783	12143	22384	3899	8887	59094
Maryland	55915	51339	101395	8043	103036	319728
Virginia	110936	116135	215046	12866	292627	747610
Kentucky	15154	17057	28922	114	12430	73677
N. Carolina	69988	77506	140710	4975	100572	393751
S. Carolina	35576	37722	66880	1801	107094	249073
Georgia	13103	14044	25739	398	29264	82548
	807094	791850	1541263	59150	694280	3893635

Total number of Inhabitants of the United States exclufive of S. Weftern and N. Teiritory.	Free white Males of 21 years and upwards.	Free Males under 21 years of age.	Free white Females.	All other Perfons.	Slaves.	Total
S.W. territory	6271	10277	15365	361	3417	35691
N. Ditto	—	—	—	—	—	—

(Source: *Return of the Whole Number of Persons in the United States.* Philadelphia: J. Phillips, 1793. Courtesy: Bureau of the Census.)

Figure 2
Manuscript Page of Census for One Section of Boston, 1790

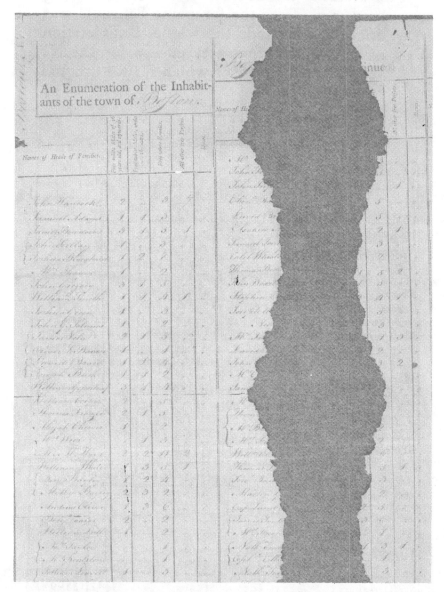

(Source: Boston, National Archives and Records Administration, Manuscript Census Schedule, 1790, State of Massachusetts, County of Suffolk, Town of Boston.)

Fugitive Documents

The following two documents are among those that might be termed fugitive or ephemeral documents. Such things as catalogs, broadsides, pamphlets, and fliers are examples of this type of source. Below is an advertisement for a slave sale that appeared in the Charleston, South Carolina, *City Gazette* on March 10, 1796. What can be learned about slavery from this document (and inferentially about other topics from similar documents)? What can be inferred about slavery from the advertisement? How useful are such documents? Would the existence of hundreds or thousands of such advertisements influence your (or the historian's) use of them as a primary source? What other sources might be necessary to follow up the clues contained in the document?

The second document, a poster that was tacked to a post in Maryland in 1800, also contains some interesting information about slavery. What does this document tell us about Peter the slave? Does the information support or refute your image of slaves and slavery? How useful might such documents be to the historian? What other documents are necessary to flesh out the picture of slavery?

FIFTY PRIME NEGROES FOR SALE. To be Sold, on Tuesday the 15th March instant, by the Subscribers, before their office near the Exchange.

About fifty prime orderly Negroes; consisting of Fellows, Wenches, Boys and Girls. This gang taken together, is perhaps as prime, complete and valuable for the number as were ever offered for sale; they are generally country born, young & able very likely; two of them capable of acting as drivers, and one of them a good jobbing carpenter. The wenches are young and improving; the boys, girls and children are remarkably smart, active and sensible: several of the wenches are fitted either for the house or plantation work; the boys and girls for trades or waiting servants. The age, descriptions and qualifications of these negroes, may be seen at the office of the Subscribers, and of Brian Cape and Son, or of Treasdale

or Kiddell, merchants, in Queen-street, who can give directions to those who desire it where the negroes may be seen.

These negroes are sold free from all incumbrances, with
warranted titles, and are sold on account of their present
Owner's declining the Planting Business, and not for any
other reason; they are not Negroes selected out of a larger
gang for the purpose of a sale, but are prime, their present
Owner, with great trouble and expence, selected them out of
many for several years past. They were purchased for stock
and breeding Negroes, and to any Planter who particularly
wanted them for that purpose, they are a very choice and
desirable gang. Any Person desirous of purchasing the whole
gang by private contract, may apply to Brian Cape and Son;
the Terms if sold together will be made convenient to the
Purchasers, and the Conditions of public sale (if not contracted for in the mean time, of which due notice will be
given) will be very easy and accommodating, and which will
be declared on the Day of Sale.

Colcock & Paterson

(Source: Charleston, South Carolina, *City Gazette,* March 10, 1796.)

THIRTY DOLLARS REWARD

Ran away last night, from the subscriber, living on the waters
of Little Pipe Creek near Westminster Town, Maryland, a tall,
well-made and active country born Negro Man, named
PETER, about 30 years of age, 5 feet 8 or 10 inches high,
wears the wool on the top of his head commonly platted, and
when loose is very long and bushy, but will likely have it cut
short: there remains the mark of a burn near the wrist, on
the back part of one of his hands, believed to be the right,
which he received when young; has a down look when spo-
ken to, but is a handsome erect figure, with smaller features
than is common for a Negro of his size and speaks German
nearly as well as English; he was brought up by me to plantation work chiefly, of which he is very capable; but can do a
little at blacksmith, shoemaking and carpenter's work, and has
some knowledge of making gun barrels—He had on and took
with him a fur hat about half worn; a homemade full'd lincy
doublet of a yellowish color, a swansdown jacket, with yellow
flannel backs and lining, a pair of tow-linnen trowsers, which

he wars very high and a pair of common half worn shoes, but as he is an artful fellow, and has money, it is expected he will soon exchange them. He also plays on the fiddle and fife tolerably well. Whoever takes up said Negro, and brings him home, shall receive if 15 miles from home 5 dollars; if 30 miles 10 dollars, if 60 miles 20 dollars, and if 100 miles or upwards the above reward, of 10 dollars if lodged in any goal, and notice given me thereof by a letter, directed to the Post Office, at Westminster, Frederick County, Maryland.

David Shriver
June 20, 1800

(Source: "The Shriver Papers," Maryland Historical Society.)

Commentaries by Foreign Visitors

Throughout our history, visitors from other countries have traveled through colonial America and the United States and have commented through letters, books, and other writings on what they observed. Jean de Crevecoeur, Alexis de Tocqueville, Fanny Trollope, and Charles Dickens, among others, were often trenchant observers of life here.

Historians have often used these sources, but these historians must deal with the following issues. First, foreign visitors may not possess the same blinders with respect to U.S. society as Americans. They may, therefore, be more objective observers or at least bring fresh comparative perspectives to those things they observe. Second, although they may possess such perspectives, they may also bring their own special biases to their observations. Third, the foreign visitors often are in the United States for only a short period of time. They therefore may see only a limited sample of cases upon which they base their conclusions. The generalizations they make may consequently be suspect.

We have included short excerpts from three such visitors to give you a sense of the variety of topics upon which they have commented.

Jean de Crevecoeur, a Frenchman who settled in New York, published a series of letters in which he commented on the process of how immigrants became transformed into "Americans." It might be interesting to compare this source with the Declaration of Principles of the Native American Convention on pp. 119–122.

It [America] is not composed, as in Europe, of great lords who possess every thing, and of a herd of people who have nothing. Here are no aristocratical families, no courts, no kings, no bishops, no ecclesiastical dominion, no invisible power giving to a few a very visible one; no great manufacturers employing thousands, no great refinements of luxury. The rich and the poor are not so far removed from each other as they are in Europe. Some few towns excepted, we are all tillers of the earth, from Nova Scotia to West Florida. We are a people of cultivators, scattered over an immense territory, communicating with each other by means of good roads and navigable rivers, united by the silken bands of mild government, all respecting the laws, without dreading their power, because they are equitable. We are all animated with the spirit of an industry which is unfettered and unrestrained, because each person works for himself. If he travels through our rural districts he views not the hostile castle, and the haughty mansion, contrasted with the clay-built hut and miserable cabbin, where cattle and men help to keep each other warm, and dwell in meanness, smoke, and indigence. A pleasing uniformity of decent competence appears throughout our habitations. The meanest of our log-houses is dry and comfortable habitation. Lawyer or merchant are the fairest titles our towns afford; that of a farmer is the only appellation of the rural inhabitants of our country. It must take some time ere he can reconcile himself to our dictionary, which is but short in words of dignity, and names of honour. There, on a Sunday, he sees a congregation of respectable farmers and their wives, all clad in neat homespun, well mounted, or riding in their own humble wagons. There is not among them an esquire, saving the unlettered magistrate. There he sees a parson as simple as his flock, a farmer who does not riot on the labour of others. We have no princes, for whom we toil, starve, and bleed: we are the most perfect society now existing in the world. Here man is free as he ought to be; nor is this pleasing equality so transitory as many others are. Many ages will not see the shores of our great lakes replenished with inland nations, nor the unknown bounds of North America entirely peopled. Who can tell how far it extends? Who can tell the millions of men whom it will feed and contain? for no European foot has as yet travelled half the extent of this mighty continent!

The next wish of this traveller will be to know whence came all these people? they are a mixture of English, Scotch, Irish, French, Dutch, Germans, and Swedes. From this promiscuous breed, that race now called Americans have arisen.

In this great American asylum, the poor of Europe have by some means met together, and in consequence of various causes; to what purpose should they ask one another what countrymen they are? Alas, two thirds of them had no country. Can a wretch who wanders about, who works and starves, whose life is a continual scene of sore affliction or pinching penury; can that man call England or any other kingdom his country? A country that had no bread for him, whose fields procured him no harvest, who met with nothing but the frowns of the rich, the severity of the laws, with jails and punishments; who owned not a single foot of the extensive surface of this planet? No! urged by a variety of motives, here they came. Every thing has tended to regenerate them; new laws, a new mode of living, a new social system; here they are become men: in Europe they were as so many useless plants, wanting vegitative mould, and refreshing showers; they withered, and were mowed down by want, hunger, and war; but now by the power of transplantation, like all other plants they have taken root and flourished!

He is an American, who leaving behind him all his ancient prejudices and manners, receives new ones from the new mode of life he has embraced, the new government he obeys, and the new rank he holds. He becomes an American by being received in the broad lap of our great Alma Mater. Here individuals of all nations are melted into a new race of men, whose labours and posterity will one day cause great changes in the world.

(Source: Ludwig Lewisohn, ed., 1904, *Letters from an American Farmer,* New York: Fox, Duffield, pp. 48–56.)

Fanny Trollope came from England in 1827 to establish a store in Cincinnati, Ohio. Her observations created a furor on both sides of the Atlantic.

In Relating all I know of America, I surely must not omit so important a feature as the cooking. . . . The ordinary mode of living is abundant, but not delicate. They consume an extraordinary quantity of bacon. Ham and beef-steaks appear morning, noon, and night. In eating, they mix things together with the strangest incongruity imaginable. I have seen eggs and oysters eaten together; the sempiternal ham with apple-sauce; beef-steak with stewed peaches; and salt fish with onions. The bread is every where excellent, but they rarely enjoy it themselves, as they insist upon eating horrible half-baked hot rolls both morning and evening. The butter is tolerable, but they have seldom such cream as every little dairy produces in England; in fact, the cows are very roughly kept, compared with ours. Common vegetables are abundant and very fine. I never saw secale or cauliflowers, and either from the want of summer rain, or the want of care, the harvest of green vegetables is much sooner over than with us. They eat the Indian corn in a great variety of forms; sometimes it is dressed green, and eaten like peas; sometimes it is broken to pieces when dry, boiled plain, and brought to table like rice; this dish is called hominy. The flour of Indian corn is made into at least a dozen different sorts of cakes; but in my opinion all bad. This flour mixed in the proportion of one third with fine wheat, makes by far the best bread I ever tasted.

I never saw turbot, salmon, or fresh cod; but the rock and shad are excellent. There is a great want of skill in the composition of sauces; not only with fish, but with every thing. They use very few made dishes, and I never saw any that would be approved by our savants. They have an excellent wild duck, called the Canvas Back, which, if delicately served, would surpass the black cock; but the game is very inferior to ours; they have no hares, and I never saw a pheasant. They seldom indulge in second courses, with all their ingenious temptations to the eating a second dinner; but almost every table has its dessert (invariably pronounced desart), which is placed on the table before the cloth is removed, and consists of pastry, preserved fruits, and creams. They are "extravagantly fond", to use their own phrase, of puddings, pies, and all kinds of "sweets", particularly the ladies; but are by no means such connoisseurs in soups and ragouts as the gastronomes of Europe. Almost every one drinks water at table; and by a strange contradiction, in the country where hard drinking is more prevalent than in any other, there is less wine taken at dinner; ladies rarely exceed one glass, and the

great majority of females never take any. In fact, the hard
drinking so universally acknowledged, does not take place at
jovial dinners, but, to speak plain English, in solitary dram-
drinking. Coffee is not served immediately after dinner, but
makes part of the serious matter of tea-drinking, which
comes some hours later. Mixed dinner parties of ladies and
gentlemen are very rare, and unless several foreigners are
present, but little conversation passes at table. It certainly
does not, in my opinion, add to the well ordering a dinner
table, to set the gentlemen at one end of it, and the ladies at
the other; but it is very rarely that you find it otherwise.

Their large evening parties are supremely dull; the men
sometimes play cards by themselves, but if a lady plays, it
must not be for money; no ecarte, no chess; very little music,
and that little lamentably bad. Among the blacks I heard some
good voices, singing in tune; but I scarcely ever heard a
white American, male or female, go through an air without
being out of tune before the end of it; nor did I ever meet
any trace of science in the singing I heard in society. To eat
inconceivable quantities of cake, ice, and pickled oysters and
to show half their revenue in silks and satins, seem to be the
chief object they have in these parties.

(Source: Frances M. Trollope, 1904, *Domestic Manners of the Americans,* New
York: Howard Wilford Bell, pp. 267–269.)

Englishman Charles Mackay commented on a number of
aspects of American life in his two-volume book of observations.

The fire system, in nearly all the principal cities of the
Union, is a peculiarity of American life. Nothing like it exists
in any European community. As yet the city of Boston appears to be the only one that has had the sense and the
courage to organize the fire brigades on a healthier plan, and
bring them under the direct guidance and control of the municipality. Everywhere else the firemen are a power in the
State, wielding considerable political influence, and uncon-
trolled by any authority but such as they elect by their own
free votes. They are formidable by their numbers, dangerous
by their organization, and in many cities, are principally composed of young men at the most reckless and excitable age
of life, who glory in a fire as soldiers do in a battle, and who
are quite as ready to fight with their fellow-creatures as with

the fire which it is more particularly their province to subdue. In New York, Philadelphia, Baltimore, and other large cities, the fire service is entirely voluntary, and is rendered for "the love of the thing," or for "the fun of the thing," whichever it may be. . . .

The firemen are mostly youths engaged during the day in various handicrafts and mechanical trades, with a sprinkling of clerks and shopmen. In New York each candidate for admission into the force must be balloted for, like a member of the London clubs. If elected, he has to serve for five years, during which he is exempt from jury and militia duty. The firemen elect their own superintendents and other officers, by ballot, as they were themselves elected; and are divided into engine companies, hook and ladder companies, and hose companies. The engine and accessories are provided by the municipality; but the firemen are seldom contented with them in the useful but unadorned state in which they receive them, but lavish upon them an amount of ornament, in the shape of painted panels, silver plating, and other finery, more than sufficient to prove their liberality, and the pride they take in their business. . . .

The men—or "boys," as they are more commonly called— not only buy their own costume and accoutrements, and spend large sums in the ornamentation of their favourite engines, or hydrants . . . but in the furnishing of their bunk-rooms and parlours at the firestations. The bunk or sleeping rooms, in which the unmarried and sometimes the married, members pass the night, to be ready for duty on the first alarm of fire, are plainly and comfortably furnished; but the parlours are fitted up with a degree of luxury equal to that of the public rooms of the most celebrated hotels. At one of the central stations, which I visited . . . , the walls were hung with portraits of Washington, Franklin, Jefferson, Mason, and other founders of the Republic; the floor was covered with velvet-pile carpeting, a noble chandelier hung from the centre, the crimson curtains were rich and heavy, while the sideboard was spread with silver claret-jugs and pieces of plate, presented by citizens whose houses and property had been preserved from fire by . . . the brigade; or by the fire companies of other cities, in testimony of their admiration for some particular act of gallantry or heroism which the newspapers had recorded.

If the firemen be an "institution," Fire itself is an institution in most American cities. . . . Into whatever city the traveller goes, he sees the traces of recent conflagration; sometimes whole blocks . . . levelled to the ground, or presenting nothing but bare and blackened walls. So constant appears to be the danger that the streets of New York, Boston, and other cities, are traversed in all directions by telegraphic wires, which centre invariably at the City Hall, and convey instantaneously to headquarters, day or night, the slightest alarm of fire. . . .

The assertion is frequently made by Americans . . . that many fires are purposely caused by the "boys" for the sake of a frolic, or a run, or in a spirit of rivalry between two or more companies. . . . In Philadelphia and Baltimore alarms of fire are regularly expected on Saturday nights, when the "boys" have received their week's wages, and are ripe for mischief.

(Source, Charles Mackay, 1857, *Life and Liberty in America,* Vol. I, pp. 48–51, 54, 55.)

Diaries

Diaries and personal journals have long been used by historians to gain insight into the lives of their writers, often highly visible public figures. Increasingly, historians are finding and using such documents to help them reconstruct the daily lives of ordinary persons in U.S. history. An excerpt from one person's diary appears below.

Samantha Barrett was a 40-year-old woman living with her 81-year-old mother (Suzanna) and her older sister (Zeloda). They lived on and ran an 85-acre farm near New Hartford, Connecticut. As you read the following excerpt, ask yourself about the quality and nature of the author's daily life. What economic and social activities does Samantha describe? What circumstances influence the way she and her family live? What other evidence would you need to help you understand Samantha's life and circumstances and in what ways it might have been (or might not have been) typical? What limitations might characterize these types of sources? How typical was Samantha's experience and what things would you have to consider in order to make a judgment about this proposition (location, type of farm, single woman, etc.)?

1828

May

1   Pleasant and warm – making soap – Mr Hamlin calld – PM Loda visited Mrs Cowles – Leister came after some milk – evening read about the Greeks

3   Clouday – some rain – Loda carried four pounds 1/2 of butter to the store, one shilling a pound – thunder shower – raind hard – Mr Tyler, Mr Butler, Mr A Loomis, Mr Lyman – Cornelia cleared of worm – Roman and William came home — heard from Grove – evening – raind hard

6   Clouday – went to Mr Masons to borrow a trap – Abijah plowd our garden – fixd some fence – took down our hog pen – got out some manure – cut off our old cows tail – Mr Barnes workd in our garden – I went to Mr Butlers on an errand – Capt G Henderson had a barn raised – evening thundered and lightened and raind hard

10 Plesant – warped and got in a piece – Loda planted peas and beans in the garden – Capt H calld to get some squash seeds – Mr Munson did a job for us. Eveline came from Mr Loomis, staid all night –

13 Clouday – Mother and Loda rode out – I went to the store, carried nine 1/2 pounds butter, nine pence per pound – bought one pound tea – had our horse shod – wove – Mr B calld – few drops of rain – a trunk pedler calld – put up some fence – evening Mrs Holcomb gone to John Hendersons wedding – I sat up till she came home 11 oclock.

15 Raind – carried Mrs Barnes bonnet home, gave her some port – went to Mr Hunts, he gave me a order of ten shillings – visited the poor families – wove – Abijah, Mr Munson calld – evening visited Mrs H–

18 Sabbath – Clouday – Loda and myself attended meeting Mr Yale preached – classed the scholars for sabbath school – Mrs Ruth Henderson, Mrs Sarah Lord, Delia Cook asked for a letter of dismission from this church – meeting Thursday evening at the center school house –

20   Plesant – washd – Abijah plowing potatoes ground –
       lost one of our sheep – Mr Hamlin calld – sold Mr
       Munson one of our calves for three dollars, eight weeks
       old – E L came to make a visit, staid all night corner
       stone laid to NE meeting house.

June

2   Plesant – wove some – Alonson Spence calld wishing
       to by our lambs – PM Mrs Barnes made us a visit –
       evening Mr. Hamlin calld, sold him four pounds twelve
       ounces pork, paid 33 cents cash – wedding at Mr.
       Marsh – began to make cheese

5   Clouday, very – growing time – washd and cleand our
       floors – Mr Barnes pold part of our peas – PM thunder
       shower – rain hard – A trunk pedler calld – Huldah and
       Loda traded with him – Roman started for Boston –
       sent a letter to Grove

6   Very warm weather – Mr Woodruf sheared our sheep
       and Mr Steel sheard Groves – borrowed some tar to
       Mr Munsons to mark our sheep – finished weaving Mrs
       Segars piece, nine yards – PM Mrs Wheeler and Laura
       Steel visited here – lent Laura my 3 to reed – evening
       constant visiter calld

7   Plesant – finished picking wool – Levi cut wood for us,
       paid him in pork and bread. Mr. Hamlin mended my
       shoes, price twenty cents – evening hard thunder
       shower –

11   In the morning clouday – rode to the carding machine –
       had my wool carded, eight pounds – Mother visited sis-
       ter Loomis – spun fifteen knots – Loda went after
       mother – PM calld

17   Clouday and very warm – Mr Barnes cut poles and
       pold our beans – let him have one gallon cider, some
       pork and cheese – Loda rode to Calvins – showers of
       rain –

July

2   Plesant – finished spinning my wool, had 21 knots –
       washed it out – PM Mrs Holcomb and myself rode to
       ward lot – salted our creatures – drank tea at Capt
       Hendersons with the Widow Ruth and she that was Ma-
       nerva Mather – evening Elmina Clark Nelson and Mr
       Hamlin here – sat up till most eleven

3   Very warm – Mrs Dowd very poor – spoold and warpd piece – Nath calld – PM Emeline made us a short visit – fixing for independence – went with her as far as Mr Munsons – raind – Abijah borrowed some grain of us, carried it to mill – evening Lucia Clee

8   Clouday part of the day – turned and raked hay – Mr Hamlin helped – got in two loads – Grove helped – drove our heifers to wardlot – drove our sheep home – paid Mr Hamlin in pork – raind – evening a hard thunder shower with sharp lightening – Mr Dowd staid all night

11   Raind very hard – Mr Butler calld – Mr Hamlin came for his pay for work – let him have four pounds seven of pork, three pounds butter, three of sheese – got in Mr Benhams piece – went to Mr. Barnes on an errand – sun shind very warm – PM Major Johnson calld – raind – Loda rode to Mr Rogers

16   Clouday and rainey – finished weaving Mr Benhams piece, fifteen yards – Nath set a trap in our orcheard to cetch a wood chuck – PM Mr Cowles calld, let him have a quart of brandy to pay for making open shed

21   Very warm — Mr Gird came after Groves lambs, came before four, bought eleven, paid twelve dollars 37 cents – Loda rode to the carding mill, got our wool carded, returned half after eight –

31   In the morning a very hard thunder shower – lightened very sharp – clear of pleasant – Loda and myself rode to Canton, bought at Mygots one fance handkerchief, 6-9, sold two pairs of socks, four shillings – one pair thread stockings

August

15   Plesant, cool wind – wove – Nath calld – I began to cross plow – PM Margaret and the babe visited here – Mrs Holcomb a while – Mrs. H. Loda and myself visited at Mr Butlers, found him sick

22   Warm weather – wove six yards and quild my quils – PM made Mrs Barnes a short visit, drank tea – evening made Mrs Holcomb a visit – Mr Hamlin there

26   To hot weather to work – wove some – cooked a wood chuck – Jason here – Grove and Jason drove red

October

2   In the morning raind – cleard of, plesant – wove – a
    great cattle show at Harwington, about seven hundred
    yoke – Mrs Steel brought me a blanket to weave –
    evening helped Mrs Holcomb husk

3   Plesant – wove nine yards – Mr Steel brought us some
    wood – Emeline came here to spin, spun two runs –
    paid our taxes to Henry Seymour, 5 dollars 64 cents –
    evening Loda and myself helped Mrs H husk – had Mr
    H company

10 Clouday – wove – Grove calld – Mr More and Lucian
    Henderson wishing to by beef chestnut – evening
    braided a foot mat –

11 Clouday – Loda and myself rode to Canton – sold my
    flannel for two and nine pence per yard – sold thirteen
    pair of socks, one and nine pence per pair – bought
    two gallons molasses, two pounds shugar, one set of
    knives and forks, five and six pence, two broms, some
    fish and one yard of mull — raind – Cornelia went
    home –

22 Warm as summer – Let Mr Hamlin have three pounds
    pork – Had three mackeril and some money – Mr H eat
    breakfast, cut us some wood – Loda went to the store
    and to Mr Yales, got some corn –

31 Warm and plesant – wove – Mother made bread out of
    our new grain – evening – Loda visited Mrs Munson – I
    spoold Mrs Steels piece

November

11 Very warm – Abijah cut and salted our pork – let Mr
    Root have eighteen pounds for a pig – Mr Ballard and
    Aunt T and Eveline made a short visit – Lydia Rogers
    brought my shoes home – PM attended the monthly
    meeting on ministers – carried Mr Yale, a stranger, Mr
    Reach a piece of fresh pork – ministers preached
    Clark, Marsh, Pierce and two more – clouday – evening
    churned

13 Plesant – went to Mrs Woodruffs – spoold and warped
    Mrs Goodwins piece – Mr Rogers brought us a load of
    wood – Made us a pig pen, banked our house – let
    him have some pork – Mr Hotchkis mended our flue – I
    went to Mr Roots and got a pig – Zachariah Spencer

warned us to do a highway tax – evening Mrs. Holcomb and myself went to Mr Hamlins, had his company back

17 Snowd, cold – wove nine yeards – a trunk pedler calld – traded nine cents – Grove got us some wood – Julia Cowles called – evening Grove helped cut sassage meat – staid all night – began to stable our creatures – frose in the house

19 Snowd hard – Loda rode to the store – got some pepper and spice, carried some butter to pay for them – wove out Mr Goodwins piece, 27-1/2 yards – filled our sassage, 45 pounds – evening Mrs H and myself went to Mr Rogers

24 Plesant and warm – washd – see a flock of wild geese – Mrs Holcomb let me have two bushels of corn to pay for an ox halve and knitting her stockins – evening knit

26 Plesant – finished Mrs Jeromes piece – Grove dressed a pig for Mrs Holcomb – Henry Seymour had a child burned today – Mr and Mrs Barnes here – evening clouday – baked our chickens pies

December

4 Warm – wove – sold Mr Smith four hundred and five pounds cheese for twenty four dollars thirty cents – Mr Hotckis came to do our chimney, took it down – traded with a trunk pedler, bought a pair of clasps to put on my cloak, gave nine pence

24 Another plesant day – carded some tow for candle wicks – knit – Loda went to Mr Hamlins – visited at Mr Loomis – Lucia calld – evening Loda watchd with Mrs Dowd

26 Plesant and warmer – made ten pounds of candles – bought one quart osters of Mr Cleveland, 16 cents – evening knit – stad with Mrs H

30 Morning plesant – Loda and myself attended Mrs Dowds funeral – Mr Yale preached – Mrs Dowd aged 38 – wind very high when we came home and continues – evening Edward Seymour brought potatoes enough to balance my account with him — I went with Huldah to Mr Masons – visited their – wind very high and very cold—

1829

January

2   Clouday – knit – Mr Barnes calld – Mrs Boot the
    mother of another son – Mr A Spencer and wife calld
    again – PM I attended the preparatory lecter Mr Yale
    Preached – snow very hard – very cold – evening knit
    – very cold night

4   Snowd – weather some warmer – evening Mrs Holcomb
    – Mr H calld again, sold him 25 cents worth of butter,
    gave him some bread and milk

11 Plesant but cold – staid from meeting on account of
    slipry going – a traviling man calld to warm, staid untill
    Monday – Mr Marsh preachd – Mr N Kelloggs babe
    died Saturday night –

23 Plesant and warm – Knit – PM I attended a meeting for
    prayer and to chose a new Deacon – made choice of
    Capt Cook – Horace Kellogg had seven votes and Se-
    lah Woodruff six – Mr Yale made two prayers, Deacon
    Goodwin one, Deacon Adams one and Capt Marsh
    some conversation respecting the low state of the
    church

29 Snowd – Abijah calld going to mill – Celestia calld with
    a subscription paper to get money to by Mr Yale some
    cloth, Loda and myself signed 25 cents – PM plesant –
    Hulday Barnes visited here – evening knit –

(Reprinted with permission of Old Sturbridge Village, Sturbridge, Massachusetts.)

Private Correspondence

Of all primary historical sources, personal letters may be the most perverse. Why perverse? On one hand, they may be documents closest in time and place to an event or to ordinary people's lives. Before the widespread (and inexpensive) use of telecommunications, most personal long-distance interaction occurred by letter. Up to current times, then, millions of letters documented people's lives. A level of intimacy and thoughtfulness often attached to letter writing as well—at least as compared with telephone conversations.

On the other hand, letters are also written for many purposes other than exchanging pleasantries and family or business information. The most obvious case might be the letter designed for the public. Letters to the newspaper editor are one type of these, but public figures often write such letters to solicit public reaction or make themselves look good. Others, aware that their papers (including letters) will be collected and deposited in archives, therefore may write letters that, again, may be self-serving and misleading.

Letters may be useful in a variety of ways. One is to gain insight into one person's thoughts or feelings. Another is to use letters more expansively "across people" who have had similar experiences, such as immigrants, slaves, or pioneers.

When we think of the westward movement before the Civil War, the image is most often of the migration into the north-western territories (Ohio, Indiana, Illinois, and Kentucky) and such trans-Mississippi states as Iowa, Kansas, and Nebraska. Less frequently, we think of a westward movement into the old south-west, especially Alabama, Mississippi, Louisiana, and Arkansas. There was, however, a substantial movement of people into those southern regions. Farming methods and cotton, the primary staple crop, led to rapid soil exhaustion. Consequently, the plantation frontier also expanded westward. The following document, a letter from Eli H. Lide to a friend in March 1936, describes the early challenges of transplanting a plantation on the Alabama frontier.

We are all very busily engaged in clearing and planting, repairing &c. having not long since gotten thro: with building as many negro houses as will answer present purposes, untill we can steal a little time from other matters, which indeed seems hard to do, for there are so many things pressing upon us and wedging themselves upon every moment of time, that some times I dislike to take the necessary time to eat. Father has a house, but I have one to build for myself or put up with rather a poor chance of a house offered me by Major Lee as a place of refuge in case I shall not find time to build. Indeed I am affraid I shall not be able to get up cabbins sufficient, for I must attend to clearing land for I have but little open, and have not been able to rent more than about

from 30 to 35 acres and some of that poor, and have to give
$4 per acre rent for a part and five dollars for a part, which
looks like buying land. My man Rowell made but a poor out
clearing land last year, that which he pretended to clear he
only fell the smallest trees, without cutting up of trimming and
deaded but very few acres and a great many trees were cut
half round and left.

I had to do all this work over and indeed what he had
done was but of little advantage, if he had done his duty I
should have been able to have cleared 75 or 80 acres more
than I shall under existing circumstances. I expect to get 80
acres under fence this week, forty of which is now ready for
the plough, on the remaining forty the logs are yet to roll and
burn. I have nearly twenty acres more cut down and am now
burning the brush. Tomorrow however I stop to plant potatoes. I have planted about 25 acres of corn on rented land
and in a few days shall plant about five acres more, on which
last mentioned I hope to make 60 or seventy bushels per
acre. I shall be obliged to plant the greater part of my land
this year in corn as it is almost all new, and of such growth
as will not die the first year say 140 acres corn and about 90
in cotton so you see I can not do much this year. I expect to
keep about four or five hands clearing all summer, by doing
this I hope to get in as much land as I can cultivate another
year.

I have been all this while holding up to your view the dark
side of the subject. I will now let you take peep at what I call
the bright side, we live in a delightful neighborhood a kind of
village place something like Society Hill not quite so dense a
population but far more numerous which in point of intelligence is inferiour to none. As to health from all the information which I can gather it must be equal to the hills of
Chesterfield the people here say equal to any in the world, of
this however I prefer to be no judge but can see no local
cause for sickness. Here is natural scenery which is grand
and sublime, entirely superior to any thing I saw on the Blue
Ridge, as to the soil it would do your very heart good to look
at it.

I have between 1800 and two thousand acres of land here
which is too much for me. I some times think of selling 480
acres but am affraid to offer it for fear some one will want to
purchase it. I put out a negro boy to learn the Blacks[mith]
trade for whom I get $150 dollars a year hire. Corn is worth
from 75/100 to 1.00 per bushel and scarce at that price.

(Source: Fletcher M. Green, ed., 1952, *The Lides Go South . . . and West. The Record of a Planter Migration in 1835,* Columbia, S.C.: U. of South Carolina Press, pp. 15–17.)

Legal Documents

L aws, as seen through law enforcement, legal opinions, and court rulings, are important sources of information about any society. Laws are rules by which people live together. As such, they are good indicators of social values—how a society views itself, what it strives to be, and the ideals that govern its day-to-day existence. Oftentimes, individual behavior does not conform to these ideals, and it is at this point that the historian can tell a great deal about what a society will or will not tolerate and what its values are.

In addition, there is often disagreement, particularly in a pluralistic society such as the United States, about what these ideals are or what the rules should be. Studying laws and their enforcement allows us to understand a great deal about a society. Accordingly, historians have long used court records and legal opinions in their research.

The following Supreme Court ruling, written by then Chief Justice John Marshall, gives us insight into the differences of opinion concerning white–native American relations as well as the conflict between state and federal government in the 1820s and 1830s. As you read this and similar documents, you should approach it using a "case study" method. That is, you should ascertain what the facts of the case are, what issues are seen as most important, what arguments are put forth to clarify the issues, and what judgment was rendered. In addition, you should be thinking about what effect this case had. President Andrew Jackson is reported to have said "John Marshall has made his opinion, now let him enforce it." Given the U.S. system of government, what was the implication of Jackson's comment? Finally, what additional information might you need to understand this episode in American history?

WORCESTER v. GEORGIA
6 Peters, 515
1832

Marshall, C. J.: This cause, in every point of view in which it can be placed, is of the deepest interest.

The defendant is a State, a member of the Union, which has exercised the powers of government over a people who deny its jurisdiction, and are under the protection of the United States.

The plaintiff is a citizen of the State of Vermont, condemned to hard labor for four years in the penitentiary of Georgia under color of an act which he alleges to be repugnant to the Constitution, laws, and treaties of the United States.

The legislative power of a State, the controlling power of the Constitution and laws of the United States, the rights, if they have any, the political existence of a once numerous and powerful people, the personal liberty of a citizen, all are involved in the subject now to be considered. . . .

We must inquire and decide whether the act of the Legislature of Georgia under which the plaintiff in error has been prosecuted and condemned, be consistent with, or repugnant to the Constitution, laws and treaties of the United States.

It has been said at the bar that the acts of the Legislature of Georgia seize on the whole Cherokee country, parcel it out among the neighboring counties of the State, extend her code over the whole country, abolish its institutions and its laws, and annihilate its political existence.

If this be the general effect of the system, let us inquire into the effect of the particular statute and section on which the indictment is founded.

It enacts that "all white persons, residing within the limits of the Cherokee Nation on the 1st day of March next, or at any time thereafter, without a license or permit from his excellency the governor . . . and who shall not have taken the oath hereinafter required, shall be guilty of a high misdemeanor, and upon conviction thereof, shall be punished by confinement to the pentientiary at hard labor for a term not less than four years." . . .

The extraterritorial power of every Legislature being limited in its action to its own citizens or subjects, the very passage of this act is an assertion of jurisdiction over the Cherokee

Nation, and of the rights and powers consequent on jurisdiction.

The first step, then, in the inquiry which the Constitution and the laws impose on this court, is an examination of the rightfulness of this claim. . . .

From the commencement of our government Congress has passed acts to regulate trade and intercourse with the Indians; which treat them as nations, respect their rights, and manifest a firm purpose to afford that protection which treaties stipulate. All these acts, and especially that of 1802, which is still in force, manifestly consider the several Indian nations as distinct political communities, having territorial boundaries, within which their authority is exclusive, and having a right to all the lands within those boundaries, which is not only acknowledged, but guaranteed by the United States. . . .

The Cherokee Nation, then, is a distinct community, occupying its own territory, with boundaries accurately described, in which the laws of Georgia can have no force, and which the citizens of Georgia have no right to enter but with the assent of the Cherokees themselves or in conformity with treaties and with the acts of Congress. The whole intercourse between the United States and this nation is, by our Constitution and laws, vested in the government of the United States.

The act of the State of Georgia under which the plaintiff in error was prosecuted is consequently void, and the judgment a nullity. . . . The acts of Georgia are repugnant to the Constitution, laws, and treaties of the United States.

They interfere forcibly with the relations established between the United States and the Cherokee Nation, the regulation of which according to the settled principles of our Constitution, are committed exclusively to the government of the Union.

They are in direct hostility with treaties, repeated in a succession of years, which mark out the boundary that separates the Cherokee country from Georgia; guarantee to them all the land within their boundary; solemnly pledge the faith of the United States to restrain their citizens from trespassing on it; and recognize the pre-existing power of the nation to govern itself.

They are in equal hostility with the acts of Congress for regulating this intercourse, and giving effect to the treaties.

The forcible seizure and abduction of the plaintiff, who was residing in the nation with its permission, and by authority of the President of the United States, is also a violation of the acts which authorize the chief magistrate to exercise this authority. . . .

Judgment reversed.

Political Platform

Political sources such as candidates' speeches and party platforms must be used with caution, but they can be rich sources of information. As you read such political documents, you should ask questions such as what can a self-consciously political document tell us about a particular period? What was the factual basis of their arguments? What implications do the authors draw from their own evidence? What kinds of people might have supported these views and programs? In what ways may historians use such political documents?

Throughout U.S. history, some Americans (their numbers have varied greatly from time to time) have been concerned about what they perceived as the negative effects of immigration. With the arrival of increasing numbers of immigrants in the 1830s and 1840s, especially the Irish and the Germans, such concern grew apace. Nativism, as such anti-immigrant feeling is called, pervades the following document. This source was the declaration of principles established by the delegates of the first national convention of the Native American party. It was a clarion call to other Americans and was designed to announce and justify a set of historical facts and political agenda for action.

We, the delegates elect to the first national convention of the Native American people of the United States, assembled at Philadelphia on the fourth day of July, 1845, for the purpose of devising a plan of concerted political action in defence of American institutions against the encroachments of foreign influence, open or concealed, we mutually pledge our lives, our fortunes, and our sacred honor.

The danger of foreign influence, threatening the gradual destruction of our national institutions, failed not to arrest the attention of the Father of his Country in the very dawn of American liberty. . . .

The influx of a foreign population, permitted, after little more than a nominal residence, to participate in the legislation of the country and the sacred right of suffrage, produced comparatively little evil during the earlier years of the republic; for that influx was then limited by the expenses of a trans-Atlantic voyage, by the existence of many wholesome re-straints upon the acquisition of political prerogatives, by the constant exhaustion of the European population in long and bloody continental wars, and by the slender inducements of-fered for immigration to a young and sparsely-peopled coun-try, contending for existence with a boundless wilderness, inhabited by savage men. Evils which are only prospective rarely attract the notice of the masses; and, until perculiar changes were effected in the political condition of Europe, the increased facilities for transportation, and the madness of par-tisan legislation, in removing all effective guards against the open prostitution of the right of citizenship, had converted the slender current of naturalization into a torrent, threatening to overwhelm the influence of the natives of the land; the far-seeing vision of the statesman only, being fixed upon the dis-tant, but steadily-approaching cloud.

"How shall the institutions of the country be preserved from the blight of foreign influence, insanely legalized through the conflicts of domestic parties?"

It is an incontrovertible truth, that the civil institutions of the United States of America have been seriously affected, and that they now stand in imminent peril from the rapid and enormous increase of the body of residents of foreign birth, imbued with foreign feelings, and of an ignorant and immoral character, who receive, under the present lax and unreason-able laws of naturalization, the elective franchise and the right of eligibility to political office.

In former years this body was recruited chiefly from the victims of political oppression, of the active and intelligent mercantile adventurers of other lands; and it then constituted a slender representation of the best classes of the foreign population, well fitted to add strength to the state, and capa-ble of being readily educated in the peculiarly American sci-ence of political self-government. Moreover, while welcoming the stranger of every condition, our laws then wisely de-manded of every foreign aspirant for political rights, a certifi-cate of practical good citizenship.

Thus tempted by the suicidal policy of these United States, and favored by the facilities resulting from the modern im-provements of navigation, numerous societies and corporate bodies in foreign countries have found it economical to trans-port to our shores, at public and private expense, the feeble, the imbecile, the idle and intractable; thus relieving the burdens resulting from the vices of the European social systems, by availing themselves of the generous errors of our own.

The mass of immigrants, formerly lost among the natives of the soil, has increased from the ratio of 1 in 40 to that of 1 in 7! A like advance in fifteen years will leave the natives of the soil a minority in their own land! Thirty years ago these strangers came by units and tens—now they swarm by thousands. (It is estimated that 300,000 will arrive within the present year.) Formerly, most of them sought only for an honest livelihood and a provision for their families, and rarely meddled with those institutions of which it was impossible they could comprehend the nature; now, each newcomer seeks political preferment, and struggles to fasten on the public purse with an avidity in strict proportion to his ignorance and unworthiness of public trust—having been SENT, as is clearly shown, for the purpose of obtaining political ascendencey in the government of the nation—having been SENT to exalt their allies to power—having been SENT to work a revolution from republican freedom to the assumed divine rights of monarchs.

From these unhappy circumstances has arisen an imperium in imperio—a body uninformed and vicious—foreign in feeling, prejudice, and manner, yet armed with a vast, and often a controlling influence over the policy of a nation whose benevolence it abuses and whose kindness it habitually insults. . . .

Whenever an attempt is made to restrain this fatal evil, native and adopted demagogues protest against it as an effort which threatens to deprive them of their most important tools; and such is the existing organization of our established political parties, that, should either of them essay the reform of an abuse which both acknowledge to be fraught with ruin, that party sinks, upon the instant, into a minority, divested of control and incapable of result.

From such causes has been derived a body, armed with political power, in a country of whose system it is ignorant, and for whose institutions it feels little interest, except for the purpose of personal advancement.

This body has formed and encouraged associations under foreign names, to promote measures of foreign policy, and to perpetuate foreign clannishness among adopted citizens of the United States, in contravention of that spirit of union and nationality, without which no people can legitimately claim a place among the nations of the earth.

It has employed the power of associations to embroil the people of this country in the political disputes of other lands with which the United States are anxious to encourage peace and amity.

It has introduced foreign emblems, not only of national, but of partisan character, in the civic processions and public displays of bodies of men, claiming the title of American citizens, and sworn to American fealty; by which means it has fomented frequent riot and murder.

It has adopted national costumes and national insignia foreign to the country, in arming and equipping military corps, constituting a part of the national guard, with its word of command in a foreign language, in open defiance of our military code; by which means it has weakened the discipline of the militia, and rendered it less available for defence in time of war.

It has formed and encouraged political combinations holding the balance of power between opposing parties; combinations which have offered their votes and influence to the highest bidder, in exchange for pledges of official position and patronage.

It has boasted of giving governors to our states and chief magistrates to the nation.

By serving as an unquestioning and uncompromising tool of executive power, it has favored a political centralism, hostile to the rights of the independent states and the sovereignty of the people.

It has facilitated the assumption by the national executive of the right to remove from office, without the consent of the senate, persons who only can be appointed with such consent; which assumption is an obvious evasion of the spirit of the constitution.

(Source: American Party, 1845, *Declaration of Principles . . . of the Native American Convention, assembled at Philadelphia, July 4, 1845*, New York: T. R. Whitney, pp. 4–7.)

Reports by Nonpublic Agencies

By 1850, New York City was occupied by 515,547 persons. Since its founding on Manhattan Island in the seventeenth century, space had always been in short supply, and consequently also housing. With substantial economic prosperity and a huge increase in immigration, especially from Ireland and Germany, the city was growing rapidly and living space became even more difficult to find. The following document was part of an 1853 report prepared by a private philanthropic organization in New York City called the Association for Improving the Condition of the Poor (AICP, founded in 1843). The report suggested the magnitude of the housing shortage in the city and three years later led to the first legislative investigation of housing in the city.

While reading this document, you should ask yourself who the people were who made up the AICP. Were they of the same or similar ethnic or racial background or of the same social class as those they studied? What were their motives for participating in AICP, altruistic or other concerns? Who actually wrote the report? Who did the research (if there was any)? What were their goals? Did their ends influence the prediction of the report? Again, what information would you like to have to cross-check this primary source?

Tenement Conditions, New York City, 1853

In the lower wards, there are thousands of poor persons, but comparatively few buildings suitable for their accommodation. Most of the houses are those which were formerly occupied by the wealthy who have removed up town. . . . Large rooms have been divided by rough partitions into dwellings for two or three families—each, perhaps, taking boarders, where they wash, cook, eat, sleep and die—many of them prematurely. . . . And in addition, night lodgers, consisting of homeless men, women and children, are not unfrequent, who for a trifling sum are allowed temporary shelter. There, huddled together, like cattle in pens, the inmates are subjected to the most debasing influences. . . . The resident poor in the First Ward have doubled since 1846; and . . . there are now . . . of that class needing relief, not less than fifteen thousand persons. . . .

When families of five, eight or ten persons . . . live in a contracted apartment, that is applied to every conceivable domestic use, and from fifteen to thirty such families in the same house—having the entry, stairway and yard in common, the last badly drained, perhaps unpaved, and the receptable of all deleterious and offensive things, it would be truly surprising if the tenants did not become filthy, reckless and debased, whatever might have been their previous habits and character. . . . How should members, often of different families and of different sex, sleep in the same room, nay often in the same bed, without danger? "I know," says one, "of nothing so demoralizing as the absence of private conveniences, and where there is a community of beds and bedrooms to all ages and both sexes." . . .

Says one witness: "The habits of a family are more depressed and deterioriated by the defect of their habitations, than the greatest pecuniary want to which they are subjected. The most cleanly and orderly female will invariably despond and relax her exertions under the influence of filth, damp and stench; and at length, ceasing to make farther effort, will probably sink into a noisy, discontented, rum-drinking slattern—the wife of a man who has no comfort in his house, the parent of children whose home is the street or the workhouse." . . . In regard to the proneness of such persons to intemperance, it is said, "That the dreadful depression consequent on ill health (the effect of crowded, filthy, badly ventilated dwellings), tempts these poor creatures with a force we cannot adequately appreciate, to have recourse to stimulating drink." . . . The connection of juvenile depravity which so fearfully abounds, with the wretched conditions of life described, is fully shown by the Chief of Police Reports, and is too obvious and direct to require remark.

(Source: Association for Improving the Condition of the Poor, 1853, *First Report of a Committee on the Sanitary Condition of the Laboring Classes in the City of New York with Remedial Suggestions,* New York, John F. Trow, pp. 7–9, 20–22.)

Songs

In trying to reconstruct the historical experience of ordinary people, historians have turned to a great variety of primary sources. One such source, not widely used, is song lyrics. The following source "Father, Dear Father, Come Home with Me Now" was a song written in 1864 by Henry C. Work. In this case, the intent of the song is fairly straightforward—it was written to promote temperance, that is, to encourage people not to drink alcohol. As you read the following lyrics, you should ask yourself the following questions. Given what song lyrics you know and sing, how seriously should we take song lyrics as a historical source? Do you think there may be a serious discrepancy between the songwriter's intent and the message or impact on the people who sing or hear the song? To what extent should song lyrics be taken literally and in what sense symbolically? Does the absence of music affect the impact of the song? Would it help to know how the song was used and who was (or was not) singing it?

"Father, Dear Father, Come Home with Me Now"

Father, dear father, come home with me now!
The clock in the steeple strikes one;
You said you were coming right home from the shop,
As soon as your day's work was done.
Our fire has gone out, our house is all dark,
and mother's been watching for you;
With poor brother Benny so sick in her arms,
Without you, oh, what can she do?
Come home! Come home! Come home!
Please, father, dear father, come home.

Father, dear father, come home with me now!
The clock in the steeple strikes two;
The night has grown colder and Benny is worse,
But he has been calling for you.
Indeed, he is worse, Ma says he will die,
Perhaps before morning shall dawn;
And this is the message she sent me to bring,
"Come quickly, or he will be gone."
Come home! Come home! Come home!
Please, father, dear father, come home.

Father, dear father, come home with me now!
The clock in the steeple strikes three;
The house is so lonely, the hours are so long,
For poor weeping mother and me.
Yes, we are alone, poor Benny is dead
And gone with the Angels of light;
And these were the very last words that he said,
"I want to kiss Papa good night."
Come home! Come home! Come home!
Please, father, dear father, come home.

Chorus

Hear the sweet voice of your own little child,
As she tearfully begs you to come!
Oh, who could resist this most pitiful pray'r,
"Please, father, dear father, come home!"

(Source: Henry C. Work, 1864, "Father, Dear Father, Come Home with Me Now.")

Testimony in Official Proceedings

Testimony given in official proceedings has been used extensively by historians. Because testimony is often given under oath, it is seen as being rather unimpeachable and less biased than other sources. But is it really? The following testimony was given by Conrad Carl to a Senate subcommittee investigating the relations between capital and labor.

A resident of New York City, Carl had been a tailor for over thirty years when he testified. From that vantage point, he personally witnessed a number of changes in his work. This document is interesting because both Carl and the subcommittee discuss the constraints he felt as he testified. Given what Carl himself says about possible reprisals by his employer, how truthful do you think his testimony was? Do you think the historical information (e.g., changes in tailoring) he mentions is more accurate than that concerning more contemporary working conditions? How accurate do you think Carl's testimony was in general? Are some aspects more likely to be accurate and representative than other aspects (speed of work versus savings)? What information would you want to have to verify his testimony? What information would you want to know about Carl himself? Do you think testimony in a court or legislative body is better information than that obtained elsewhere? Do you think the things he mentions were typical of workers in the late nineteenth century? If this was the only document with which you had to work, what could you say about the impact of machinery on working conditions?

TESTIMONY OF CONRAD CARL

Sen. Pugh: Please give us any information that you may have as to the relation existing between the employers and the employees in the tailoring business in this city, as to wages, as to treatment of the one by the other class, as to the feeling that exists between the employers and the employed generally, and all that you know in regard to the subject that we are authorized to inquire into?

A. During the time I have been here the tailoring business is altered in three different ways. Before we had sewing machines we worked piecework with our wives, and very often our children. We had no trouble then with our neighbors, nor with the landlord, because it was a very still business, very quiet; but in 1854 or 1855, and later, the sewing machine was invented and introduced, and it stitched very nicely, nicer than the tailor could do; and the bosses said: "We want you to use the sewing machine; you have to buy one." Many of the tailors had a few dollars in the bank, and they took the money and bought machines. Many others had no money, but must help themselves; so they brought their stitching, the coat or vest, to the other tailors who had sewing machines, and paid them a few cents for the stitching. Later, when the money was given out for the work, we found out that we could earn no more than we could without the machine; but the money for the machine was gone now, and we found that the machine was only for the profit of the bosses; that they got their work quicker, and it was done nicer. . . . The machine makes too much noise in the place, and the neighbors want to sleep, and we have to stop sewing earlier; so we have to work faster. We work now in excitement—in a hurry. It is hunting; it is not work at all; it is a hunt.

Q. You turn out two or three times as much work per day now as you did in prior times before the war?

A. Yes, sir; two or three times as much; and we have to do it, because the wages are two-thirds lower than they were five or ten years back. . . .

Sen. Blair: What proportion of them are women and what proportion men, according to your best judgment?

A. I guess there are many more women than men.

Q. The pay of the women is the same as the pay of the men for the same quantity of work, I suppose?

A. Yes; in cases where a manufacturer—that is, a middleman—gets work from the shop and brings it into his store and employs hands to make it, women get paid by the piece also. If the manufacturer gets $.25 for a piece, he pays for the machine work on that piece so many cents to the machine-worker, he pays so many cents to the presser, so many cents to the finisher, and so many to the button-sewer—so much to each one—and what remains is to pay his rent and to pay for the machinery.

Q. What is your knowledge as to the amount that workers of that class are able to save from their wages?

A. I don't know any one that does save except those manufacturers.

Q. As a class, then, the workers save nothing?

A. No.

Q. What sort of house-room do they have? . . .

A. They live in tenement houses four or five stories high, and have two or three rooms.

Q. What is the state of feeling between the employers and their employees in that business? How do you workingmen feel towards the people who employ you and pay you?

A. Well, I must say the workingmen are discouraged. If I speak with them they go back and don't like to speak much about the business and the pay. They fear that if they say how it is they will get sent out of the shop. They hate the bosses and the foremen more than the bosses, and that feeling is deep. . . .

Q. But can you explain why they hate the foremen, as you say they do, more than bosses, when the bosses keep the foremen there and could discharge them and get better ones in their places if they desired?

A. Gentlemen, if I say all this here—if it is made public I come out of work.

Sen. Pugh: Then you are testifying here under the apprehension of punishment for what you have stated?

A. Well, I have no fear for anyone, you know, and if you think it is better that I say it, I do so.

Q. What is your feeling of restraint in testifying? What injury would you be subjected to for telling the truth? Would the workingmen in your business testify under a fear of being punished by their employers for telling the truth?

A. Yes, It is nothing but fear. . . .

Sen. Blair: . . . This committee desires to obtain such information as you can give in regard to the condition of those engaged in your trade, and if there is any attempt to punish you for giving such information I think you can find protection from the country, or from some source. We cannot compel you to give the information, but we desire you to state, if you will, the names of some of these bosses and foremen, so that if they do not think proper to come here and speak for themselves the country will understand that you have told us the truth.

A. Now, sir, if I lose my work who can give me another work? I am an old man now, you know, and the young ones, they get the work and they say, "He is an old man; what can he do?" . . .

(Source: U.S. Congress, Senate Committee on Education and Labor, 1885, *Report of the Committee of the Senate Upon the Relations Between Labor and Capital,* Washington, D.C.: U.S. Government Printing Office, vol. 1, pp. 413–421.)

Newspapers

As you are well aware, newspapers contain many different sections and features. Some of these are fairly recent additions as, for example, the sports section. Although newspapers have changed over time, they have usually contained advertising (as we saw above), journalistic accounts of contemporary events, and editorial comment. Because of the wealth of information newspapers contain and their wide reading audience, historians have used newspapers as major primary sources. However, the various types of information in newspapers must be approached with different cautions.

Two excerpts from newspapers follow. One is a report written by journalist Tomas Kettell for *The Democratic Review* in 1850. The second is an editorial, which appeared in *The New York Evening Post* on January 26, 1866. As you read these documents, you should consider how to approach each document. What is the bias of each author? Is one more biased than the other? Can one source be said to be more objective than the other? Are reports always better information and less biased than editorials? How might one discern the bias of these sources? Is the bias systematic?

Internal Transportation

The business portion of the city is necessarily crowded within a small space, because . . . economy of time requires that all the places to which merchants and dealers are called many times each day . . . should be readily accessible. . . . Where the means of travel between these localities and [homes] are few and costly, the utmost economy of room is practised. In European cities, lofty buildings without yards, in narrow streets, contain the family above, and the office below, and until about twenty years since, New-York was cramped in a similar manner. At that time the omnibus system commenced running. By that plan coaches pass every five minutes through the principal avenues, carrying business men to their homes at night, and to their offices in the morning. This im-mediately permitted an expansion of the surface occupied by dwellings, and houses multiplied rapidly in the upper part of the city, which spreads from the business section in a fan-like form over the island. . . .

While the omnibus system has thus expanded the city sur-face, steam has greatly reduced the cost of fuel and food.
. . . Railroads . . . enable the perishable fruits and vegetables of summer to reach the market from considerable distances, and by so doing, not only place within the reach of citizens, fresh and cheap garden stuffs, but . . . confer on a larger number of farmers the profits of garden culture. The article of milk, as an instance, requires to be placed within the reach of the consumers in a very brief period from the time of its yield, necessarily, the circle of country which supports cows for the supply of city milk, must be very contracted; all cities have seriously felt the inconvenience of this fact. New-York dairies were established, in which swill-fed cows, diseased through constant confinement and unnatural food, yielded an abundant but deleterious fluid, having none of the properties of milk, although sold as such to the deluded citizens. The railroads now bring fresh milk every morning from a distance of sixty miles in time for use, and consequently the propor-tion of healthy milk used, has much increased, while the price at which it is afforded to citizens has been proportionally re-duced. . . .

Without these means of communication, one of two things must have happened . . . the city must have ceased to grow, or its general business must have yielded such profits as

would have enabled citizens to pay extravagant prices for
food and fuel. . . .

(Source: Tomas Kettell, 1850, "Internal Transportation," *The Democratic Review,* vol. 27, August, pp. 148–152.)

Editorial

[The Metropolitan Health Bill] unites the territory now included in the Metropolitan Police District in a "Metropolitan
Sanitary District." It constitutes four men versed in sanitary
science and the four Metropolitan Police Commissioners . . .
this Board . . . has authority by the bill to enforce cleanliness
in all parts of the city. . . . Ten of [the] inspectors are to be
medical men of several years' experience in the city, and the
others must be specially qualified. . . . To enforce its measures, the Board of Health has the full co-operation of the
police. This secures at once economy and efficiency. . . .

The bill . . . removes the care of the city's health entirely
from political office-holders and places it in the hands of men
of science; it does not propose an untried experiment, for in
its main features advantage has been taken of the experience
of London, Liverpool, Paris and Philadelphia, all which cities
have boards of health similarly constituted with that proposed
for New York. In London the creation of such a board of
health, with adequate powers, has resulted in reducing the
mortality from one in twenty to one in forty-five. . . .

If we are to prepare ourselves against cholera . . . we have
no time to lose. . . . The gentlemen named in the bill as
commissioners of health have been chosen . . . because they
have made the sanitary care of large cities a special study,
and are known to be capable and distinguished in that branch
of science. The co-operation of the police force is necessary
to the effective cleansing of the city; it saves enormous
waste, does away with a multitude of petty officeholders, who
corrupt the city elections, and substitutes for these incapable
persons a thoroughly disciplined sanitary force. . . . It is a
reform in the right direction—towards economy and the con-
centration of necessary authority in the hands of competent
persons.

(Source: *The New York Evening Post,* January 26, 1866.)

Directory of Organizations, Associations, and Government Agencies

LITERALLY HUNDREDS—if not thousands—of organizations have interests in U.S. history. Obviously, not all of those organizations or agencies could be listed here; we have tried to list all the major national organizations and agencies, as well as representative specialized agencies. We have listed organizations and agencies in three categories. First are those with general interests in the field of U.S. history; they may specialize in a particular region, such as the South, or topic, such as education, but their interests cover the entire span of our nation's history.

State historical societies are the second category. Other state resources that might be of assistance include state archives, state humanities councils, and state preservation offices. Note that many localities also have historical societies providing a range of services. These may be accessed through local telephone directories.

The third category includes agencies or organizations specializing in U.S. history to 1865. These organizations can be particularly helpful in researching events or developments in that time span.

We have not included organizations focusing on the study of one individual (e.g., Abigail Adams Historical Society, Jefferson Davis Association), organizations devoted to the study of one immigrant group (e.g., Polish-American Historical Society, Swedish-American Historical Society), and museums or restorations (e.g., Colonial Williamsburg, Old Sturbridge Village, Lincoln's New Salem), although all of these organizations can be helpful to teachers and students. Information about these types of organizations can be found in such other reference works as the *Encyclopedia of Associations* (Detroit, MI: Gale Research, annual) or *The Living History Sourcebook* (Nashville, TN: American Association for State and Local History, 1985).

General information for teachers and students can also be obtained through college and university departments of history, obviously too numerous to list here. A call to the department of a local institution can yield information on the specialties of faculty members and requirements for non–college students' use of the history library.

General Organizations and Agencies

Agricultural History Society (AHS)
Economic Research Service
U.S. Department of Agriculture
Washington, DC 20250
(202) 447-8183
Wayne D. Rasmussen, Executive Secretary

The Agricultural History Society has 1,400 members, composed of historians, geographers, agricultural economists, farmers, and others interested in the history of agriculture. The organization presents awards for writing on agricultural history and sponsors an annual symposium in April in conjunction with the meeting of the Organization of American Historians.

PUBLICATIONS: AHS publishes a quarterly, *Agricultural History,* as well as the proceedings of its annual symposium.

American Association of Museums (AAM)
1225 I Street, NW, Suite 200
Washington, DC 20005
(202) 289-1818
Ed Able, Director

This national association has 9,000 members, including history museums, historic houses and societies, and preservation projects, among other types of museums. The association accredits museums and studies all aspects of collection development, maintenance, and management. Its annual meeting is held in June.

PUBLICATIONS: AAM publishes a monthly newsletter, *Aviso;* a bimonthly journal, *Museum News;* and an annual museum directory. It also publishes books on such topics as caring for collections, museums and the humanities, and museum accreditation.

American Association for State and Local History (AASLH)
174 Second Avenue, North
Nashville, TN 37204
(615) 255-2971
Gerald George, Director

The stated purpose of this membership organization is "advancing knowledge, understanding, and appreciation of local history in the United States and Canada," but it also works in the areas of state, regional, and even national and international history, particularly in relation to public education about history. The association offers seminars, workshops, and consultant services; its annual meeting is held in September.

PUBLICATIONS: AASLH publishes the monthly journal *History News;* the monthly newsletter *History News Dispatch;* and a series of technical reports on "everyday problems faced by museum and historical agency personnel." Other publications include the biennial *Directory of Historical Agencies in North America,* as well as numerous bibliographies, technical leaflets, guides, and educational materials, including videotapes.

American Folklore Society (AFS)
Maryland State Arts Council
15 West Mulberry Street
Baltimore, MD 21201
(301) 685-6740
Charles Camp, Executive Secretary

With more than 3,000 individual and institutional members, the American Folklore Society supports the collection, discussion, and publication of folklore. Although folklore from throughout the world is of interest to the society, North America is emphasized. The AFS annual meeting is held in October.

PUBLICATIONS: AFS publishes the *American Folklore Newsletter* six times per year; the quarterly *Journal of American Folklore;* and several irregular series, including *Memoirs Series.*

American Historical Association (AHA)
400 A Street, SE
Washington, DC 20003
(202) 544-2422
Samuel R. Gammon, Executive Director

The 13,000 members of this association include professional historians, educators, and others interested in historical study. The association holds an annual meeting in December, maintains an extensive library, and offers seminars on various historical topics.

PUBLICATIONS: AHA publishes the journal *American Historical Review* five times per year. It also publishes the proceedings of its annual meetings, as well as pamphlets on historical subjects.

American Indian Historical Society (AIHS)
1493 Masonic Avenue
San Francisco, CA 94117
(415) 626-5235
Jeanette Henry Costo, Executive Secretary

The American Indian Historical Society was founded in 1964 to promote study and understanding of the history of Native Americans. The organization sponsors classes, forums, and lectures; evaluates how Native Americans are depicted in textbooks; and supports the rights of Indians. The society sponsors a triennial meeting.

PUBLICATIONS: The society publishes an annual volume entitled *The Indian Historian.* It also publishes a newspaper on an irregular basis and occasional books.

Association for Living Historical Farms and Agricultural Museums (ALHFAM)
National Museum of American History
Smithsonian Institution
Washington, DC 20650
(202) 357-2813
John T. Schlebecker, Secretary

Despite its title, this organization is now recruiting as members all museums or other organizations interested in the use of "living history" techniques to increase public understanding of the past. The association provides assistance to its members in living history interpretation through regional workshops. It also maintains an information bank and develops standards for living historical farms and museums.

PUBLICATIONS: ALHFAM publishes a bimonthly *Bulletin,* an annual convention proceedings, and a variety of booklets on topics of concern to members.

**Association for the Study of Afro-American Life and History
(ASALH)**
1407 14th Street, NW
Washington, DC 20005
(202) 667-2822
Karen Robinson, Executive Director

The 12,000 members of this organization include historians, scholars, and students interested in the study of black American history and culture. The organization, which sponsors Afro-American History Month, collects manuscripts, promotes research and writing, and works for interracial harmony. The association's annual meeting is held in October. Its publishing arm holds a media festival every November.

PUBLICATIONS: ASALH publishes two quarterlies, *Journal of Negro History* and *Negro History Bulletin*. Its publishing arm also issues textbooks and monographs on related topics.

Bureau of the Census
U.S. Department of Commerce
Washington, DC 20233
(301) 763-4040
John G. Keane, Director

Calling itself "America's Fact Finder," the Bureau of the Census conducts the decennial census of U.S. population. It also conducts economic, agricultural, and government censuses every five years, as well as up to 250 smaller surveys each year. Topics covered include manufacturing, mining, retail trade, wholesale trade, service industries, transportation, and construction. The Bureau also collects data on other nations.

PUBLICATIONS: The Bureau of the Census publishes as many as 2,000 reports each year, in printed, microfiche, and computer tape form. It also publishes a variety of wall maps and educational materials. Help finding appropriate census information can be obtained by contacting the regional offices listed below.

California
Census Bureau Regional Office
11777 San Vicente Boulevard
Los Angeles, CA 90049
(213) 209-6612

Colorado
Census Bureau Regional Office
7655 West Mississippi Avenue
Denver, CO 80226
(303) 236-2200

Georgia
Census Bureau Regional Office
1365 Peachtree Street, NE
Atlanta, GA 30309
(404) 881-2274

Illinois
Census Bureau Regional Office
55 East Jackson Boulevard
Chicago, IL 60604
(312) 353-0980

Kansas
Census Bureau Regional Office
One Gateway Center
4th and State Streets
Kansas City, KS 66101
(913) 236-3731

Massachusetts
Census Bureau Regional Office
441 Stuart Street
Boston, MA 02116
(617) 565-7078

Michigan
Census Bureau Regional Office
231 West Lafayette
Detroit, MI 48226
(313) 226-4675

New York
Census Bureau Regional Office
26 Federal Plaza
New York, NY 10278
(212) 264-4730

North Carolina
Census Bureau Regional Office
230 South Tryon Street

Charlotte, NC 28202
(704) 371-6144

Pennsylvania
Census Bureau Regional Office
600 Arch Street
Philadelphia, PA 19106
(215) 597-8313

Texas
Census Bureau Regional Office
1100 Commerce Street
Dallas, TX 75242
(214) 767-0625

Washington
Census Bureau Regional Office
1700 Westlake Avenue, N
Seattle, WA 98109
(206) 442-7080

**ERIC Clearinghouse for Social Studies/Social Science Education
(ERIC/ChESS)**
2805 East Tenth Street, Suite 120
Indiana University
Bloomington, IN 47405
(812) 335-3838
John Patrick, Director

The ERIC Clearinghouse for Social Studies/Social Science Education
provides comprehensive information services in the area of social
science and history education. These services include low-cost user
service products, computer searches, and information-answering
services.

PUBLICATIONS: The clearinghouse publishes a free newsletter,
Keeping Up, as well as reference sheets and digests on current topics.
The clearinghouse also publishes information analysis products, in-
cluding the recent *Teaching History in the Elementary School.*

History of Science Society (HSS)
35 Dean Street
Worcester, MA 01609
(617) 793-5363
Michael Sokal, Executive Secretary

The 4,000 members of this society include educators, historians, scientists, and others studying the history of science and its influence on other aspects of culture. The organization presents several annual awards and meets annually in the fall.

PUBLICATIONS: HSS publishes a quarterly entitled *Isis,* as well as a quarterly newsletter and an annual publication, *Osiris.*

Immigration History Society (IHS)
Balch Institute
18 South Seventh Street
Philadelphia, PA 19106
(215) 925-8090
M. Mark Stolarik, Editor

This organization encourages interchange among historians, sociologists, economists, and others doing research in the field of human migration, particularly migration to the United States. Members meet twice each year in conjunction with the meetings of the Organization of American Historians and American Historical Association.

PUBLICATIONS: IHS publishes a semiannual *Immigration History Newsletter* as well as the semiannual *Journal of American Ethnic History.*

Library of Congress
10 First Street, SE
Washington, DC 20540
(202) 287-5000
Daniel J. Boorstin, Librarian of Congress

One of the world's largest libraries, the Library of Congress contains more than 50 million items. Its collection on U.S. history is one of the finest anywhere and includes the papers of 23 U.S. presidents. The library answers reference questions that cannot be handled by other libraries and provides referrals for questions on the history of science and technology.

PUBLICATIONS: One of the key resources for historical researchers is the Library of Congress publication *The National Union Catalog,* which lists every publication issued a Library of Congress card and the libraries that have it in their holdings. The Library of Congress has also published printed subject guides, which are of great assistance in historical research. Library of Congress bibliographic resources are computerized and are made available in microfiche form.

National Archives and Records Administration (NARA)
Pennsylvania Avenue and Eighth Street
Washington, DC 20408
(202) 523-3298
Don Wilson, Archivist

An independent agency of the federal government, the National Archives and Records Administration is the official depository for records of all federal agencies. As such, it has a huge collection of documentary materials related to U.S. history, going back to records of the Continental Congress in 1774.

PUBLICATIONS: NARA's key publication for the historical researcher is *Guide to the National Archives of the United States,* which describes the Archives' holdings. For many categories of records, NARA has published special guides and listings; examples include *Black History: A Guide to Civilian Records in the National Archives* and *Civil War Maps in the National Archives.* Microfilm reels of many records in the National Archives can be purchased from the Archives or can be viewed at Archives branches. Branches are found at the following locations:

California
National Archives Branch
Federal Records Center
24000 Avila Road
Laguna Niguel, CA 92677
(714) 831-4220

National Archives Branch
Federal Records Center
1000 Commodore Drive
San Bruno, CA 94066
(415) 876-9001

Colorado
National Archives Branch
Federal Records Center
Building 48, Federal Center
Denver, CO 80225
(303) 234-3187

Georgia
National Archives Branch
Federal Records Center
1557 St. Joseph Avenue

East Point, GA 30344
(404) 526-7477

Illinois
National Archives Branch
Federal Records Center
7358 South Pulaski Road
Chicago, IL 60629
(312) 353-8541

Massachusetts
National Archives Branch
Federal Records Center
380 Trapelo Road
Waltham, MA 02154
(617) 223-2657

Missouri
National Archives Branch
Federal Records Center
2306 East Bannister Road
Kansas City, MO 64131
(816) 926-7271

New Jersey
National Archives Branch
Federal Records Center
Building 22—MOT Bayonne
Bayonne, NJ 07002
(201) 858-7245

Pennsylvania
National Archives Branch
Federal Records Center
5000 Wissahickon Avenue
Philadelphia, PA 19144
(215) 438-5200

Texas
National Archives Branch
Federal Records Center
P.O. Box 6216
Fort Worth, TX 76115
(817) 334-5515

Washington
National Archives Branch
Federal Records Center
6125 Sand Point Way, NE
Seattle, WA 98115
(206) 442-4502

National Council on Public History (NCPH)
Department of History
West Virginia University
Morgantown, WV 26506
(304) 293-2421
Barbara J. Howe, Executive Secretary

This organization aims to encourage broader interest in history and
to stimulate interest in history by promoting its use in society. The
focus is nonacademic history—history that is brought to the public
through museums and public displays. The organization serves as a
clearinghouse, conducts training programs, and advises those seeking
information on public history. The group has an annual spring
conference.

PUBLICATIONS: NCPH publishes a quarterly newsletter, a quarterly journal, *The Public Historian,* and an irregular publication entitled *Directory of Academic and Training Programs.*

National Council for the Social Studies (NCSS)
3501 Newark Street, NW
Washington, DC 20016
(202) 966-7840
Frances Haley, Executive Director

The purpose of the National Council for the Social Studies is to
improve social studies education, including history education, by setting guidelines and standards for the profession, providing leadership
and leadership training opportunities, and by encouraging research.
Consultant and workshop services are provided at negotiated fees.
Letter and phone information requests are answered at no charge. An
annual conference is held in November.

PUBLICATIONS: NCSS journals include *Social Education* and *Theory and Research in Social Education.* It also publishes a newsletter,
The Social Studies Professional, a "How to Do It" series for teachers, and bulletins on topics of interest to the membership. Two bulletins of special note are *Teaching American History: New Directions*
and *History in the Schools.*

National Endowment for the Humanities (NEH)
1100 Pennsylvania Avenue, NW
Washington, DC 20506
(202) 786-0435
Lynne V. Cheney, Chairman

This relatively new federal agency (established in 1965) aims to increase the influence of the humanities—primarily literature, history, and philosophy—on American thinking and life. It fulfills its mission by funding research, enhancement of proven humanities programs at the higher education level, and educational programs. Each year, NEH funds a number of summer institutes for elementary and secondary teachers of history; lists of these institutes are available from the agency.

PUBLICATIONS: Six times annually, NEH publishes the journal *Humanities*. It also publishes occasional reports such as the recent *American Memory: A Report on the Humanities in the Nation's Public Schools,* which helped to spark a resurgence of interest in history education. NEH also supports the development of many other works, although it does not publish these items.

National History Day
11201 Euclid Avenue
Cleveland, OH 44106
(216) 421-8803
Lois Scharf, Executive Director

This organization sponsors a program in which secondary students prepare projects for submission in local, state, and national competitions. The projects are judged by professional historians and teachers; winners are recognized at all levels. Each year's competition has a particular theme that students must address.

PUBLICATIONS: The organization annually publishes a collection of the winning papers from the competition.

National Park Service (NPS)
U.S. Department of the Interior
C Street between 18th and 19th, NW
Washington, DC 20240
(202) 343-1100
William Penn Mott, Director

In addition to administering the national park system, the National Park Service also oversees national monuments (e.g., Aztec Ruins in New Mexico), battlefields (e.g., Fort Necessity, the site of a

Pennsylvania battle in the French and Indian War), historic sites and parks (e.g., San Jose Mission in Texas), memorials and memorial parks (e.g., Roger Williams memorial in Rhode Island), and military parks (e.g., Gettysburg, Pennsylvania).

PUBLICATIONS: NPS publishes informational brochures on all of the sites it administers, as well as other educational materials.

National Women's History Project (NWHP)
P.O. Box 3716
Santa Rosa, CA 95402
(707) 526-5974
Molly MacGregor, Director

As its name implies, this organization promotes education on the history of women through such activities as publication of resource catalogs on women's history, sponsorship of National Women's History Week in March, and publication of teaching materials on women's history. The staff conducts workshops and other training programs and offers internships. The organization also sponsors the Women's History Network.

PUBLICATIONS: The National Women's History Project publishes a variety of materials, including resource catalogs, a community organizing guide, bibliographies, curriculum guides, lesson plans, and posters.

Oral History Association (OHA)
P.O. Box 13734, NTSU Station
Denton, TX 76203
(817) 387-1021
Ronald E. Marcello, Executive Secretary

The Oral History Association has 1,400 individual and institutional members interested in the exchange of information on oral history, in encouraging the growth of oral history materials, and in the improvement of the discipline's techniques. The organization holds an annual colloquium in the fall.

PUBLICATIONS: Periodic publications include a quarterly newsletter, an annual membership directory, and the annual *Oral History Review*. OHA also publishes bibliographies, evaluation guidelines, and papers of special interest to its members.

Organization of American Historians (OAH)
112 North Bryan Street
Bloomington, IN 47401

(812) 335-7311
Joan Hoff-Wilson, Executive Secretary

The Organization of American Historians' mission is to promote historical research, study, and writing. It sponsors several award programs for historical writing, as well as maintaining a speakers bureau and operating a job registry. An annual meeting is held in April.

PUBLICATIONS: OAH publishes the bimonthly *Magazine of History*, targeted at teachers of American history; the quarterly *Journal of American History*, intended for a scholarly audience; and a newsletter.

Smithsonian Institution
1000 Jefferson Drive, SW
Washington, DC 20560
(202) 357-1300
Robert McCormick Adams, Secretary

The Smithsonian is perhaps best known for the museums it maintains, including the National Museum of American History and the National Air and Space Museum. The Smithsonian also conducts original research in the sciences, humanities, arts, and education and prepares and distributes many publications. The Smithsonian also offers educational programs for adults and children, with special emphasis given to preservice and in-service teacher training.

PUBLICATIONS: The Smithsonian publishes many books and reports. It publishes the monthly journal *Smithsonian*, as well as a quarterly newsletter for schools, *Art to Zoo*. This newsletter promotes the use of community resources in the classroom and contains ready-to-use instructional materials.

Social Science Education Consortium (SSEC)
855 Broadway
Boulder, CO 80302
(303) 492-8154
James R. Giese, Executive Director

The SSEC is dedicated to the improvement of social studies/social science education, including history education. Activities designed to implement that goal include curriculum development, teacher training, and dissemination of new teaching ideas and materials. The SSEC's Resource and Demonstration Center houses one of the nation's largest collections of curriculum materials in social studies and history, as well as the archives of many curriculum development projects of the 1960s and 1970s.

PUBLICATIONS: The SSEC publishes teacher resource and curriculum planning materials. Representative titles include *Lessons on the Constitution, The Causes of the American Revolution,* and *A Humanities Approach to Early National U.S. History.*

Society of American Historians (SAH)
610 Fayerweather Hall
Columbia University
New York, NY 10027
(212) 280-2555
Kenneth T. Jackson, Executive Secretary

This society includes as members authors who have written at least one book on U.S. history that is recognized as being of high literary and scholarly quality. The society awards several prizes in the area of historical writing. Its annual meeting is held in April.
PUBLICATIONS: None

Society for History Education
California State University, Long Beach
Long Beach, CA 90840
(213) 985-4503
Augustus Cerillo, Jr., President

Members of this organization include high school and college teachers and librarians. The organization's goal is to support the work of historians who choose to teach by offering reprint, workshop, and other services.
PUBLICATIONS: The society publishes a newsletter, *Network News Exchange,* as well as a quarterly journal, *The History Teacher.*

Society for the History of Technology (SHOT)
Department of History
Duke University
Durham, NC 27706
(919) 684-2434
Aarne Vesilind, Secretary

This organization counts among its members 2,600 scholars, engineers, and institutions (including libraries and museums). Its purpose is to "encourage the study of the development of technology and its relations with society and culture." Through its training and award programs, SHOT encourages an interdisciplinary approach to study of the area. The organization's annual meeting is held in December.

PUBLICATIONS: SHOT publishes two quarterlies—a newsletter and the journal *Technology and Culture.*

Southern History Association (SHA)
Department of History
University of Georgia
Athens, GA 30602
(404) 542-8848
William F. Holmes, Secretary

This organization promotes the study of Southern history through research, preservation of historical records, and encouragement of state and local historical societies. The organization bestows awards for work in the area of Southern history. An annual meeting is held in November.

PUBLICATIONS: SHA publishes a quarterly journal, *Journal of Southern History.*

State Historical Societies

Each of the 50 states, as well as the District of Columbia, has a state historical society that offers services ranging from maintenance of museums, to publishing of newsletters, journals, and educational materials, to providing various training programs. The historical periods for which the state societies have extensive collections may vary from state to state. However, all are likely to have at least some material relevant to the period covered in this volume.

Alabama
Alabama Department of Archives and History
624 Washington Avenue
Montgomery, AL 36130
(205) 832-6510

Alaska
Alaska Historical Society
P.O. Box 100299
Anchorage, AK 99510
(907) 346-2410

Arizona
Arizona Historical Society
949 East Second Street
Tucson, AZ 85719
(602) 628-5774

Arkansas
Arkansas History Commission
1 Capitol Mall
Little Rock, AR 72201
(501) 682-6900

California
California Historical Society
2090 Jackson Street
San Francisco, CA 94109
(415) 567-1848

Colorado
Colorado Historical Society
1300 Broadway
Denver, CO 80203
(303) 866-3682

Connecticut
Connecticut Historical Society
1 Elizabeth Street
Hartford, CT 06105
(203) 236-5621

Delaware
Historical Society of Delaware
505 Market Street Mall
Wilmington, DE 19801
(302) 655-7161

District of Columbia
Columbia Historical Society
1307 New Hampshire Avenue, NW
Washington, DC 20036
(202) 785-2068

Florida
Florida Historical Society
University of South Florida Library
Tampa, FL 33620
(813) 974-3815

Georgia
Georgia Historical Society
501 Whitaker Street
Savannah, GA 31401
(912) 651-2128

Hawaii
Hawaiian Historical Society
560 Kawaiahao Street
Honolulu, HI 96813
(808) 537-6271

Idaho
Idaho State Historical Society
610 North Julia Davis Drive
Boise, ID 83702
(208) 384-2120

Illinois
Illinois State Historical Society
Old State Capitol
Springfield, IL 62706
(217) 782-4836

Indiana
Indiana Historical Society
315 West Ohio Street
Indianapolis, IN 46202
(317) 232-1882

Iowa
State Historical Society of Iowa
402 Iowa Avenue
Iowa City, IA 52240
(319) 335-3916

Kansas
Kansas State Historical Society
120 West Tenth Street
Topeka, KS 66612
(913) 296-3251

Kentucky
Kentucky Historical Society
300 West Broadway
Frankfort, KY 40601
(502) 564-3016

Louisiana
Louisiana Historical Society
203 Carondelet Street
New Orleans, LA 70130
(504) 588-9044

Maine
Maine Historical Society
485 Congress Street
Portland, ME 04101
(207) 774-1822

Maryland
Maryland Historical Society
201 West Monument Street
Baltimore, MD 21201
(301) 685-3750

Massachusetts
Massachusetts Historical Society
1154 Boylston Street
Boston, MA 02215
(617) 536-1608

Michigan
Historical Society of Michigan
2117 Washtenaw Avenue
Ann Arbor, MI 48104
(313) 769-1828

Minnesota
Minnesota Historical Society
690 Cedar Street
St. Paul, MN 55101
(612) 296-6980

Mississippi
Mississippi Historical Society
100 South State Street
Jackson, MI 39205
(601) 354-6218

Missouri
State Historical Society of Missouri
Hitt and Lowry Streets
Columbia, MO 65201
(314) 882-7083

Montana
Montana Historical Society
225 North Roberts
Helena, MT 59601
(406) 449-2681

Nebraska
Nebraska State Historical Society
1500 R Street
Lincoln, NE 68506
(402) 432-2793

Nevada
Nevada Historical Society
1650 North Virginia Street
Reno, NV 89503
(702) 789-0190

New Hampshire
New Hampshire Historical Society
30 Park Street
Concord, NH 03301
(603) 225-3381

New Jersey
New Jersey Historical Society
230 Broadway
Newark, NJ 07104
(201) 483-3939

New Mexico
Historical Society of New Mexico
P.O. Box 5819
Santa Fe, NM 87502

New York
New York Historical Society
170 Central Park West
New York, NY 10024
(212) 873-3400

North Carolina
Historical Society of North Carolina
University of North Carolina, Wilson Library
Chapel Hill, NC 27514
(919) 962-1345

North Dakota
State Historical Society of North Dakota
North Dakota Heritage Center
Bismarck, ND 58505
(701) 224-2666

Ohio
Ohio Historical Society
I-71 and Seventeenth Avenue
Columbus, OH 43211
(614) 466-1500

Oklahoma
Oklahoma Historical Society
2100 North Lincoln Boulevard
Oklahoma City, OK 73105
(405) 521-2491

Oregon
Oregon Historical Society
1230 Southwest Park Avenue

Portland, OR 97205
(503) 222-1741

Pennsylvania
Historical Society of Pennsylvania
1300 Locust Street
Philadelphia, PA 19107
(215) 732-6200

Rhode Island
Rhode Island Historical Society
52 Power Street
Providence, RI 02906
(401) 331-8575

South Carolina
South Carolina Historical Society
100 Meeting Street
Charleston, SC 29401
(803) 723-3225

South Dakota
South Dakota State Historical Society
Soldiers' and Sailors' Memorial Building
East Capitol Avenue
Pierre, SD 57501
(605) 773-3458

Tennessee
Tennessee Historical Society
War Memorial Building, Ground Floor
Nashville, TN 37219
(615) 742-6717

Texas
Texas Historical Commission
P.O. Box 12276, Capitol Station
Austin, TX 78711
(512) 475-3092

Utah
Utah State Historical Society
307 West Second Street

Salt Lake City, UT 84102
(801) 533-5961

Vermont
Vermont Historical Society, Inc.
State Street
Montpelier, VT 05602
(802) 828-2291

Virginia
Virginia Historical Society
428 North Boulevard
Richmond, VA 23221
(804) 358-4901

Washington
Washington State Historical Society
315 North Stadium Way
Tacoma, WA 98403
(206) 593-2830

West Virginia
West Virginia Historical Society
Department of Culture and History
State Capitol Complex
Charleston, WV 25305
(304) 348-2277

Wisconsin
State Historical Society of Wisconsin
816 State Street
Madison, WI 53706
(608) 262-9580

Wyoming
Wyoming State Archives and Historical Department
Barrett Building
Cheyenne, WY 82002
(307) 777-7518

Agencies or Organizations Specializing in U.S. History to 1865

American Antiquarian Society (AAS)
185 Salisbury Street
Worcester, MA 01609
(617) 755-5221
Marcus A. McCorison, Director

The purpose of this organization is to "collect, preserve, and encourage serious study of the materials of American history and life through 1876." The society has an active publications program as well as a large research library. It sponsors fellowships, research, and educational programs. Semiannual meetings are held in April and October.

PUBLICATIONS: AAS publishes a newsletter, books and pamphlets on topics related to U.S. history through 1876, and the proceedings of its semiannual meetings.

American Society for Eighteenth-Century Studies (ASECS)
St. Olaf College
Northfield, MN 55057
(507) 663-3488
Richard G. Peterson, Executive Secretary

This organization was founded to advance study and research on the eighteenth century. Its 1,500 members include scholars and others interested in cultural history. The society gives awards for published works on the history of the eighteenth century. An annual spring meeting is held.

PUBLICATIONS: ASECS publishes two quarterlies, *Eighteenth-Century Studies* and *News Circular,* as well as an annual directory and a second annual volume, *Studies in Eighteenth-Century Culture.*

Bostonian Society
Old State House
206 Washington Street
Boston, MA 02109
(617) 242-5610
Joan Hull, Director

The Bostonian Society is dedicated to the history of Boston and antiques associated with it. The society maintains a museum with exhibits related to the Revolution and early Boston; it also maintains a marine collection showing the city's relation to the sea. The society's library contains many historic photographs and manuscripts. The society holds an annual meeting.

PUBLICATIONS: The society publishes the proceedings of its meetings on an irregular basis.

Colonial Society of Massachusetts (CSM)
87 Mt. Vernon Street
Boston, MA 02108
(617) 227-2782
Frederick S. Allis, Jr., Editor

The 250 members of this society are interested in the history of the New England colonies, particularly Plymouth and Massachusetts Bay colonies.

PUBLICATIONS: CSM is the copublisher of the journal *New England Quarterly.*

Commission on the Bicentennial of the United States Constitution
736 Jackson Place, NW
Washington, DC 20503
(202) 653-5196
Warren Burger, Chairman

This special government commission was established to organize the national celebration of the bicentennial of the Constitution and Bill of Rights. The commission funds a national competition on the bicentennial, as well as a number of smaller state programs. Each year between 1987 and 1991, the commission is focusing on a different aspect of the Constitution's history, such as ratification, establishment of the first Congress, and so on. Every state also has a bicentennial commission.

PUBLICATIONS: The commission publishes a newsletter, *We the People,* and has funded the development of numerous publications on the Constitution.

Council of the Thirteen Original States (CTOS)
485 Ocean Avenue
Stratford, CT 06497
(203) 377-1520
Frederick Biebel, Executive Director

This council organizes and supports activities that focus on the importance of the 13 original states in the founding and development of the United States. The organization sponsors debates and an annual meeting.

PUBLICATIONS: CTOS publishes a yearbook on a theme related to the founding of the United States.

Early American Industries Association (EAIA)
P.O. Box 2128
Empire State Plaza Station
Albany, NY 12220
Douglas R. Hough, President

EAIA has 2,800 members, including collectors, museums, dealers, libraries, and historical societies. All of the members are interested in studying early American industry on the farm, at home, at sea, and in the shop. The organization helps members identify unknown tools and devices. Spring and fall meetings are held each year.

PUBLICATIONS: In addition to a membership directory and books on topics of interest to members, the association publishes a quarterly journal, *The Chronicle,* and a newsletter, *Shavings from the Chronicle.*

Institute of Early American History and Culture (IEAHC)
P.O. Box 220
Williamsburg, VA 23187
(804) 253-5117
Thad W. Tate, Director

This institute is "dedicated to the furtherance of study, research, and publications bearing upon American history approximately to the year 1815." The institute maintains a large collection of pre-1800 American newspapers. It also sponsors awards and fellowships.

PUBLICATIONS: The institute publishes monographs, biographies, and other works on the period of interest. It also makes new editions of out-of-print works available and publishes a newsletter on an irregular basis.

Lewis and Clark Trail Heritage Foundation (LCTHF)
5054 Southwest 26th Place
Portland, OR 97201
(503) 244-2486
Robert E. Lange, Editor

LCTHF supports activities that enhance public knowledge of the Lewis and Clark expedition and the contributions of the expedition and its members to U.S. history. The foundation encourages efforts of local groups to coordinate long-range planning of activities, particularly those related to preservation of historic sites along the route traveled by the expedition. An annual meeting is held in August.

PUBLICATIONS: The foundation publishes a quarterly journal, *We Proceeded On,* as well as papers from its annual meeting and a membership directory.

Museum Association of the American Frontier
HC74, P.O. Box 18
Chadron, NE 69337
(308) 432-3843
Charles E. Hanson, Jr., Director

This organization includes as members 1,400 universities, historical societies, and scholars. The association acts as a clearinghouse for disseminating information on the North American fur trade. Other services provided include consultation for museums and publishers, professional training, and other educational activities. An annual meeting is held.

PUBLICATIONS: The association publishes a periodical entitled *Museum of the Fur Trade Quarterly.*

Project '87
American Political Science Association and
   American Historical Association
1527 New Hampshire Avenue, NW
Washington, DC 20036
(202) 483-2512
Sheilah Mann, Director

This joint project of the APSA and AHA began to prepare for the bicentennial of the U.S. Constitution in the early 1980s by looking at the state of education on the Constitution in U.S. schools. It has supported other research, as well as writing on the Constitution.

PUBLICATIONS: Project '87 has published or supported publication of such works as *Lessons on the Constitution* and *Teaching About the Constitution in American Secondary Schools.* It also publishes a journal, *This Constitution: A Bicentennial Chronicle.*

Society for Historians of the Early American Republic (SHEAR)
History Department
Lebanon Valley College
Annville, PA 17003
(717) 867-4411
James H. Broussard, Secretary

This society's 1,000 members are primarily scholars interested in the period 1789–1848. The society presents awards for historical writing and sponsors an annual meeting in July.

PUBLICATIONS: SHEAR publishes a quarterly, *Journal of the Early Republic.*

Reference Works

Atlases

America in Maps Dating from 1500 to 1856.
Egon Klemp, ed. New York: Holmes and Meier, 1976.
290 pp. $495. ISBN 0-8419-0200-3.

This oversized (and costly) volume contains excellent reproductions of historic maps dating from 1500 to 1856.

American Expansion: A Book of Maps.
Randall D. Sale and Edwin D. Karn. Lincoln, NE: University of Nebraska Press, 1979.
28 pp. $4.95. ISBN 0-8032-9104-3.

This brief atlas contains one map for each census year. The maps show political boundaries at the time of the census, extension of settlement, exploration, and location of land offices.

Atlas of American History.
James T. Adams, ed. New York: Scribner, 1985.
360 pp. $50. ISBN 0-684-18411-7.

This classic reference volume, now in its second revised edition, contains maps prepared under the supervision of historians. Topics covered in the maps include discovery, exploration, frontier posts, settlement, territorial organization, and the extension of communications. An index contains variant spellings of place names.

Atlas of the Lewis and Clark Expedition.
Gary E. Moulton, ed. Lincoln, NE: University of Nebraska Press, 1983.
196 pp. $100. ISBN 0-8032-2861-9.

Based on the journals of the Lewis and Clark expedition, this volume presents maps of the complete journey of exploration across "Lousiana."

Battlefield Atlas of the American Revolution.
Craig L. Symonds. Annapolis, MD: Nautical and Aviation Publishing, 1986.
110 pp. $15.95. ISBN 0-933852-53-3.

This volume, prepared by a history professor at the Naval Academy, presents an overview of the engagements of the American Revolution. Maps of the various battles are accompanied by essays explaining the most important information presented and telling the outcome of the battle.

Battlefield Atlas of the Civil War.
Craig L. Symonds. Annapolis, MD: Nautical and Aviation Publishing, 1985.
106 pp. $15.95. ISBN 0-933852-49-5.

This volume contains an overview of the battles of the Civil War, along with 50 maps. Each map is accompanied by a brief essay explaining the most important information on the map.

Early Maps of North America.
Robert M. Lunny. Newark, NJ: New Jersey Historical Society, 1961.
48 pp. $6.95. ISBN 0-686-81821-0.

This resource is especially helpful to those interested not only in history, but also in the development of cartography. The author traces the history of American cartography to 1810.

Historical Atlas of the United States.
Clifford L. Lord and Elizabeth H. Lord. New York: Johnson Reprint, 1969 (reprint of 1953 ed.).
312 pp. $39. ISBN 0-384-33650-7.

The first section of this atlas contains general maps, the second focuses on the colonial period, and the third covers maps from 1775 to 1865. Political, economic, and social data are presented.

Historical Atlas of United States Congressional Districts, 1789–1983.
Kenneth C. Martis. New York: Free Press, 1982.
302 pp. $150. ISBN 0-02-920150-0.

This volume contains maps of congressional districts from the first Congress to the 97th. The members of each Congress are listed.

Railroad Maps of North America: The First Hundred Years.
Andrew M. Modelski. Washington, DC: Library of Congress, 1984. *186 pp. $28. ISBN 0-8444-0396-2.*

This volume contains 92 maps related to the development of railroads in the United States. The maps are all historical maps from the Library of Congress collection.

These States United.
Chicago, IL: Rand McNally, 1985. *64 pp. $3. ISBN 0-528-17701-X.*

This atlas, specifically designed for student use, includes 96 maps covering U.S. history from the pre-Columbian period to the present. The volume also includes tables, graphs, and an index.

United States History Atlas.
Maplewood, NJ: Hammond, 1985. *64 pp. $4.49. ISBN 0-8437-7465-7.*

An atlas designed especially for students, the *United States History Atlas* aims to help students "discover the geographic and political influences underlying our nation's history and growth." Graphs on presidential elections, charts on the economy, and other materials supplement the maps.

Bibliographies and Printed Indexes

This listing of bibliographies and printed indexes is necessarily very selective. The bibliographies that are annotated are currently in print and cover a range of topics and periods in U.S. history. Hundreds more bibliographies and bibliographic guides are listed in the volumes we have included in the "Handbooks for Conducting Historical Research" section of this chapter. Students and teachers doing research should consult those handbooks for additional "leads" in searching for information. Note also that we have not listed print versions of indexes covered in the "Online

Databases" section of the chapter. To determine whether those databases are available in print form, contact the suppliers.

The American Electorate: A Historical Bibliography.
Santa Barbara, CA: ABC-CLIO, 1984.
388 pp. $32.50. ISBN 0-87436-372-1.

More than 1,400 works are annotated in this bibliography, which covers the electoral process, the changing nature of the electorate, and reasons for voting.

American History: A Bibliographic Review.
Carol B. Fitzgerald, ed. Westport, CT: Meckler Publishing, annual.
Approx. 200 pp. $49.95.

This annual review publishes articles on bibliographic subjects of interest to historians, special bibliographies, and some reviews of books.

American Maritime History: A Bibliography.
Susan K. Kinnell and Suzanne R. Ontiveros, eds. Santa Barbara, CA: ABC-CLIO, 1986.
260 pp. $32.50. ISBN 0-87436-471-X.

This volume annotates 919 works on U.S. and Canadian maritime history. Topics include shipbuilding, piracy, sea disasters, the sea in literature, famous voyages, and many more.

The American Presidency: A Historical Bibliography.
Santa Barbara, CA: ABC-CLIO, 1984.
376 pp. $65.50. ISBN 0-87436-370-5.

This resource focuses not only on the presidency, but on the lives of the presidents, presidential elections, and the growth of the bureaucracy. More than 3,000 works are annotated.

America's Military Past: A Guide to Information Sources.
Jack C. Lane, ed. Detroit, MI: Gale, 1980.
280 pp. $62. ISBN 0-8103-1205-0.

This guide covers major "works dealing with American land and air forces without including any naval sources." Among the annotated works are government publications, books, and articles. The guide is arranged chronologically.

Bibliographic Guide to North American History.
Boston, MA: G. K. Hall, annual.
$150/year.

This guide lists the monographs and serials cataloged by the Research Libraries of the New York Public Library and the Library of Congress on an annual basis. Topic coverage includes Canada and the United States.

Bibliographies in American History: Guide to Materials for Research.
Henry P. Beers, ed. Woodbridge, CT: Research Publications, 1982.
978 pp. $260. ISBN 0-89235-038-5.

The first portion of this work is a standard bibliography originally published in 1942. The second part, which covers the years from 1942 to 1978, picks up where the first left off. Separately published books, bibliographies appearing in journals, and bibliographies appearing as parts of larger books are all included in this massive work.

Bibliography of American Naval History.
Paolo E. Coletta, ed. Annapolis, MD: Naval Institute Press, 1981.
453 pp. $15.95. ISBN 0-87021-105-6.

The author has annotated more than 4,500 books, documents, dissertations, theses, articles, essays, interviews, and works of fiction. The materials are arranged chronologically.

Bibliography on Southern Women.
Memphis, TN: Memphis State University Center for Research on Women, 1986.
37 pp. $2.50.

This bibliography is divided into three sections: scholarly historical works, personal narratives, and research studies on social conditions and indicators. The publisher plans to update the bibliography periodically.

Biography Index.
Bronx, NY: H.W. Wilson, quarterly.
$75/yr.

This index is a guide to biographical material appearing in periodicals and books. It serves both general and scholarly reference needs.

Book Review Digest.
Bronx, NY: H.W. Wilson, monthly except February and July.
Subscription rate is on a service basis; minimum rate is $95.

This subject and title index provides excerpts of and citations to reviews of fiction and nonfiction published in the United States. Reviews of books on history for the general reader are included, making the index especially useful for teachers.

Civil War Books: A Critical Biography.
Allan Nevins, James I. Robertson, and Bell I. Wiley, eds. Wilmington, NC: Broadfoot, 1984 (reprint of 1967 ed.).
2 vols. $50 for set. ISBN 0-916107-09-4.

The first volume in this set lists books and pamphlets on military aspects of the war, prisons and prisoners of war, blacks, the navies, and diplomacy. The second volume focuses on general works on the Union and Confederacy.

The Democratic and Republican Parties in America: A Historical Bibliography.
Santa Barbara, CA: ABC-CLIO, 1984.
290 pp. $28. ISBN 0-87436-364-0.

This volume includes abstracts of more than 1,000 journal articles organized into five sections: party politics in America, the two-party system, the Republican ascendancy, the Democratic resurgence, and redefinitions and realignments.

Dickinson's American Historical Fiction.
Virginia B. Gerhardstein, ed. Methuen, NJ: Scarecrow, 1986.
368 pp. $27.50. ISBN 0-8108-1867-1.

This volume will be useful to teachers wishing to use historical fiction in their U.S. history courses. Students can also use the book to locate novels for pleasure reading or to deepen their understanding of a particular period.

Education Index.
Bronx, NY: H.W. Wilson, monthly (September–June).
Annual subscription rate determined by subscriber's periodical holdings; minimum rate is $80.

This index covers articles on education in English-language periodicals. Teachers can use this index to locate reviews of books, classroom materials, and teaching ideas.

The Female Experience in Eighteenth- and Nineteenth-Century America: A Guide to the History of American Women.
Jill Conway, ed. Princeton, NJ: Princeton University Press, 1985.
314 pp. $14.50. ISBN 0-691-00599-0.

This guide provides extensive annotated listings related to women's history in the 1700s and 1800s. The volume is a useful resource for those researching social history, as well as women's history.

Goldentree Bibliographies in American History.
Arthur Link, general ed. Arlington Heights, IL: Harlan Davidson, 1969–1981.
Variable lengths and prices.

Generally regarded as some of the finest bibliographies on particular periods or topics, this series includes the following titles of interest to teachers of early U.S. history:

American Social History Before 1860
American Economic History Before 1860
American Diplomatic History Before 1890
The American Colonies in the Seventeenth Century
The American Colonies in the Eighteenth Century
The American Revolution
Confederation, Constitution, and Early National Period
The Era of Good Feeling and the Age of Jackson
Manifest Destiny and the Coming of the Civil War
The Nation in Crisis
American Negro History
The Old South

Introduction to United States Documents.
Joe Morehead, ed. Littleton, CO: Libraries Unlimited, 1983.
309 pp. $19.50. ISBN 0-87287-362-5.

This resource, a library school text, is a reference source for anyone interested in acquiring or gathering information via the numerous publications produced by the federal government.

Labor in America: A Historical Bibliography.
Santa Barbara, CA: ABC-CLIO, 1984.
307 pp. $69. ISBN 0-87436-397-7.

This resource contains more than 2,750 annotations of journal articles on the history of labor in the United States. Students researching labor or social history will find this source helpful.

The Living History Sourcebook.
Jay Anderson. Nashville, TN: American Association for State and Local History, 1985.
469 pp. $19.95. ISBN 0-910050-75-9.

This resource contains extensively annotated listings of museums, events, books, articles, magazines, organizations, suppliers, sketchbooks, films, and simulations related to living history and reenactments. Anecdotes from the author's own experience make this more interesting reading than a typical bibliography or resource guide.

Pamphlets in American History: A Bibliographic Guide to the Microform Collections.
Henry Barnard, ed. Sanford, NC: Microfilming Corporation of America, 1979–1984.
5 volumes of varied length. $150 each.

This series serves as a bibliography of selected pamphlet literature, as well as a guide to the collection at the State Historical Society of Wisconsin. The volumes are topically organized.

Religious Conflict in America.
Albert J. Menendez. New York: Garland Publishing, 1985.
500 pp. $20. ISBN 0-8240-8904-9.

This work lists books and articles dealing with religious conflict in our nation's history. The entries are arranged chronologically.

Review of Resources: Teaching Law and the Constitution.
Mary Elizabeth Glade, ed. Boulder, CO: Social Science Education Consortium, 1987.
149 pp. $14.95. ISBN 0-89994-320-9.

This publication provides analyses of 160 sets of materials on the Constitution, Bill of Rights, and the law. Also included are bibliographies of children's literature and films with constitutional content.

Revolutionary America 1763–1789: A Bibliography.
Ronald M. Gephard, comp. Washington, DC: Government Printing Office, 1984.
2 volumes. $38 for set. ISBN 0-8444-0359-8 and 0379-2.

This two-volume set is a guide to the Library of Congress's collection of materials on revolutionary America published since 1972. The organization combines chronological and topical approaches; nearly 15,000 items are listed.

Selected Ethnic Literature: An Annotated Bibliography of Twelve Ethnic Groups.
Sharon Zirbes Fuller and H. Virginia Chacon, comps. Greeley, CO: Ukapress, 1986.
67 pp. $3.

This guide contains 329 briefly annotated entries on American ethnic groups. It also lists additional resources and ethnic holidays.

Slave Life in America: A Historiography and Selected Bibliography.
James S. Olson. Lanham, MD: University Press of America, 1983.
119 pp. $19.75. ISBN 0-8191-3285-3.

This resource annotates approximately 75 sources related to the religious, family, and cultural life of slaves. The author also provides a great deal of background information about slave life.

Sources for American Studies.
Jefferson B. Kellogg and Robert H. Walker, eds. Westport, CT: Greenwood Press, 1983.
766 pp. $45. ISBN 0-313-22555-9.

This volume contains a series of bibliographic essays on such topics as Afro-American studies, architectural history, economic history, folklore, immigration, and many more. Full citations are given for all sources mentioned in the essays.

Travels in America from the Voyages of Discovery to the Present: An Annotated Bibliography of Travel Articles in Periodicals.
Garold Cole. Norman, OK: University of Oklahoma Press, 1984.
291 pp. $48.50. ISBN 0-8061-1791-5.

The majority of travel narratives cited in this volume are from the eighteenth and nineteenth centuries. The more than 1,000 entries are grouped by region and date and are extensively indexed.

U.S. Cultural History: A Guide to Information Sources.
Philip I. Mitterling. Detroit, MI: Gale, 1980.
581 pp. $62. ISBN 0-8103-1369-3.

This volume contains numerous annotations of books and journal articles, all relating to cultural history. Sections include architecture and the arts, biography, economic, political and social thought, education, historiography, literature, and science and medicine, among others.

The War of the American Revolution: A Selected Annotated Bibliography of Published Sources.
Richard L. Blanco. New York: Garland Publishing, 1984.
654 pp. $49. ISBN 0-8240-9171-X.

This volume includes more than 3,500 books, articles, dissertations, and public documents related to the Revolution, with attention given to women, Native Americans, and other often neglected topics.

Women's Studies: A Recommended Core Bibliography.
Catherine R. Loeb, Susan E. Searing, and Esther F. Stineman. Littleton, CO: Libraries Unlimited, 1987.
238 pp. $23.50. ISBN 0-87287-598-9.

This broadly focused bibliography includes a section on history, as well as listings in such other subjects related to historical research as autobiography and other memoirs, language, and sociology.

Writings on American History: A Subject Bibliography of Books and Monographs.
James R. Masterson, comp. White Plains, NY: Kraus International, 1985.
10 volumes of varying length. $1,300 for set. ISBN 0-527-98268-7.

Along with the previously published *Writings on American History: A Bibliography of Articles,* this massive set of guides provides comprehensive coverage of materials published between 1962 and 1973. Earlier editions of *Writings on American History* provided coverage of works from 1902 to 1962.

Biographical Dictionaries

American Historians: 1600–1865.
Clyde N. Wilson, ed. Detroit, MI: Gale, 1984.
382 pp. $88. ISBN 0-8103-1144-5.

This resource offers lengthy essays on 46 writers of American history who worked in the period between 1600 and 1865. Bibliographies of writings by these historians are included.

Biographical Dictionary of Indians of the Americas.
Newport Beach, CA: American Indian Publications, 1984.
570 pp. $140. ISBN 0-317-17420-7.

This volume provides biographies of Native Americans from both
North and South America.

Complete Book of U.S. Presidents.
William A. DeGregorio. New York: Dembner Books, 1984.
691 pp. $22.50. ISBN 0-934878-36-6.

This resource describes the U.S. presidents, devoting ten to twenty
pages to each. Standard information is presented on each individual,
along with interesting and unusual facts.

Concise Dictionary of American Biography.
New York: Scribner, 1980.
1,280 pp. $75. ISBN 0-684-16631-3.

Abridged from a much longer eight-volume work, this volume contains brief biographies of thousands of Americans, none of whom
were alive at the time the volume was published. Notable people in
all walks of life are included.

Dictionary of American Negro Biography.
Rayford W. Logan and Michael R. Winston. New York: Norton,
1983.
$50. ISBN 0-393-01513-0.

This lengthy volume provides biographies of prominent black Americans from all periods of history.

Directory of American Scholars, Volume I: Historians.
Jacques Cattell Press, ed. New York: Bowker, 1982.
$90. ISBN 0-8352-1478-8.

One of four volumes in the series, this book contains biographical
information on some 9,000 historians. Personal information and data
on publications and areas of specialization are provided.

**Famous American Women: A Biographical Dictionary from Colonial
Times to the Present.**
Robert McHenry, ed. New York: Dover, 1983.
482 pp. $9.95. ISBN 0-486-24523-3.

This volume contains more than 1,000 biographical sketches of women in American history. The listings are presented alphabetically but are indexed by field and by women's organization.

Mujeres Celebres: A Biographical Encyclopedia of Hispanic Women.
Martha P. Cotera, ed. Santa Rosa, CA: National Women's History Project, 1988.
$19.95.

This volume contains biographies and pictures of Hispanic women in history. Women from the United States, Latin America, the Caribbean, and Spain are included.

Notable American Women: 1607–1950.
Edward T. James and Janet W. James, eds. Cambridge, MA: Harvard University Press, 1971.
2,141 pp. $32.50. ISBN 0-674-62734-2.

This work was specifically written to fill in the gaps left by other biographical dictionaries, which tended to emphasize males. More than 1,300 women in various periods of U.S. history are included in this work.

Webster's American Biographies.
Springfield, MA: Merriam-Webster, 1984.
1,233 pp. $18.95. ISBN 0-87779-253-4.

This well-known reference contains more than 3,000 entries covering prominent Americans from all historical periods. Native Americans, women, and western pioneers are among the traditionally neglected groups paid close attention in this book.

Who Was Who in America: A Series Providing Concise Biographies of the Outstanding Individuals of America's Past . . . from 1607 to the Present, Volume I: 1607–1897.
Chicago, IL: Marquis, 1963.
1,396 pp. $67.50. ISBN 0-8379-0201-0.

The first in a series of nine volumes, this resource treats public figures in U.S. history from 1607 to 1897. The descriptions are somewhat more detailed than those provided in the *Concise Dictionary of American Biography* or *Webster's American Biographies.*

Dictionaries

Concise Dictionary of American History.
New York: Scribner, 1983.
1,140 pp. $70. ISBN 0-684-17321-2.

This greatly condensed version of the *Dictionary of American History* contains more than 6,000 entries covering U.S. history from prehistoric times to the 1980s.

Dictionary of American History.
Michael Martin and Leonard Gelber. Boston: Littlefield, Adams, 1981.
714 pp. $9.95. ISBN 0-8226-0124-9.

This compact reference includes more than 4,000 entries related to political, military, social, technological, and intellectual history. Slogans and sayings are also included.

Dictionary of Historical Terms.
Chris Cook. New York: Peter Bedrick Books, 1983.
304 pp. $22. ISBN 0-911745-16-5.

This book includes 2,000 terms used in examining U.S. and world history. Extensive cross-references are provided.

Dictionary of the Social Sciences.
Hugo F. Reading. New York: Methuen, 1977.
$21.95. ISBN 0-7100-8642-3.

Terms related to research methodologies will be useful to students and teachers interested in developing skill in historical research.

The Encyclopedic Dictionary of American History.
Sluice Dock, CT: Dushkin, 1986.
344 pp. $9.95. ISBN 0-87967-605-1.

This volume includes more than 1,500 entries arranged alphabetically and extensively cross-referenced. Includes entries on people, events, and developments.

Encyclopedias, Almanacs, and Chronologies

The Abraham Lincoln Encyclopedia.
Mark E. Neely, Jr. New York: McGraw-Hill, 1982.
416 pp. $39.96. ISBN 0-07-046145-7.

This reference work includes 300 alphabetically arranged articles on Lincoln and his views on such topics as economics, race, Thomas Jefferson, and others. The volume is illustrated with photographs, cartoons, lithographs, and engravings.

The Almanac of American History.
Arthur M. Schlesinger, ed. New York: Putnam, 1983.
623 pp. $7.98. ISBN 0-399-51082-6.

This volume traces important events in U.S. history from the early arrival of European settlers to 1982. Each chronological section is introduced by a prominent U.S. historian. Events covered include not only military and political history, but also art, culture, intellectual history, labor history, and more.

Annals of America: 1493–1973.
Mortimer Adler, ed. Chicago: Encyclopaedia Britannica Educational Corporation, 1976.
23 vols. of various lengths. $459 for set. ISBN 0-87827-199-6.

The volumes in this series are arranged chronologically. Each volume presents a chronology of important events enhanced with primary source material related to those events.

The Discoverers: An Encyclopedia of Explorers and Explorations.
Helen Delpar. New York: McGraw-Hill, 1979.
$49.95. ISBN 0-07-016264-6.

This single-volume resource treats explorers and their discoveries in more depth than a traditional encyclopedia. The volume is a good starting point for research on the topic.

Encyclopaedia Britannica.
Chicago: Encyclopaedia Britannica Educational Corporation, 1987.
$1,049 (includes free rolling book cart). ISBN 0-85229-444-1.

The *Encyclopaedia Britannica* is a sound general encyclopedia to use for broad summaries of historical topics and events.

Encyclopedia of American Economic History.
Glenn Porter, ed. New York: Scribner, 1980.
1,286 pp. $200. ISBN 0-684-16271-7.

This three-volume reference work includes entries on important events, people, and policies in American economic history.

Encyclopedia of American Facts and Dates.
Gorton Carruth and Associates. New York: Crowell, 1979.
1,015 pp. $14.95. ISBN 0-690-01669-7.

A standard reference work, this volume is arranged chronologically. Topics covered include politics and government, war, books, art, architecture, science, economics, education, folklore, and many more.

Encyclopedia of American Foreign Policy.
Alexander De Conde, ed. New York: Scribner, 1978.
1,201 pp. $200. ISBN 0-684-15503-6.

This three-volume work contains 95 essays on "concepts, themes, large ideas, theories, and distinctive policies in the history of American foreign relations." Bibliographies, cross-references, and a biographical dictionary are included.

Encyclopedia of American History.
Richard B. Morris, ed. New York: Harper and Row, 1982.
1,285 pp. $29.45. ISBN 0-06-181605-1.

A standard work that is frequently revised, this volume is divided into four main parts: a basic chronology, a topical chronology, biographical sketches of 500 notable Americans, and a section on the structure of the federal government.

Encyclopedia of American Political History.
Jack P. Greene, ed. New York: Scribner, 1984.
1,420 pp. $200. ISBN 0-683-17003-5.

This three-volume work presents approximately 90 scholarly articles on "major issues, themes, institutions, processes, and developments as they have been manifest through the whole of United States history." Each article includes a bibliography.

Encyclopedia Americana.
Danbury, CT: Grolier, 1987.
$799 plus $23 shipping.

The *Encyclopedia Americana* is an excellent source of general information on history. It contains broad summaries of historical events
and biographical sketches of important Americans suitable for use by
students.

Encyclopedia of Black America.
W. Augustus Low and Virgil A. Clift. New York: McGraw-Hill, 1980.
992 pp. $76. ISBN 0-07-038834-2.

This work, arranged alphabetically, covers the black American experience from the colonial period to 1980. Education, employment,
politics, agriculture, labor, medicine, literature, music, and many
other topical areas.

Harvard Encyclopedia of American Ethnic Groups.
Stephan Thernstrom, ed. Cambridge, MA: Harvard University Press,
1980.
2,001 pp. $70. ISBN 0-674-37512-2.

This massive work provides an alphabetical listing of American ethnic groups. Topics covered for each group are origins, migration,
arrival, settlement, economic life, social structure, social organization,
family and kinship, behavior and personal/individual characteristics,
culture, religion, education, politics, intergroup relations, group maintenance, and individual ethnic commitment. A bibliography is also
provided for each group.

International Encyclopedia of the Social Sciences.
New York: Free Press, 1977.
$310. ISBN 0-02-895700-8.

This reference work contains signed articles dealing with the social
sciences and history. The articles contain illustrations, bibliographies,
and cross-references. Contributors include leading scholars in their
respective fields.

The Oxford History of the American People.
Samuel Eliot Morison. New York: New American Library, 1965.
*3 volumes of varying length. $3.95–$4.95 each. ISBN 0-451-62192-1,
62408-4, and 62446-7.*

These volumes cover the history of the United States from the pre-Columbian period to the 1963 assassination of John F. Kennedy. Political, social, cultural, military, and economic history are covered.

The Timetables of American History.
Laurence Urdang, ed. New York: Simon and Schuster, 1981.
470 pp. $13.95. ISBN 0-671-25246-1.

This volume presents a chronology of U.S. history in tabular form. Columns cover history and politics, the arts, science and technology, and miscellaneous. The fact that events outside the United States are also included will help students gain a global perspective.

Handbooks for Conducting Historical Research

Handbook for Research in American History: A Guide to Bibliographies and Other Reference Works.
Francis Paul Prucha. Lincoln, NE: University of Nebraska Press, 1987.
302 pp. $9.95. ISBN 0-8032-8719-4.

This is an extensive guide to information sources in U.S. history. The first part of the book deals with sources by type: library catalogs and guides, general bibliographies, book review indexes, and so on. The second part of the book is organized by subject area: political history, foreign affairs, military history, and so on.

Harvard Guide to American History.
Frank Freidel, ed. Cambridge, MA: Harvard University Press, 1974.
1,312 pp. $15. ISBN 0-674-37555-6.

A classic reference, this volume is organized into four sections: research methods and materials, biographies and personal records, comprehensive and area histories, and histories of special subjects.

Historian's Handbook: A Descriptive Guide to Reference Works.
Helen J. Poulton with Marguerite S. Howland. Norman, OK: University of Oklahoma Press, 1986.
300 pp. $10.95. ISBN 0-8061-1009-0.

The subtitle of this book accurately sums up its purpose and contents. It is somewhat different from other handbooks because the items cited are described, a feature that will make it useful to newcomers to historical research.

History: A Student's Guide to Research and Writing.
Robert Skapura and John Marlowe. Littleton, CO: Libraries Unlimited, 1988.
48 pp. $30 for set of 10. ISBN 0-87287-649-7.

This brief guide is designed to give students direction in beginning their research for reports and term papers. Steps in preparing a paper are also given.

The Modern Researcher.
Jacques Barzun and Henry F. Graff. New York: Harcourt Brace Jovanovich, 1985.
480 pp. $13.95. ISBN 0-15-562512-8.

This book focuses in detail on the process of conducting research and writing results. Students and teachers who use it not only will get direction in conducting their own research, but also will have a deeper understanding of how historians work.

A Student's Guide to History.
Jules R. Benjamin. New York: St. Martin's Press, 1987.
175 pp. $7.95. ISBN 0-312-77004-9.

This small handbook focuses not only on historical research, but also on the use of history, reading history assignments and taking notes in class, studying for exams, writing book reviews and short papers. Thus it is a complete guide to the study of history and may be an especially suitable introduction for high school students.

Online Databases

The databases cited in this section are available through one or all of the following vendors:

Bibliographic Retrieval Services (BRS) Information Technologies
1200 Route 7

Latham, NY 12110
(800) 345-4BRS

DIALOG Information Services, Inc.
3460 Hillview Avenue
Palo Alto, CA 94304
(800) 3-DIALOG

Unisys Corporation
2400 Colorado Avenue
Santa Monica, CA 90406
(213) 829-7511

Academic American Encyclopedia Database (AAED)
Supplier: Grolier Electronic Publishing
Availability: BRS: $20/hr.; citations: $.37 online, no offline charges

DIALOG: $45/hr.; citations: no online charge, $.25 off-line

This online edition of Grolier's academic encyclopedia provides teachers and students with 30,000 full-text entries, including tables, charts, cross-references, and bibliographic entries from the print version.

America: History and Life
Supplier: ABC-CLIO
Availability: DIALOG: $65/hr.; citations: no online charge, $.15 off-line

This database indexes articles from almost 2,000 journals published worldwide. Books, book reviews, and dissertations are also indexed. The focus is the history and culture of the United States and Canada from prehistoric times to the present.

Arts and Humanities SEARCH
Supplier: The Institute for Scientific Information
Availability: BRS: $60/hr.; citations: $.39 online, no offline charges

This database focuses on arts and the humanities, including archaeology, architecture, dance, film, television, radio, folklore, history, language, linguistics, literature, music, philosophy, theater, and religion.

Biography Master Index
Supplier: Gale Research Company
Availability: DIALOG: $63/hr.; citations: $.55 online, $.65 offline

This is an index to biographical information from more than 600 publications, including biographical dictionaries, directories, and various kinds of handbooks.

Cendata
Supplier: U.S. Bureau of the Census
Availability: DIALOG: $36/hr.; citations: no online charge, $.20 offline

Cendata is a full-text database providing demographic and economic information from the Bureau of the Census. Also available via Cendata are the 20 most recent press releases from the Bureau of the Census.

Congressional Record Abstracts
Supplier: National Standards Association
Availability: DIALOG: $96/hr.; citations: $.15 online, $.25 offline

This database presents abstracts for each issue of the Congressional Record, the official journal of the legislative branch. This database will be of most interest to history students as a source of information on how current debates reflect enduring issues.

Dissertation Abstracts Online
Supplier: University Microfilms International
Availability: BRS: $34/hr.; citations: $.26 online, no offline charges

DIALOG: $72/hr.; citations: $.25 online, $.25 offline

This database provides access to virtually all doctoral dissertations accepted at North American universities since 1861. Only those dissertations added since 1980 have been abstracted, however. Information on ordering copies of the actual dissertations is supplied.

Educational Resources Information Center (ERIC)
Supplier: Office of Educational Research and Improvement
Availability: BRS: $16–$35/hr.; citations: $.11 online, no offline charge

DIALOG: $30/hr.; citations: $.10 online, $.14 offline

Unisys: $35/hr.; citations: $.10 online, $.14 offline

ERIC provides coverage of all areas of education, including history. Focus is on journal literature and "fugitive" documents not readily available elsewhere; these include locally developed materials, research reports, and conference papers, among others.

GPO Publications Reference File
Supplier: U.S. Government Printing Office
Availability: BRS: $26–$35/hr.; citations: $.07 online, no offline
charge

DIALOG: $35/hr.; citations: no online charge, $.10 off-
line

This database lists all documents for sale by the GPO. It can be
used to locate and order government publications dealing with
history, such as reports from the National Endowment for the Humanities or the U.S. Bureau of the Census.

Historical Abstracts
Supplier: ABC-CLIO
Availability: DIALOG: $65/hr.; citations: no online charge, $.15 off-
line

Articles from nearly 2,000 journals published worldwide are summarized and indexed. Focus is on history, social sciences, and humanities. Also cited are books and dissertations. Although the focus is not
strictly the United States and Canada, students of U.S. history can
use the database to gather information about events that impacted
the United States.

Social SciSearch
Supplier: Institute for Scientific Information
Availability: BRS: $43.50–$64.50/hr.; citations: $.23 online, $.15 off-
line

DIALOG: Nonsubscribers—$159/hr.; citations: $.20 online, $.25 offline. Subscribers—$62/hr.; citations: $.20
online, $.25 offline

This database allows researchers to trace citations both forward (i.e.,
find those works cited in a later work) and backward (i.e., find those
works that have cited a particular previous work). Social and behav-
ioral sciences are covered, as are interdisciplinary areas of study and
approaches to history.

Periodicals

American Heritage: The Magazine of History
American Heritage (division of Forbes)
60 Fifth Avenue

New York, NY 10011
Bimonthly, plus issues in April and November. $24/yr.

This popular and lavishly illustrated journal covers a wide range of topics. For example, among the features in a recent issue were an analysis of the letters of General William Tecumseh Sherman; an article about the discovery of Machu Picchu; a memoir by historian Annie Dillard, who as a child was already intrigued by the French and Indian War; an article on the battle for Wake Island in World War II; and never-before-published photographs of FDR.

American Historical Review
American Historical Association
400 A Street, SE
Washington, DC 20003
5 times/yr. $43/yr.

This scholarly journal covers all periods of U.S. history as well as world history. Each issue contains five lengthy articles and a number of scholarly reviews.

American West
American West Publishing
3033 North Campbell Avenue
Tucson, AZ 85719
Bimonthly. $15/yr.

The official journal of the Western History Association, *American West* is written for both scholars and the general public. Each issue includes eight or nine articles on topics related to the West. The journal is illustrated.

Aztlan—International Journal of Chicano Studies Research
University of California, Los Angeles
Chicano Studies Research Center
405 Hilgard Avenue
Los Angeles, CA 90024
Semiannual. Individuals: $15/yr.; institutions: $20/yr.

Although the focus of this journal is broader than history, looking at contemporary concerns as well, it is of interest to students and teachers researching the history of Hispanics in the United States.

Civil War History: A Journal of the Middle Period
Kent State University Press
Kent, OH 44242
Quarterly. Individuals: $15/yr.; institutions: $25/yr.

Each issue of this quarterly journal includes four or five articles on topics related to the Civil War and Reconstruction. Critical book reviews are also featured.

Ethnohistory
American Society for Ethnohistory
Arizona State Museum
University of Arizona
Tucson, AZ 85721
Quarterly. $10/yr.

This illustrated journal is "devoted to original research in the documentary history of the culture and movements of primitive peoples and related problems." Book reviews are included.

Great Plains Quarterly
Center for Great Plains Studies
1214 Oldfather Hall
University of Nebraska
Lincoln, NE 68588
Quarterly. $15/yr.

This journal focuses on issues related to the history and culture of the Great Plains, from earliest times to the present. Relevant books are reviewed.

Hispanic American Historical Review
Duke University Press
P.O. Box 6697
Durham, NC 27708
Quarterly. Individuals: $28/yr.; institutions: $45/yr.

Every issue of this scholarly journal includes four or five articles, with emphasis on the period from the seventeenth to nineteenth centuries. Critical book reviews are provided.

History News
American Association for State and Local History
172 Second Avenue North
Nashville, TN 37201
Monthly. Individuals: $40/yr.; students: $25/yr.; institutions: varies depending on annual budget (all rates include membership in AASLH)

History News includes articles on a range of topics of interest to museums, historians, and educators. Numerous announcements of programs and publications are included in the journal.

The History and Social Science Teacher
Grolier Publications
16 Overlea Boulevard
Toronto, Ontario, Canada M4H 1A6
Quarterly. Individuals: $16/yr.; students: $12/yr.; institutions: $19/yr.

This journal publishes articles on "curricular issues related to history, social sciences and social studies." For example, a recent issue included articles on the educational use of museums, local history, using pre-Columbian art to teach history, and researching social issues using databases.

Humanities
National Endowment for the Humanities
Superintendent of Documents
Government Printing Office
Washington, DC 20402
Bimonthly. $9/yr.

This journal, prepared by the National Endowment for the Humanities, carries scholarly articles, comments from prominent Americans on the value of the humanities in their own educations, and announcements of various NEH programs.

Journal of American History
Organization of American Historians
112 North Bryan Street
Bloomington, IN 47401
Quarterly. Individual: depends on income; students: $12/yr.; institutions: $80/yr. (all rates include membership in OAH)

This scholarly journal focuses exclusively on U.S. history, providing several scholarly articles and a large number of critical book reviews in each issue.

Journal of the History of Ideas
Temple University
Philadelphia, PA 19122
Quarterly. Individuals: $15/yr.; institutions: $25/yr.

This scholarly journal is devoted to intellectual and cultural history. Subjects treated include the history of philosophy, literature and the arts, the natural and social sciences, and religious, political, and social movements. At the secondary level, this journal is likely to be useful for advanced placement classes only.

Journal of Interdisciplinary History
MIT Press
28 Carleton Street
Cambridge, MA 02142
Quarterly. Individuals: $26/yr.; institutions: $60/yr.

This journal presents scholarly articles on interdisciplinary approaches to the study of history. Book reviews are included.

Journal of Social History
Carnegie-Mellon University Press
Schenley Park
Pittsburgh, PA 15213
Quarterly. $22/yr.

This scholarly journal includes interdisciplinary articles on social history topics, including women's history, history of the family, and history of various ethnic groups. Book reviews are included.

Journal of Southern History
Southern Historical Association
Rice University
P.O. Box 1892
Houston, TX 77251
Quarterly. $20/yr.

This highly regarded journal presents three or four scholarly articles in each issue. The focus is, as the title suggests, the history of the southern United States. Book reviews are also included.

Labor History
New York University
Bobst Library
70 Washington Square South
New York, NY 10012
Quarterly. Individuals: $21/yr.; institutions: $28/yr.

This journal focuses on the study of the history of work and the labor movement in the United States. Although a majority of the articles treat periods after 1865, some articles do relate to the early years of U.S. history.

Magazine of History for Teachers of American History
Organization of American Historians
112 North Bryan Street

Bloomington, IN 47401
Quarterly. Individuals: $12/yr.; institutions: $17/yr.

This relatively new journal is designed to "address the interests and concerns of secondary history and social studies teachers." Each issue has a particular theme (e.g., development of nationalism, slavery, the frontier, the Constitution), presenting two or three articles on the theme along with three or four lesson plans complementing the articles. An interesting feature is a column in which secondary students discuss history topics.

Negro History Bulletin
Association for the Study of Afro-American Life and History
1407 14th Street, NW
Washington, DC 20005
Quarterly. Individuals: $25/yr.; institutions: $30/yr.

This journal treats the history of black Americans in three to six long articles per issue. Critical book reviews are also included in every issue.

New England Quarterly: A Historical Review of New England Life and Letters
New England Quarterly
Meserve Hall, 2nd Floor
Boston, MA 02115
Quarterly. $15/yr.

New England Quarterly is another highly regarded regional journal focusing on the history and culture of the region. In addition to four or five scholarly articles per issue, the journal provides critical book reviews.

Prologue: Journal of the National Archives
National Archives and Records Administration
Pennsylvania Avenue and Eighth Street
Washington, DC 20408
Quarterly. $12/yr.

This journal publishes scholarly articles based on records in the National Archives. Announcements of National Archives programs are also included in the journal.

Reviews in American History
Johns Hopkins University Press
701 West 40th Street

Baltimore, MD 21211
Quarterly. Individuals: $18/yr.; students: $16/yr.; institutions: $45/yr.

This journal is devoted to reviews of scholarly historical writings, including 20 or more in each issue.

Signs: Journal of Women in Culture and Society
University of Chicago Press
P.O. Box 37005
Chicago, IL 60637
Quarterly. Individuals: $29/yr.; institutions: $58/yr.

This interdisciplinary journal treats new scholarship about women. Although the journal has a broad scope, many articles are of interest to students and teachers of early U.S. history. For example, a special issue recently focused on women and the Constitution.

Social Education
National Council for the Social Studies
3501 Newark Street, NW
Washington, DC 20016
7 times/yr. Individuals: $40/yr.; students: $20/yr. (rates include membership in NCSS)

The official journal of NCSS, *Social Education* contains analytical articles as well as articles focusing on what and how to teach. All of the content areas comprising social studies are covered; several special sections in recent years have focused particularly on history.

Teaching History: A Journal of Methods
Emporia State University
Emporia, KS 66801
Semiannually. Individuals: $5/yr.; institutions: $10/yr.

This journal focuses on the teaching of history, in both high schools and colleges. The articles cover world history, as well as U.S. history. Critical book reviews are provided.

Technology and Culture
University of Chicago Press
P.O. Box 37005
Chicago, IL 60637
Quarterly. Individuals: $23.40/yr.; students: $16.15/yr.; institutions: $42.50/yr.

Prepared by the Society for the History of Technology, this journal focuses on "the development of technology and its relation with society and culture." Each issue includes two or three scholarly articles, reviews of museum exhibits related to technology, reports on conferences, and critical book reviews.

William and Mary Quarterly
Institute of Early American History and Culture
P.O. Box 220
Williamsburg, VA 23187
Quarterly. $15/yr.

This scholarly journal focuses on American history and culture prior to 1815. It thus is perhaps the journal best focused for study of early American history. It includes both scholarly articles and critical book reviews.

Women's Studies Quarterly
The Feminist Press
City University of New York
311 East 94th Street
New York, NY 10128
Quarterly. Individuals: $25/yr.; institutions: $35/yr.

This interdisciplinary journal covers issues and events related to women's studies and feminist education at all levels. Two issues each year have special themes (e.g., women and art; women and history; women, race and culture) and two are general. In addition to articles, course descriptions, and book reviews, the journal provides announcements of grants, scholarships, and other programs of interest.

Resources on Teaching History

The resources listed in this section are varied in their intent. Some were written to provide guidance or assistance to history teachers in improving their courses. Others, written in an attempt to reshape the curriculum in our schools, are usually not as directly helpful to teachers, but should be on the professional shelf of every school library because of the public debate and inquiry they have prompted.

Abrams, Eileen. **A Curriculum Guide to Women's Studies for the Middle School, Grades 5–9.**
New York: The Feminist Press, 1981.
60 pp. Paperbound. $6.95. ISBN 0-912670-94-0.

This guide for teaching about women in history and society can be used to plan a course on women or to plan for infusion into U.S. history and other courses.

Academic Preparation in Social Studies: Teaching for Transition from High School to College.
New York: College Entrance Examination Board, 1986.
112 pp. Softbound. $6.95. ISBN 0-87447-224-5.

One of six sequels to the College Board's *Academic Preparation for College* (1983), this book suggests three changes in the content of social studies: (1) use of new findings in social history, (2) adoption of a worldwide perspective, and (3) more thorough incorporation of social studies concepts. The book describes how these three changes might be made in a program based on a core of world history, U.S. history, and American government.

Banks, James A. **Multiethnic Education: Theory and Practice.**
Lexington, MA: Allyn and Bacon, 1981.
300 pp. Hardbound. $22.86. ISBN 0-205-07293-3.

This resource, by a leading proponent of multiethnic education, describes the history, rationale, and goals of multiethnic education; presents methodological issues and models; discusses characteristics and curricular reform; examines relationships to specific areas of the curriculum; and includes curriculum guidelines applicable to all areas.

Cheney, Lynne V. **American Memory: A Report on the Humanities in the Nation's Public Schools.**
Washington, DC: National Endowment for the Humanities, 1987.
35 pp. Paperbound. $4.

One of the reports contributing to the debate on the place of history in the curriculum, this booklet looks at problems with the current curriculum—too much emphasis on process, poor textbooks, and ill-prepared and overworked teachers. Three recommendations linked to these perceived problems conclude this essentially political document.

Commission on the Humanities. **The Humanities in American Life.**
Berkeley, CA: University of California Press, 1980.
205 pp. Paperbound. $5.95. ISBN 0-520-04183-6.

This report assesses the status of the humanities in the schools, in higher education, and in community and private life. It then makes recommendations for priorities and suggests methods of garnering support for the humanities.

Downey, Matthew T., ed. **"The Children of Yesterday."** *Social Education* 50 no. 4 (April–May 1986): 260–293.
$5 for back issue of journal.

This special section of *Social Education* focuses on teaching about children in history. It includes an introduction to the benefits and possible pitfalls of teaching about children, several articles describing programs in which children are incorporated into the study of history, and an extensive annotated bibliography on the history of childhood.

Downey, Matthew T., ed. **History in the Schools.**
Washington, DC: National Council for the Social Studies, 1985.
54 pp. Paperbound. $7.25. ISBN 0-87986-049-9.

This document, the product of a one-day conference on the status of history education, looks at the place of history in the curriculum and concludes that it is still the dominant social studies subject. Problems in the curriculum, the methods and materials used in history classes, and preparation of history teachers are examined.

Downey, Matthew T., ed. **Teaching American History: New Directions.**
Washington, DC: National Council for the Social Studies, 1982.
115 pp. Paperbound. $8.75. ISBN 0-87986-043-X.

This volume looks at five areas of historical scholarship and their implications for the teaching of U.S. history. These areas are women, family, labor, Native Americans, and social history. For each, an essay on research in the area is followed by suggestions for classroom practice.

Finn, Chester E., Jr., Diane Ravitch, and Robert T. Fancher, eds. **Against Mediocrity: The Humanities in America's High Schools.**
New York: Holmes and Meier, 1984
287 pp. Paperbound. $11.50. ISBN 0-8419-0945-8.

This collection examines the importance of humanities to education as a whole and discusses and provides case studies on the teaching of English, foreign languages, and history. Several articles are devoted to the education of teachers and improvement of teaching.

FitzGerald, Frances. **America Revised.**
New York: Random House, 1980.
256 pp. Paperbound. $5.95. ISBN 0-394-74439-X.

The author of this best-seller, a journalist, provides an analysis and critique of U.S. history textbooks and compares texts from different eras. FitzGerald's thesis is that national and educational politics have more influence on texts than historical scholarship.

Haynes, Charles C. **Religious Freedom in America: A Teacher's Guide.**
Silver Spring, MD: Americans United Research Foundation.
108 pp. Paperbound. $2. ISBN 0-9617164-0-1.

This publication provides teachers with a variety of source materials for integrating the story of religious liberty into the curriculum. Background essays on religious freedom are followed by annotated lists of classroom materials for teaching about various topics and lists of other resources.

Hirsch, E.D., Jr. **Cultural Literacy: What Every American Needs to Know.**
Boston, MA: Houghton Mifflin, 1987.
268 pp. Hardbound. $16.59. ISBN 0-395-43095-X.

Hirsch's best-seller has four major components: a review of the research on reading, emphasizing the need for background information to read effectively; a discussion of why national language and culture are important in a pluralistic society; an analysis of how and why the schools have failed to develop cultural literacy and suggestions for addressing the problem; and the "list of what literate Americans know."

History–Social Science Framework for California Public Schools.
Sacramento, CA: California State Department of Education, 1988.
136 pp. Paperbound. $6. ISBN 0-8011-0712-1.

This new framework, which many expect to be a model for other states as well, proposes a substantially different curriculum arrangement than has been traditional for more than 50 years. Key differences include more emphasis on history and integration of biography, literature, and art with the teaching of history.

Howard, James, and Thomas Mendenhall. **Making History Come Alive.**
Washington, DC: Council for Basic Education.
99 pp. Paperbound. $5.50.

Yet another study on the status of history in the schools, this report concludes that "history is in trouble." The authors suggest reasons why history is important, why it is not taught as extensively as they believe it ought to be, and what the "irreducible minimum" of history instruction ought to be. Appendices provide various aids for history teachers.

Keller, Clair W., and Denny L. Schillings, eds. **Teaching About the Constitution.**
Washington, DC: National Council for the Social Studies, 1987.
122 pp. Paperbound. $10.95. ISBN 0-87986-055-3.

This volume includes four brief scholarly essays on the origins and development of the Constitution, along with teaching activities related to the content in the essays. Most valuable are teaching activities on constitutional change, an area in which there is still room for additional instructional materials.

Kyvig, David E., ed. **Nearby History Series.**
Nashville, TN: American Association for State and Local History, 1986– .
3 books, 124–176 pp. Paperbound. $11.95 each. ISBN 0-910050-82-1, 84-8, and 88-0.

To date, this series includes three titles, although more will be published in the future. Each volume is subtitled "Exploring Their History" and focuses on one kind of place that can be explored in "doing" and teaching about local history. The first volume looks at local schools, the second at houses and homes, and the third at public places, such as parks, streets, and government buildings.

Metcalf, Fay D., and Matthew T. Downey. **Teaching Local History: Trends, Tips, and Resources.**
Boulder, CO: Social Science Education Consortium, 1977.
104 pp. Paperbound. $12.95. ISBN 0-89994-215-6.

This publication contains a variety of suggestions to help teachers introduce the study of local history. Topics covered include using the community as a historical resource; social, economic, and family history; architecture and public art; and folklore and cultural journalism.

Patrick, John J., ed., **"The U.S. Constitution and American Values,"** *Social Education* 51 no. 5 (September 1987): 328–355.
$5 for back issue of journal.

This special section of *Social Education* examines the values of democratic government and the place of the Constitution in citizen education. An essay by William Bennett on James Madison as a role model for today's students and a piece on the use of debates to develop understanding and values are also included, as is an annotated bibliography of educational materials. This issue of *Social Education* is also of interest because it contains a special insert on the Northwest Ordinance, prepared by Patrick.

Patrick, John J., Richard Remy, and Mary Jane Turner. **Education on the Constitution in Secondary Schools.**
Bloomington, IN: Social Studies Development Center, 1986.
91 pp. Paperbound. $10.

The authors provide an overview of the status of education on the Constitution as of 1986, describe six generic teaching strategies for teaching about the Constitution, apply these generic strategies to constitutional topics, and describe bicentennial programs and materials.

Ravitch, Diane, and Chester E. Finn, Jr. **What Do Our 17-Year-Olds Know? A Report on the First National Assessment of History and Literature.**
New York: Harper and Row, 1987.
302 pp. Hardbound. $15.95. ISBN 0-06-015849-2.

This much-publicized book reports the findings of a national assessment of what 17-year-olds know about history and literature. It describes how and why the assessments were done and presents the learning objectives for the assessments. It describes how students did on the questions; looks at correlations between such factors as parent education, sex, and ethnic background and performance; and presents recommendations for remedying the problem the assessment revealed—that students appear to know little about history and literature.

Rosenzweig, Linda W., **"Teaching About Social History,"** *Social Education* 46 no. 5 (May 1982): 321–336.
$5 for back issue of journal.

This special section of *Social Education* presents two especially useful articles. One presents an approach to integrating social history into history courses, and the other looks at the use of social history in social science courses. Two lists of resources for teaching social history are included.

Sewall, Gilbert T. American History Textbooks: An Assessment of Quality.
New York: Educational Excellence Network, Teachers College, 1987.
82 pp. Paperbound. $4.

Like several other reports listed in this section, this volume has provoked considerable controversy. It provides a scathing critique of history textbooks and suggests recommendations for their improvement. It should be noted that no specific criteria for evaluating the texts were provided to the reviewers, severely limiting the value of the study; still, the report is worth reading because of the debate it has engendered.

Women's History Curriculum Guide.
Santa Rosa, CA: National Women's History Project, n.d.
63 pp. Paperbound. $7.95. ISBN 0-938625-6920-7.

This K–12 curriculum guide provides background information for educators unfamiliar with the history of women in the United States, along with numerous suggestions for classroom use. Recommended supplementary instructional materials are listed.

Classroom Materials

7

Computer Software

America, An Early History
Source: Aquarius Instructional
            P.O. Box 128
            Indian Rocks Beach, FL 34635
Cost: Complete series of 6 disks: $150; individual disks: $29.95
Type: Simulation
Grades: 6–12
Systems: Apple family; TRS-80

This series develops student understanding of social, religious, economic, and political influences on early American life. Titles in the series are *A New Continent Is Discovered; Jamestown, An Early Settlement; The Thirteen Colonies; The Struggle for Independence; American Explorers;* and *Western Expansion.*

American History Decades Games
Source: Social Studies School Service
            P.O. Box 802
            Culver City, CA 90232
            (developed by BrainBank)
Cost: Complete series of 3 disks and guides: $110; individual
            disk with guide: $39
Type: Game
Grades: 7–10
Systems: Apple family

Each disk contains five games that quiz students on the decades in which particular events in U.S. history occurred. Events related to politics, economics, science, technology, folklore, and art are included. The game can accommodate one to four players.

American History Explorer Series
Source: Mindscape
            3444 Dundee Road
            Northbrook, IL 60062
Cost: Complete series of 4 disks and 4 guides: $150; individual
            disks and guides: $39.95
Type: Tutorial
Grades: 5–8
Systems: Apple II family (64K), IBM PC/PCjr, Tandy 1000

The explorers in the title of this series are students, who "explore a
specific historical event, identify the event taking place, and give
clues to support their conclusions." Titles in the series are *Revolution and Constitution, Discovery and Exploration, Westward Expansion,* and *Civil War.*

American History Keyword Series
Source: Focus Media
            P.O. Box 865
            Garden City, NY 11530
Cost: 2 disks and guides: $45 each
Type: Drill and practice
Grades: 7–12
Systems: Apple II family

These two disks help students review important vocabulary terms
related to the Civil War and westward expansion. A variety of clues,
such as definitions, examples, synonyms, and historical references,
are provided to help students identify the terms.

The American People
Source: Focus Media
            P.O. Box 865
            Garden City, NY 11530
Cost: $45
Type: Game
Grades: 5–12
Systems: Apple II family; Commodore 64 and 128

Students compete to identify well-known Americans in the following
categories: explorers, women, inventors, sports, the arts, and military
leaders.

The American Revolution
Source: BLS Tutorsystems
2503 Fairlee Road
Wilmington, DE 19810
Cost: Complete series of 3 disks and guide: $165
Type: Tutorial
Grades: 7–12
Systems: Apple family

This three-part program helps students more fully understand the American Revolution. Titles in the series are *The Age of Discord, The War of Independence,* and *Saratoga and the French Alliance.*

Choice or Chance?
Source: Rand McNally
P.O. Box 7600
Chicago, IL 60680
Cost: Complete series of 3 disks, guide, and masters for student workbook: $111
Type: Simulation
Grades: 7–9
Systems: Apple II family; Atari 800

This program focuses on the relationship between geography and history. Students take the roles of such explorers as DeSoto and Hudson, making decisions on scenarios faced by the explorers and comparing the results they achieved with what actually happened.

The Civil War
Source: Hartley Courseware
P.O. Box 419
Dimondale, MI 48821
Cost: $89.95
Type: Simulation
Grades: 10–12
Systems: Apple (64K); IBM PC (256K)

This simulation allows students to plan strategy for the North and South in the Civil War, accounting for each side's strengths and weaknesses. The aim is to give students "greater understanding of why the Civil War took place and how it affected all Americans."

The Constitution and the Government of the United States
Source: Educational Activities
            P.O. Box 392
            Freeport, NY 11520
Cost: Complete series of 3 disks and 5 booklets: $179
Type: Tutorial
Grades: 7–12
Systems: Apple family

This tutorial program uses a case study approach to help students develop their understanding of the Constitution. Actual Supreme Court cases illustrate how the meaning of the Constitution has changed over time.

The Constitution of the United States
Source: BLS Tutorsystems
            2503 Fairlee Road
            Wilmington, DE 19810
Cost: Complete series of 5 disks and guide: $255
Type: Tutorial
Grades: 7–12
Systems: Apple family

This series of lessons uses a variety of techniques to teach about the Constitution. Titles in the series are *The Age of the Constitution; The Preamble and Article I; The Legislative Branch, Article I; Articles II–VII;* and *The Amendments to the Constitution.*

Creating the U.S. Constitution
Source: Educational Activities
            P.O. Box 392
            Freeport, NY 11520
Cost: $59.95
Type: Simulation
Grades: 7–12
Systems: Apple family

This interactive simulation is a single-disk introduction to the workings of the constitutional convention. Students assume the role of one of six important members of the convention, interacting with other delegates and voting on issues as their "role" would have voted.

Decisions, Decisions: American History Series
Source: Tom Snyder Productions
         90 Sherman Street
         Cambridge, MA 02140
Cost: 2 programs, each containing 1 disk and guide: $89.95 each
Type: Simulation
Grades: 7–12
Systems: Apple family; IBM PC

These two simulations involve students in decision making about historical issues. The two programs are titled *Colonization: Exploring the New World* and *Revolutionary Wars: Choosing Sides.* Connections are drawn between historical and contemporary or future issues.

EasySearch: American Inventions
Source: Focus Media
         P.O. Box 865
         Garden City, NY 11530
Cost: Disk, guide, and workbook: $49
Type: Database
Grades: 5–9
Systems: Apple family

This database program allows students to search for information about important inventions developed in the United States. Types of information included are the inventor, the primary use and purpose of the invention, and its original source of power.

Explorer Series
Source: Hartley Courseware
         P.O. Box 419
         Dimondale, MI 48821
Cost: 3 programs, each containing 2 disks, 2 workbooks, and
         guide: $89.95 each
Type: Simulation
Grades: 5–10
Systems: Apple (64K); IBM PC (256K)

Titles in this series include *Discover the World,* in which students search for routes to the Orient circa 1412; *Race for the West,* in which students compete against the English and French to claim land in the northwestern United States; and *The 49'ers,* which involves a simulated covered wagon journey to California, followed by the setting up of a mining operation.

Facts and Fallacies
Source: Hartley Courseware
P.O. Box 419
Dimondale, MI 48821
Cost: 2 disks and guide: $39.95 (Apple) or $49.95 (IBM)
Type: Drill and practice; game
Grades: 7–9
Systems: Apple family; IBM PC

This game provides a review of history facts. Questions are of varying difficulty, with more points awarded for more difficult questions.

Great American History Knowledge Race
Source: Focus Media
P.O. Box 865
Garden City, NY 11530
Cost: 2 disks, guide: $85
Type: Game
Grades: 9–12
Systems: Apple family; Commodore 64 and 128; IBM PC

This set of programs helps students review important historical facts. Categories related to early U.S. history include "Colonial Period," "New Nation," "The Civil War," and "The Nation Expands."

The HBJ Historian
Source: Harcourt Brace Jovanovich
School Department
6277 Sea Harbor Drive
Orlando, FL 32821
Cost: 5 programs, each containing 2 disks, guide, copy masters: $156.60
Type: Tutorial
Grades: 7–12
Systems: Apple family (64K)

This series of programs puts students in the role of historical researchers, exploring hypotheses related to the following topics: "Boom Towns," "The Spaniards and California," "Lincoln and Fort Sumter," "Anasazi Civilization," and "The Labor Movement Before 1915."

History 1 and History 2 (High School Skills Social Studies Instructional Series [Plato])

Source: Control Data Publishing
          3111 Sibley Memorial Drive
          Eagan, MN 55121
Cost: $115
Type: Tutorial; drill and practice
Grades: 9–12
Systems: IBM PC

This two-part program is designed to improve high school students' social studies skills. The first program deals with colonization, founding the nation, and sectionalism; the second covers geographic expansion, economic expansion, and social expansion. (A third program on later U.S. history is also available.)

The History of the U.S. Democomp Package

Source: Focus Media
          P.O. Box 865
          Garden City, NY 11530
Cost: Set of 6 disks, guide, and workbook: $259
Type: Database (maps)
Grades: 5–12
Systems: Apple family (color monitor recommended)

This series of six programs includes dozens of colorful historical maps, many with overlays that show change over time. Graphs and charts are also included in the database, which is divided into the following six segments: *Explorers of North America, The Thirteen Colonies, Ownership of North America, Territorial Expansion of the U.S., America Moves West,* and *European Immigration to the U.S.* The workbooks help students use the programs independently.

The Indian Wars

Source: Hartley Courseware
          P.O. Box 419
          Dimondale, MI 48821
Cost: Set of 2 disks, guide, and 2 manuals: $89.95
Type: Simulation; tutorial
Grades: 10–12
Systems: Apple (64K); IBM (256K)

This simulation requires students to play the role of someone in the U.S. Army or the Native American groups opposing them. They plan strategy and answer questions to gain strength.

Industrialism in America: An Economic History
Source: Focus Media
             P.O. Box 865
             Garden City, NY 11530
Cost: Set of 2 disks and guide: $99
Type: Tutorial
Grades: 7–12
Systems: Apple family

This three-part program looks at the following topics: "The Industrial Revolution Comes to the U.S.," "The Age of Big Business," and "Industrial America in the 20th Century." Economic vocabulary and concepts are stressed as students learn about the historical development of our economic system.

Lincoln's Decisions
Source: Educational Activities
             P.O. Box 392
             Freeport, NY 11520
Cost: $63
Type: Tutorial
Grades: 7–12
Systems: Apple family; IBM PC; TRS 80

This program presents students with dilemmas faced by President Lincoln at several major turning points in his life and administration. The aim is to deepen students' understanding of "the values, conflicts, and tribulations of Civil War times."

Living History
Source: Aquarius Instructional
             P.O. Box 128
             Indian Rocks Beach, FL 34635
Cost: 2 programs, each consisting of 1 disk and guide: $59.95
             each
Type: Tutorial; drill and practice; game
Grades: 6–12
Systems: Apple family

These two programs present actual documents from U.S. history, along with vocabulary exercises, a game, and other activities designed to help students understand the importance of the documents presented.

MECC Dataquest: The Presidents
Source: MECC
            3490 Lexington Avenue North
            St. Paul, MN 55126
Cost: $49
Type: Database
Grades: 7–12
Systems: Apple (64K)

This package includes facts about the 40 U.S. presidents, their administrations, and events that took place while they were in office. Students must develop their own questions and the criteria the computer will use to search for answers.

The Medalists Series
Source: Hartley Courseware
            P.O. Box 419
            Dimondale, MI 48821
Cost: 3 packages, each containing 1 disk and guide: $39.95 (Apple) or $49.95 (IBM) each
Type: Game; drill and practice
Grades: 6–8
Systems: Apple family; IBM PC

Titles of interest in this series include *Presidents, Black Americans,* and *Women in History.* The title *The Medalists* refers to the designation given students when they achieve a designated score on the quiz/games.

Meet the Presidents
Source: Perfection Form
            1000 North Second Avenue
            Logan, IA 51546 (developed by Versa)
Cost: 2 disks, guide: $39.95
Type: Game; drill and practice
Grades: 4–9
Systems: Apple family

This program uses a game-show format to test students' knowledge of facts about the presidents. Entertaining graphics and music are designed to stimulate student interest.

Oregon Trail
Source: MECC
3490 Lexington Avenue North
St. Paul, MN 55126
Cost: $29.95
Type: Simulation
Grades: 4–12
Systems: Apple (64K)

Perhaps the best-known piece of social studies software, *Oregon Trail* invites students to "relive the days of pioneers and covered wagons." Students make decisions and observe the consequences as they attempt to reach their destination—Oregon Territory.

Presidential Profiles
Source: Opportunities for Learning
20417 Nordhoff Street
Chatsworth, CA 91311
Cost: $49.95
Type: Game
Grades: 5–12
Systems: Apple II family

This set of three games encourages students to learn, in-depth, about our nation's presidents. Timelines, facts about presidents, and visuals are incorporated into the games.

Quest for Files: Social Studies Series
Source: Mindscape
3444 Dundee Road
Northbrook, IL 60062
Cost: Complete series of 3 disks and guide: $125; individual programs: $49.95
Type: Database; tutorial
Grades: 7–12
Systems: Apple II family (64K); IBM PC/PCjr

Titles of the three programs in this database series are *Families of the World: The Melting Pot; The American Presidency: Hail to the Chief;* and *The First U.S. Congress: Dawn's Early Light.* The programs encourage students to use the databases to test various hypotheses about the topics.

The Research Companion: Supreme Court Decisions
Source: Focus Media
            P.O. Box 865
            Garden City, NY 11530
Cost: 3 disks and guide: $119
Type: Simulation; database
Grades: 9–12
Systems: Apple (64K)

Part 1 of this program asks students to play roles of law students or legal assistants to a Supreme Court justice. With access to 60 landmark Supreme Court cases, students research important constitutional issues. The second part of the program gives students access to all the details of the relevant cases and allows the information to be printed.

Revolutions: Past, Present, and Future
Source: Opportunities for Learning
            20417 Nordhoff Street
            Chatsworth, CA 91311
Cost: 5 disks and guide: $169
Type: Tutorial
Grades: 10–12
Systems: Apple II family

This program introduces the nature of political revolutions, with particular focus on the American, French, and Russian revolutions. Three historical models are used to analyze these revolutions, on which timelines, graphs, and text material are presented. Students use their understanding of historical influences to predict present and future areas of unrest.

Santa Fe Trail
Source: Educational Activities
            P.O. Box 392
            Freeport, NY 11520
Cost: $59.95
Type: Simulation
Grades: 7–12
Systems: Apple family

This simulation uses graphics, animation, and sound effects to motivate students as they make their way from Missouri to New Mexico on the Santa Fe Trail. As in *Oregon Trail,* students must make decisions and suffer the consequences as they try to reach their destination.

Settling America

Source: Social Studies School Service
         P.O. Box 802
         Culver City, CA 90232 (developed by World Book)
Cost: $39.95
Type: Simulation
Grades: 4–9
Systems: Apple family

The focus of this simulation is life in the Ohio valley in the late 1700s. Students use provided background information to make decisions about their farms and community life. They are awarded points on the basis of their decisions.

Social Studies Data Bases

Source: Scholastic
         P.O. Box 7501
         Jefferson City, MO 65102
Cost: 3 disks, guide, student handbook: $79.95
Type: Database
Grades: 7–12
Systems: Apple (64K); IBM PC; Tandy 1000

This program contains content files, instructions on how to create original files, and activities that teach students how to use databases. Topics covered in the existing files are "The Expanding American Frontier, "Inventions and Technology," and "Twentieth Century America." The activities help students build files on American presidents, local history, and pop culture and history.

Timeliner

Source: Tom Snyder Productions
         90 Sherman Street
         Cambridge, MA 02140
Cost: $59.95
Type: Graphics
Grades: 5–12
Systems: Apple family

This program allows students or teachers to create their own timelines for display in the classroom by simply entering the dates and events they wish to display. The computer then produces a timeline drawn to scale. Several timelines can be combined for comparison and analysis.

Time Tunnel: American History
Source: Focus Media
P.O. Box 865
Garden City, NY 11530
Cost: 2 programs, each containing 1 disk and guide: $99 each
Type: Tutorial
Grades: 7–12
Systems: Apple family; Commodore 64; IBM PC; TRS-80

In each of these programs, the first segment focuses on people from the period 1760–1860, including such notables as Harriet Beecher Stowe, Eli Whitney, George Washington, Dolly Madison, Robert Fulton, Thomas Paine, and Elizabeth Cady Stanton. Students are given clues and must determine which historical figure these clues describe.

U.S. Adventure
Source: K-12 MicroMedia
6 Arrow Road
Ramsey, NJ 07446
Cost: $39.95
Type: Game
Grades: 5–12
Systems: Apple family; Commodore 64; IBM PC

This program takes students on a cross-country geographic and historic tour starting in Delaware in 1787. Students travel to the 50 states in the order of their admittance to the nation, discovering facts about each state and the nation as they proceed.

U.S. History
Source: Hartley Courseware
P.O. Box 419
Dimondale, MI 48821
Cost: $39.95 (Apple) or $49.95 (IBM)
Type: Drill and practice; game
Grades: 10–12
Systems: Apple family; IBM PC

This program provides a history review in a game format. Categories range from the early explorers to the present. The program can be used by individuals or groups.

U.S. History: The Young Republic and Growth of a Nation
Source: Focus Media
P.O. Box 865
Garden City, NY 11530
Cost: 2 programs, each containing 2 disks and guide: $99 each
Type: Tutorial; drill and practice
Grades: 7-12
Systems: Apple family; Commodore 64; TRS-80

These two programs review important concepts and facts from U.S. history. The first program covers colonial life and the American Revolution, and the second looks at the periods before and after the Civil War.

Voyages of Discovery
Source: K-12 MicroMedia
6 Arrow Road
Ramsey, NJ 07446
Cost: $49
Type: Simulation
Grades: 3-8
Systems: Apple family; Commodore 64

This package includes two simulations: one of the voyage of Christopher Columbus, the other of the Lewis and Clark expedition. Students must plan for the voyages, make decisions along the way, and track their progress.

Washington's Decisions
Source: Educational Activities
P.O. Box 392
Freeport, NY 11520
Cost: $63
Type: Tutorial
Grades: 7-12
Systems: Apple family

This program presents students with major decisions in George Washington's life as a mechanism for developing understanding of the Revolutionary and early national periods. Students also develop a deeper understanding of Washington as an individual and as a leader.

Filmstrips, Slide Programs, and Media Kits

This section lists a selection of filmstrips, slide programs, recordings, and media kits covering the early years of U.S. history. Teachers should note that many filmstrips are now available on videocassette as well; the number is increasing rapidly. Check with the publisher regarding the availability of programs of interest in other formats. Also check before purchasing video materials that you do not already have the program in the filmstrip format.

America: Colonization to Constitution
Type:　5 color filmstrips, 5 cassette tapes, and 5 guide booklets
Grades:　5–12
Length:　13 min. each
Cost:　$111.95
Source:　National Geographic Society
　　　　　Educational Services
　　　　　17th and M Streets, NW
　　　　　Washington, DC 20036
Date:　1972

These five programs cover five segments of early U.S. history: *Penetrating the Wilderness; The Colonies Mature; Road to Independence; Years of War: Lexington to Valley Forge;* and *Victory and Constitution.* The filmstrips are largely made up of important artwork depicting the period described in the tapes. Each guide contains a synopsis of the program, key points for students to look for, discussion questions, and follow-up activities.

America Divided: The Civil War and Reconstruction
Type:　4 color filmstrips, 4 cassettes, guide
Grades:　5–9
Length:　15 min. each
Cost:　$140
Source:　Encyclopaedia Britannica Educational Corporation
　　　　　425 North Michigan Avenue
　　　　　Chicago, IL 60611
Date:　1984

Titles in this series show its focus: *Sectional Differences and Slavery; The Civil War: 1861–1864; The Civil War: 1864–1865;* and *Reconstruction.* The discussion guide will aid teachers in developing student understanding of the causes and effects of the Civil War.

America Grows: A Nation Builds

Type:	4 color filmstrips, 4 cassettes, guide
Grades:	5–9
Length:	17 min. each
Cost:	$140
Source:	Encyclopaedia Britannica Educational Corporation
	425 North Michigan Avenue
	Chicago, IL 60611
Date:	1984

Prints, documents, cartoons, and drawings are used to illustrate the growth of the nation from the adoption of the Constitution to the gold rush of 1849. Titles in the series are *Early National Growth; New Ways, New Tools, New Ideas; New Technology in Transportation and Communication;* and *America's Early Westward Movement.*

America Rises: From Colonies to Nation

Type:	5 color filmstrips, 5 cassettes, guide
Grades:	5–9
Length:	15 min. each
Cost:	$140
Source:	Encyclopaedia Britannica Educational Corporation
	425 North Michigan Avenue
	Chicago, IL 60611
Date:	1984

This series looks at the three regions of the colonies, the Revolutionary War, and the Constitution. The discussion guide will help teachers develop student understanding of the differences among the colonial regions and the reasons for resistance to British rule.

The American Revolution: History Through Art

Type:	2 color filmstrips, 2 cassettes, guide
Grades:	7–12
Length:	Approx. 15 min. each
Cost:	$48
Source:	Random House/Educational Enrichment Materials
	400 Hahn Road
	Westminster, MD 21157
Date:	1982

These two filmstrips use the visuals that the colonists used to communicate their resistance to develop student understanding of the causes and events of the American Revolution. The guide will assist teachers unfamiliar with art, as it presents biographies of the artists and a glossary of art terms.

The American Woman: A Social Chronicle
Type: 6 color filmstrips, 6 cassettes, guide
Grades: 7–12
Length: Approx. 15 min. each
Cost: $32 each or $150 for program
Source: Random House/Educational Enrichment Materials
           400 Hahn Road
           Westminster, MD 21157
Date: 1976

The six filmstrips together provide a chronological view of the history of women in America. Of particular interest to teachers of early American history are the following titles from the series: *Puritans and Patriots; "Mill Girls," Intellectuals, and the Southern Myth;* and *Pioneer Woman and Belles of the Wild West.*

America's Beginnings: Indians and Explorers
Type: 5 color filmstrips, 5 cassettes, guide
Grades: 5–9
Length: 14 min. each
Cost: $140
Source: Encyclopaedia Britannica Educational Corporation
           425 North Michigan Avenue
           Chicago, IL 60611
Date: 1984

This series looks at pre-Columbian life in the Americas, the voyages of discovery, and the role of the Spanish, French, and English in the New World. Photographs of pre-Columbian art are among the visuals used in the filmstrips.

America's Frontier Trails West
Type: 4 color filmstrips, 4 cassettes, guide
Grades: 7–12
Length: Approx. 15 min. each
Cost: $101

Source: Random House/Educational Enrichment Materials
400 Hahn Road
Westminster, MD 21157
Date: 1982

This series looks at trails and those who blazed the trails across the western United States following the Lewis and Clark expedition at the beginning of the nineteenth century. Titles in the series are *Trails to the Northwest, Trails of the Rockies, Trails of the Southwest,* and *Exploring the Grand Canyon and Colorado River.*

America's 19th Century Wars: Triumph and Tragedy
Type: 6 color filmstrips, 6 cassettes, guide
Grades: 7–12
Length: Approx. 15 min. each
Cost: $32 each or $150 for program
Source: Random House/Educational Enrichment Materials
400 Hahn Road
Westminster, MD 21157
Date: 1979

This series covers the War of 1812, the Mexican-American War, the Civil War (two filmstrips), the Indian wars, and the Spanish-American War. For each war, information is provided on the background, the conflict itself, the way in which a resolution was negotiated, and the effects of that war on the United States.

America's Past
Type: 4 captioned color filmstrips
Grades: 5–8
Length: Approx. 10 min. each
Cost: $17 each or $60 for program
Source: Clearvue
5711 North Milwaukee Avenue
Chicago, IL 60646
Date: 1965

Titles in this series include *James Oglethorpe and Georgia, Roger Williams and Rhode Island, Mark Twain's America,* and *Famous American Women.* By looking at these individuals, the series examines the principles on which the nation was founded and the changes that took place over its first hundred years.

The Battle of Bunker Hill
Type: 1 color filmstrip, 1 cassette, guide
Grades: 7–12
Length: 20 min.
Cost: $49
Source: The Associated Press/Center for Humanities
            P.O. Box 1000
            Mount Kisco, NY 10549
Date: 1984

This program focuses on the Battle of Bunker Hill as a turning point in U.S. history. It describes the events leading up to the battle, the conflict itself, and the effects.

Biographies of Great Americans
Type: 6 color filmstrips, 3 cassettes
Grades: 5–9
Length: Approx. 12 min. each
Cost: $149 for program
Source: Eye Gate Media
            3333 Elston Avenue
            Chicago, IL 60618
Date: 1978

These six programs present biographies of the following Americans: Benjamin Banneker, Eli Whitney, Harriet Tubman, Robert Fulton, Harriet Beecher Stowe, and Frederick Douglass. The focus is on each individual's contribution to the nation.

Black History in America
Type: 5 color filmstrips, 5 cassettes, guide
Grades: 7–12
Length: 20 min. each
Cost: $139
Source: Educational Design
            47 West 13th Street
            New York, NY 10011
Date: 1971

This five-part series is intended to provide a complete course in the history of black Americans. Two programs are of special interest to teachers of early American history: *The Era of Black Slavery, 1681–1860,* which looks at the African cultures from which black Americans came, the conditions of the slave trade, treatment of blacks in the colonial and revolutionary periods, slave revolts, abolitionism, and the underground railroad; and *The Black Man in the Late 19th Century,* which covers the Civil War, reconstruction, and subsequent events in the 1800s.

Black Studies Resources
Type: 465 slides, guide
Grades: 7–college
Length: Not applicable
Cost: $349
Source: Educational Design
47 West 13th Street
New York, NY 10011
Date: 1971

This massive slide collection includes primary-source documents, prints, drawings, engravings, and early photographs covering black history in the United States. Annotations are provided in the accompanying guide.

The Civil War
Type: 2 color filmstrips, 2 cassettes, guide
Grades: 7–12
Length: 18 min. each
Cost: $84
Source: Educational Dimensions
P.O. Box 126
Stamford, CT 06904
Date: 1979

These two filmstrips provide an overview of the Civil War—the events that led to it, the military and political thinking related to the war itself, and the consequences of Lincoln's assassination.

The Civil War
Type: 3 color filmstrips, 3 cassettes
Grades: 5–12
Length: 14–16 min. each
Cost: $85.95
Source: National Geographic Society
Educational Services
17th and M Streets, NW
Washington, DC 20036
Date: 1979

The three titles in this program cover three sets of events related to the Civil War: the events leading to the war, the war itself, and the aftermath of the war. Historical photographs are integrated into the filmstrips.

The Civil War

Type:	8 color filmstrips, 8 cassettes, guide, duplicating masters
Grades:	7–12
Length:	8–12 min. each
Cost:	$225
Source:	United Learning
	6633 West Howard Street
	Niles, IL 60648
Date:	1980

This series provides a comprehensive unit on the Civil War, focusing on the effects of the war on civilians, as well as soldiers. The filmstrips cover events from Fort Sumter to Appomattox. Visuals include historical artifacts, historical photographs, lithographs, paintings, and sketches of battlefields.

Colonial America

Type:	5 color filmstrips, 5 cassettes, guide
Grades:	7–12
Length:	Approx. 20 min. each
Cost:	$138
Source:	Random House/Educational Enrichment Materials
	400 Hahn Road
	Westminster, MD 21157
Date:	1984

Titles in this series, which spans the period from the landing of the Pilgrims at Plymouth to the eve of the American Revolution, are *England Stakes a Claim, Religious Havens, The American Melting Pot, Expansion and Conflict,* and *War for Empire.*

The Constitution: The Compromise That Made a Nation

Type:	2 color filmstrips, 2 cassettes, guide
Grades:	7–9
Length:	10–12 min. each
Cost:	$69
Source:	Clearvue
	5711 North Milwaukee Avenue
	Chicago, IL 60646
Date:	1978

This program focuses primarily on the conflict between large and small states and how the Great Compromise, which resolved this conflict, was achieved.

Declaration of Independence

Type:	1 color filmstrip, 1 cassette
Grades:	5–12
Length:	17 min.
Cost:	$32.95
Source:	National Geographic Society
	Educational Services
	17th and M Streets, NW
	Washington, DC 20036
Date:	1979

This introduction to the Declaration of Independence looks at its drafting and adoption, as well as analyzing its main points and the list of grievances it presents.

Diary of the American Revolution

Type:	2 cassettes or long-playing records
Grades:	7–12
Length:	Not applicable
Cost:	$27
Source:	Educational Audio Visual
	Pleasantville, NY 10570
Date:	1967

These recordings present material taken from newspapers, diaries, and other primary sources written during the American Revolution. The materials cover military, political, and social aspects of the revolution.

Digging Up America's Past

Type:	5 color filmstrips, 5 cassettes
Grades:	5–12
Length:	13–17 min. each
Cost:	$111.95
Source:	National Geographic Society
	Educational Services
	17th and M Streets, NW
	Washington, DC 20036
Date:	1977

This program examines techniques used to learn about the past, including both archaeological and historical research methodology. Titles in the series are *North America Before Columbus, Middle America Before Cortes, South America Before Pizarro, The First Europeans in the Americas,* and *Colonization and After.*

Discovery and Exploration

Type:	5 color filmstrips, 5 cassettes, guide
Grades:	7–12
Length:	Approx. 20 min. each
Cost:	$138
Source:	Random House/Educational Enrichment Materials
	400 Hahn Road
	Westminster, MD 21157
Date:	1984

This program examines why humans explore new lands, using such explorers as Columbus, da Gama, Cartier, and Hudson, and conquistadors as examples. Maps and paintings of the period are a special feature of the filmstrips.

Famous Patriots of the American Revolution

Type:	6 color filmstrips, 6 cassettes, guide
Grades:	7–8
Length:	Approx. 20 min. each
Cost:	$28 each or $133 for program
Source:	Random House/Educational Enrichment Materials
	400 Hahn Road
	Westminster, MD 21157
Date:	1973

This series focuses on the lives of Patrick Henry, Crispus Attucks, Nathanael Greene, Haym Salomon, Molly Pitcher, and John Paul Jones. Through coverage of events in these individuals' lives, the series provides an overview of the American Revolution.

Famous Trailblazers of Early America

Type:	6 color filmstrips, 6 cassettes, guide
Grades:	7–8
Length:	Approx. 20 min. each
Cost:	$28 each or $133 for program
Source:	Random House/Educational Enrichment Materials
	400 Hahn Road
	Westminster, MD 21157
Date:	Not available

This series looks at the motivations and achievements of Daniel Boone, Lewis and Clark, Zebulon Pike, William Becknell, Jedediah Smith, and Brigham Young. The filmstrips attempt to portray these six men as real humans with failings but striving for greatness.

Famous Women of the West
Type: 1 color filmstrip, 1 cassette, guide
Grades: 7–12
Length: 13 min.
Cost: $25
Source: Multi-Media Productions
            P.O. Box 5097
            Stanford, CA 94305
Date: 1974

This program focuses on the women who helped settle the land west of the Mississippi. A range of outstanding women, including entertainers, politicians, teachers, and guides, are featured.

Farming Was Family Work
Type: 1 color filmstrip, 1 cassette
Grades: 7–adult
Length: 20 min.
Cost: $30
Source: Old Sturbridge Village
            Sturbridge, MA 01566
Date: Not available

This filmstrip looks at farming in the 1830s, using photos of a recreated farm to emphasize the seasonal nature of the work. The narration is based on the diaries of a man, a woman, and two children.

Federalists Versus Republicans
Type: 1 filmstrip, 1 long-playing record, guide, duplicating masters, and multiple copies of a booklet
Grades: 7–12
Length: Not applicable
Cost: $144
Source: Educational Audio Visual
            Pleasantville, NY 10570
Date: 1971

This kit is designed to help students examine the conflicts between Federalists and Republicans in the period from 1789 to 1815. The relationship between the debates of that era and current issues is stressed through a booklet titled *The Debate Today*.

The First Americans: Culture Patterns
Type: 4 color filmstrips, 4 cassettes, guide
Grades: 6–9
Length: Approx. 15 min. each
Cost: $30 each or $103 for program
Source: Clearvue
            5711 North Milwaukee Avenue
            Chicago, IL 60646
Date: 1974

This series covers Native Americans from the first prehistoric people in North America to the time of the Spanish explorers. Titles of the programs in the series are *The Paleo-Indians, The Arctic Indians, The Southwest Indians,* and *The Mound Builders*.

The First People of North America: Indians and Inuit
Type: 6 color filmstrips, 6 cassettes, guide
Grades: 5–9
Length: 15–17 min. each
Cost: $160
Source: United Learning
            6633 West Howard Street
            Niles, IL 60648
Date: 1979

This series presents a historical overview of various native cultures in North America. Variations in lifestyle based on geographic and environmental differences are stressed. Groups studied in the series are the Woodland Indians, Southwestern Indians, Great Plains Indians, Indians of the Pacific Northwest, and the Inuit.

French Explorers of the New World
Type: 4 captioned color filmstrips
Grades: 5–9
Length: Approx. 10 min. each
Cost: $27 each or $94 for program
Source: Encyclopaedia Britannica Educational Corporation
            425 North Michigan Avenue
            Chicago, IL 60611
Date: 1961

The explorers covered in this series are LaSalle, Joliet, Cartier, and Champlain. Their motivations and accomplishments are emphasized.

From Farm to Factory
Type: 70 slides, cassette
Grades: 7–adult
Length: 20 min.
Cost: $30
Source: Old Sturbridge Village
             Sturbridge, MA 01566
Date: Not available

This slide-tape program focuses on three farm girls who took jobs working in the mills at Lowell, Massachusetts. The narration is based on actual diaries and letters of "mill girls."

The French and Indian Wars: Road to the American Revolution?
Type: 2 filmstrips, 1 cassette
Grades: 11–12
Length: 15–17 min. each
Cost: $49
Source: Eye Gate Media
             3333 Elston Avenue
             Chicago, IL 60618
Date: 1975

These two filmstrips examine such questions as: "Why were the English colonies in America so much more successful than those of France? Did the French and Indian wars make our revolution inevitable?" The years 1689–1762 provide the subject matter for the programs.

Indian Cultures of the Americas
Type: 6 captioned color filmstrips
Grades: 7–12
Length: Approx. 12 min. each
Cost: $27 each or $140 for program
Source: Encyclopaedia Britannica Educational Corporation
             425 North Michigan Avenue
             Chicago, IL 60611
Date: 1963

Based on the American Heritage *Book of Indians,* this series looks at the cultures of the Incas, Mayas, and Aztecs; Indians of the Southeast; Indians of the Southwest; Indians of the Northeast; Indians of the Plains; and Eskimos and other Indians of the Northwest.

Indians of North America
Type: 5 color filmstrips, 5 cassettes
Grades: 5–12
Length: 13–14 min. each
Cost: $111.95
Source: National Geographic Society
             Educational Services
             17th and M Streets, NW
             Washington, DC 20036
Date: 1973

The first filmstrip in this series looks at the first Americans. The next three titles look at the history of Indian groups in the Eastern woodlands, on the Plains, and in the West. The final filmstrip looks at Indians today.

Indians View Americans, Americans View Indians
Type: 2 color filmstrips, 1 long-playing record, picture charts, 21 duplicating masters, and 25 copies of a student book, *Indian Readings*
Grades: 7–12
Length: Not applicable
Cost: $144
Source: Educational Audio Visual
             Pleasantville, NY 10570
Date: 1971

This unit is designed to help students "analyze their own cultural biases through studying Indian-white relations during the Colonial and immediate post-Colonial period." To meet that goal, the kit provides readings, recordings, and visual materials to examine these relations. Students participate in a simulation and use anthropological and historical methods to examine how biases affect perceptions.

Legacies: An Audio Introduction to the History of Women and the Family in America
Type: 9 audiocassettes, book, guide
Grades: 9–adult
Length: 9 hr.
Cost: $50

Publisher: The Annenberg/CPB Project
             1111 16th Street, NW
             Washington, DC 20036
Date: 1987

This series of programs looks at the history of women and the family in the years from 1607 to 1870. Because of the social history approach taken, these materials would be valuable supplements to texts taking a political/military approach.

The Louisiana Purchase
Type: 1 color filmstrip, 1 cassette, guide
Grades: 7–12
Length: 13 min.
Cost: $25
Source: Multi-Media Productions
            P.O. Box 5097
            Stanford, CA 94305
Date: 1986

The focus of this filmstrip is the effect of the U.S. purchase of the land known as Louisiana, including the changing view Americans had of themselves, the intensification of the conflict between slave and free states, and the shifts in the balance of power within the U.S. government.

The Loyalists in the American Revolution
Type: 1 color filmstrip, 1 cassette, guide
Grades: 7–12
Length: 14 min.
Cost: $25
Source: Multi-Media Productions
            P.O. Box 5097
            Stanford, CA 94305
Date: 1975

This filmstrip looks at the thousands of colonists who remained loyal to Great Britain, examining who remained loyal and what happened to them during and after the American Revolution.

The Making of the Nation
Type: 5 color filmstrips, 5 cassettes
Grades: 7–12
Length: Approx. 20 min. each
Cost: $138

Source: Random House/Educational Enrichment Materials
400 Hahn Road
Westminster, MD 21157
Date: 1984

This series looks at events in the establishment of the new nation, the United States of America. Individual titles in the series are *George Washington and the New Nation; Adams and Jefferson; New Wars, New Frontiers; Jackson and the "Common Man"; and Expansion and Change.*

Manifest Destiny

Type: 2 color filmstrips, 1 cassette
Grades: 11–12
Length: Approx. 17 min. each
Cost: $49
Source: Eye Gate Media
3333 Elston Avenue
Chicago, IL 60618
Date: 1971

This program surveys expansionist policies from 1781 to the closing of the frontier, looking particularly at why the United States chose to advance its boundaries.

The Mayflower Compact

Type: 1 color filmstrip, 1 cassette, guide
Grades: 7–12
Length: 20 min.
Cost: $49
Source: The Associated Press/Center for the Humanities
P.O. Box 1000
Mount Kisco, NY 10549
Date: 1983

This filmstrip looks at the first document providing for self-government in North America. The effects of the document on American history are stressed.

The Monroe Doctrine Applied: U.S. Policy Toward Latin America

Type: 2 color filmstrips, 2 cassettes, guide
Grades: 7–12
Length: Approx. 20 min. each
Cost: $97

Source: Associated Press/Center for the Humanities
            P.O. Box 1000
            Mount Kisco, NY 10549
Date: 1986

This program provides background on President Monroe's decision to issue the Monroe Doctrine and looks at how subsequent U.S. involvement in Latin America has been shaped by the doctrine.

A New Nation: The Struggle to Survive
Type: 2 color filmstrips, 2 cassettes, guide
Grades: 5–12
Length: Approx. 20 min. each
Cost: $119
Source: Social Studies School Service
            P.O. Box 802
            Culver City, CA 90232 (produced by Benchmark)
Date: 1982

This filmstrip set uses reenactments, period art, and contemporary photography to help students understand some of the crises faced by the nation in the period from 1789 to 1815. These include the Whiskey Rebellion, the "Genet Affair," feuds between Hamilton and Jefferson, the Alien and Sedition Acts, and the War of 1812, among others.

The Origins of America's Economy
Type: 1 color filmstrip, 1 cassette, guide
Grades: 7–12
Length: 11 min.
Cost: $25
Source: Multi-Media Productions
            P.O. Box 5097
            Stanford, CA 94305
Date: 1979

This program focuses on the War of 1812 and the economic and social changes it created, purporting that these changes are keys to the development of an urbanized and industrialized economy. Also covered are the regional aspects of the U.S. economy, transportation, and development of unions.

People of the American Revolution
Type: 3 color filmstrips, 3 cassettes
Grades: 4–9

Length: 15–19 min. each
Cost: $85.95
Source: National Geographic Society
             Educational Services
             17th and M Streets, NW
             Washington, DC 20036
Date: 1986

This set of filmstrips looks at both famous patriots, such as Thomas Jefferson, George Washington, and Molly Pitcher, and lesser known participants, such as Caesar Rodney and Henry Knox. Titles of the filmstrips are *Signers of the Declaration, Soldiers of the Revolution,* and *Women of the Revolutionary Era.*

The Presidency: Decisions of Destiny
Type: 5 color filmstrips, 5 cassettes, guide
Grades: 7–12
Length: Approx. 20 min. each
Cost: $178
Source: Random House/Educational Enrichment Materials
             400 Hahn Road
             Westminster, MD 21157
Date: 1982

These five filmstrips look at key decisions faced by five early presidents. The titles reveal the decisions examined: *Washington Refuses a Crown, Jefferson Buys Louisiana, Jackson Defeats the Bank, Polk Expands the Nation,* and *Lincoln Emancipates the Slaves.* A second set of filmstrips looking at decisions made by twentieth-century presidents is also available.

Presidents and Precedents
Type: 10 filmstrips, 10 cassettes, guide, 10 duplicating masters,
             wall chart
Grades: 7–12
Length: Approx. 20 min. each
Cost: $214
Source: Random House/Educational Enrichment Materials
             400 Hahn Road
             Westminster, MD 21157
Date: 1976

This multimedia kit pairs early and later presidents, examining how decisions became models for future problem solving and decision making. Pairs covered are Washington and Truman, Jackson and

Lincoln, Jefferson and Wilson, the two Roosevelts, and Monroe and Kennedy.

Presidents of the United States
Type: 9 filmstrips, 9 cassettes
Grades: 5–12
Length: 16–17 min. each
Cost: $247.30
Source: National Geographic Society
             Educational Services
             17th and M Streets, NW
             Washington, DC 20036
Date: 1979

These programs look at the personalities, early lives, families, and administrations of the following presidents: Washington, J. Adams, Jefferson, Madison, Monroe, J. Q. Adams, Jackson, Lincoln, A. Johnson, and Grant. A later series looks at presidents of the twentieth century.

Ragamuffins and Redcoats
Type: 4 color filmstrips, 4 cassettes, 4 guides, duplicating masters
Grades: 5–9
Length: 12–15 min. each
Cost: $129
Source: Educational Activities
             P.O. Box 392
             Freeport, NY 11520
Date: 1975

This program takes an "irreverently reverent" look at the Revolution, providing many anecdotes and debunking popular myths. Students should enjoy the humor used to convey information about such events and people as Tories, Hessians, Washington, colonial protests, and frontier campaigns.

Settling the West
Type: 6 color filmstrips, 6 cassettes, guide
Grades: 7–9
Length: Approx. 15 min. each
Cost: $28 each or $133 for program
Source: Random House/Educational Enrichment Materials
             400 Hahn Road
             Westminster, MD 21157
Date: 1971

This series looks at how the land gained through the Louisiana Purchase was settled in the years from 1803 to 1869. Individual filmstrips look at *The Trailblazers, The Miners, Wagon Trains to Railroads, The Cattlemen, The Farmers,* and *Growth of Towns and Cities.*

The 1770's: When America Was Born
Type: 6 filmstrips, 3 cassettes, guide
Grades: 7–12
Length: Approx. 10 min. each
Cost: $165
Source: United Learning
             6633 West Howard Street
             Niles, IL 60648
Date: 1975

One of the *American Decades Series,* this set of filmstrips looks at daily life in the colonies, colonial grievances against England, colonial leaders, organizing for revolt, the Declaration of Independence, and the war itself.

Slavery: America's Peculiar Institution
Type: 2 color filmstrips, 2 cassettes, guide
Grades: 7–12
Length: Approx. 20 min. each
Cost: $52
Source: Social Studies School Service
             P.O. Box 802
             Culver City, CA 90232 (produced by Zenger Productions)
Date: Not available

This program traces the origins of slavery, examines the slave trade, and discusses the lives of slaves in the United States. The aim of the program is to "offer insight into present day problems by helping students gain a better understanding of the period in U.S. history when slavery was a legal and political institution."

Songs of Colonial and Revolutionary America
Type: 4 color filmstrips, 4 cassettes, guide
Grades: 4–8
Length: Approx. 9 min. each
Cost: $37 each or $140 for program

Source: Encyclopaedia Britannica Educational Corporation
425 North Michigan
Chicago, IL 60611
Date: 1984

This series looks at songs sung by the early settlers, the colonists, sailors, and soldiers. The origins of the songs and ways in which colonists adapted them to reflect their changing lifestyles are explained.

Supreme Court Decisions That Changed the Nation
Type: 6 color filmstrips, 6 cassettes, 6 guides
Grades: 7–12
Length: Approx. 20 min. each
Cost: $59 each or $277 for program
Source: Center for Humanities
P.O. Box 1000
Mount Kisco, NY 10549
Date: 1986

This series examines seven landmark Supreme Court cases. Of particular interest to teachers of early U.S. history are programs on *Marbury* v. *Madison, McCulloch* v. *Maryland,* The Dred Scott case, and *Plessy* v. *Ferguson.* Students learn not only about the substance of the cases and their impact on the United States, but also about the workings of the Supreme Court.

U.S. History Through Architecture
Type: 4 color filmstrips, 4 cassettes, guide
Grades: 7–12
Length: Approx. 20 min. each
Cost: $154
Source: Social Studies School Service
P.O. Box 802
Culver City, CA 90232 (produced by McIntyre)
Date: 1977

This series looks at four periods of U.S. history by examining the architecture of each. The periods covered are the colonial, federal, eclectic, and international.

Voices of the American Revolution
Type: 1 cassette
Grades: 7–12
Length: Not applicable

Cost: $15
Source: Educational Audio Visual
Pleasantville, NY 10570
Date: 1967

This recording includes dramatic readings of the work of prominent participants in the American Revolution—John Adams, Tom Paine, General Burgoyne, Alexander Hamilton, and George Washington. A script is included.

The War with Mexico
Type: 2 color filmstrips, 1 cassette, guide
Grades: 7–12
Length: Approx. 14 min. each
Cost: $30
Source: Multi-Media Productions
P.O. Box 5097
Stanford, CA 94305
Date: 1975

This set of two filmstrips provides an overview of the Mexican-American War, looking at the reasons why the war was controversial in both countries. The long-term effects are also examined.

Westward Movement
Type: 5 color filmstrips, 5 cassettes, guide, duplicating masters
Grades: 5–9
Length: Approx. 15 min. each
Cost: $170
Source: United Learning
6633 W. Howard Street
Niles, IL 60648
Date: 1985

This unit includes filmstrips with the following titles: *The First Frontier, Early Frontier Life, Moving Deep into the Interior, Settling Western Lands,* and *Sodbusters, Cowboys, and Indians.* An interesting feature is the use of folk songs to illustrate aspects of pioneer life.

Where Historians Disagree
Type: 3 sets, each including 2 color filmstrips, 2 cassettes, and guide
Grades: 7–12
Length: Approx. 20 min. each

Cost: $60 per set
Source: Random House/Educational Enrichment Materials
            400 Hahn Road
            Westminster, MD 21157
Date: 1986

Each two-filmstrip set in this series looks at an event in U.S. history about which historians have differing theories or interpretations. Topics applicable to the early years of U.S. history are the origins of the American Revolution, the background of the Constitution (whether it was needed, whether the founders acted out of self-interest), and the reasons why the Civil War was fought.

Women in American History
Type: 6 color filmstrips, 6 cassettes, 6 guides, duplicating masters
Grades: 7–12
Length: Approx. 15 min. each
Cost: $139
Source: Educational Activities
            P.O. Box 392
            Freeport, NY 11520
Date: 1973

This series looks at women's contributions, as well as their struggles for equality and justice. Vignettes from the lives of well-known women, as well as excerpts from primary source documents, give students a firsthand look at women's roles in various periods of history.

Women in the American Revolution
Type: 2 color filmstrips, 1 cassette
Grades: 11–12
Length: Approx. 20 min. each
Cost: $49
Source: Eye Gate Media
            3333 Elston Avenue
            Chicago, IL 60618
Date: 1975

This two-part program looks at why Revolutionary heroines were so rare. It also examines how the move to America and the Revolution itself broadened perceptions of women's roles.

Games, Simulations, and Dramatizations

American History Re-creations
Grades: 8–12
Playing time: 3–4 hours for each re-creation
Participants: 15–35
Cost: $35 for each set of 5 re-creations
Publisher: Interact
                 P.O. Box 997
                 Lakeside, CA 92040

Students re-create such historical events as the trial of Anne Hutchinson, the Second Continental Congress, the Virginia Ratification Convention, the election of 1828, the Seneca Falls Convention, and John Brown's trial.

Civil War Map Game: 1861–1865
Grades: 4–12
Playing time: Flexible
Participants: 2–30
Cost: $20
Publisher: Social Studies School Service
                 P.O. Box 802
                 Culver City, CA 90232
                 (developed by Educational Materials Associates)

This board game reinforces map skills as students learn more about important events in the Civil War. A pre/posttest is provided, as are ten activity masters.

Discovery 2
Grades: 5–8
Playing time: 15–23 hours
Participants: 15–35
Cost: $40
Publisher: Interact
                 P.O. Box 997
                 Lakeside, CA 92040

Students simulate colonization of the New World in the seventeenth century. Students must select an appropriate site, establish the colony, and make daily decisions.

Division
Grades:	8–12
Playing time:	10–19 hours
Participants:	18–35
Cost:	$16
Publisher:	Interact
	P.O. Box 997
	Lakeside, CA 92040

This simulation focuses on the crises of the 1850s and the election of 1860. Students are involved in research, writing, and debating.

Games and Strategies for Teaching U.S. History
Grades:	8–12
Playing time:	Variable
Participants:	Variable
Cost:	$15
Publisher:	J. Weston Walch
	P.O. Box 658
	Portland, ME 04104

This book includes a number of games and simulations for use in U.S. history classes. Among these are team games, board games, debates, and mock trials.

Gold Rush
Grades:	4–8
Playing time:	10–13 hours
Participants:	20–35
Cost:	$40
Publisher:	Interact
	P.O. Box 997
	Lakeside, CA 92040

Students form mining companies and head for mid-nineteenth-century western gold fields. The simulation develops a range of skills, with emphasis on outlining.

Great American Confrontations
Grades:	7–12
Playing time:	1 day for each confrontation

Participants: 10–35
Cost: $12 for each confrontation
Publisher: Interact
                   P.O. Box 997
                   Lakeside, CA 92040

Each confrontation involves students in presenting a "television show"—panel, debate, interview, game show competition—on an event from U.S. history. Explorers debate who discovered America, Jeffersonians and Hamiltonians participate in a "family feud" quiz show, and John C. Calhoun and William Lloyd Garrison are guests on a talk show.

Great American Lives
Grades: 7–12
Playing time: 1–2 hours for each biography
Participants: 10–35
Cost: $10 for each biography
Publisher: Interact
                   P.O. Box 997
                   Lakeside, CA 92040

This series uses a "This is Your Life" format to familiarize students with the lives of Benjamin Franklin, Thomas Jefferson, John Charles Fremont, Abraham Lincoln, and Elizabeth Cady Stanton.

Great Women Biographical Card Games
Grades: 3–adult
Playing time: 20 min.
Participants: 3–6
Cost: $7 for each set
Publisher: National Women's History Project
                   P.O. Box 3716
                   Santa Rosa, CA 95402

Three sets of cards acquaint players with the lives of *Foremothers* (e.g., Susan B. Anthony, Harriet Tubman, Sojourner Truth), *Founders and Firsts* (e.g., Clara Barton, Elizabeth Blackwell, Amelia Earhart), and *Poets and Writers* (e.g., Louisa May Alcott, Harriet Beecher Stowe, Phillis Wheatley).

Honor
Grades: 4–8
Playing time: 10–15 hours
Participants: 10–35

Cost: $25
Publisher: Interact
              P.O. Box 997
              Lakeside, CA 92040

Students explore the lifestyle of Native Americans before they began to use the horse, with a focus on coming-of-age rituals.

Independence
Grades: 8–12
Playing time: 10–15 hours
Participants: 20–35
Cost: $16
Publisher: Interact
                P.O. Box 997
                Lakeside, CA 92040

Students take the roles of colonists—Loyalists, Patriots, or Neutralists—and decide whether to adopt the Declaration of Independence. Individuals increase their power by demonstrating increased knowledge of the issues.

Involvement Part I: 1785–1865
Grades: 9–12
Playing time: 1–2 hours per simulation
Participants: 20–30
Cost: $10
Publisher: Social Studies School Service
                P.O. Box 802
                Culver City, CA 90232

This resource includes instructions for brief simulations of Federalist–Anti-Federalist debates, the War of 1812, debates over sectionalism, war with Mexico, immigration questions, and reconstruction.

The Lewis and Clark Expedition
Grades: 7–12
Playing time: 5 hours
Participants: 6–40
Cost: $21.50
Publisher: History Simulations
                P.O. Box 2775
                Santa Clara, CA 95051

Working in groups, students conduct research to develop their understanding of U.S. geography, events surrounding the Louisiana Purchase and the Lewis and Clark expedition, and the lifestyle and contributions of Native Americans in the early American West.

Mahopa
Grades: 5–8
Playing time: 12–15 hours
Participants: 15–35
Cost: $16
Publisher: Interact
                   P.O. Box 997
                   Lakeside, CA 92040

Students take on the identities of three imaginary Native American tribes, read about Native American history, write diary entries that relate their tribal identities to events they read about, and present dramatizations.

Making the Constitution
Grades: 9–12
Playing time: 9–12 hours
Participants: 15–30
Cost: $21.95
Publisher: Social Science Education Consortium
                   855 Broadway
                   Boulder, CO 80302

This unit provides complete instructions and materials for conducting a simulation of the Constitutional Convention, along with readings and activities that help students put the convention in its historical context, analyze the document that resulted, and learn about ratification.

People v. *Coronel*
Grades: 7–12
Playing time: 5 hours
Participants: 15–30
Cost: $3.95
Publisher: Constitutional Rights Foundation
                   601 South Kingsley Drive
                   Los Angeles, CA 90005

People v. *Coronel* is a mock trial set in the days of the California gold rush. Students learn about state sovereignty, federalism, immigration, nativism, and criminal case procedures.

Pioneers

Grades:	5–8
Playing time:	10–15 hours
Participants:	15–35
Cost:	$40
Publisher:	Interact
	P.O. Box 997
	Lakeside, CA 92040

Students take the roles of wagon trains heading for Oregon in 1846. They must choose goods to take with them, write diary entries, and make group decisions on such issues as which fork in a trail to follow.

Radicals vs. Tories

Grades:	7–12
Playing time:	3 hours
Participants:	24–100
Cost:	$14.50
Publisher:	History Simulations
	P.O. Box 2775
	Santa Clara, CA 95051

This simulation of the Second Continental Congress involves students in deciding whether to vote for or against independence.

1787: A Simulation Game

Grades:	7–9
Playing time:	3–10 hours
Participants:	20+
Cost:	$69
Publisher:	Social Studies School Service
	P.O. Box 802
	Culver City, CA 90232
	(developed by Olcott Forward)

This flexible simulation provides opportunities for students to play fictional delegates to the Constitutional Convention, thus allowing them to examine the conflicting interests that shaped our Constitution. Included with the game are an audiocassette, teacher's guide, role cards, and worksheets.

Skins

Grades: 5–12
Playing time: 8+ hours
Participants: 15–35
Cost: $16
Publisher: Interact
                  P.O. Box 997
                  Lakeside, CA 92040

Skins is a simulation of the Rocky Mountain fur trade from 1826 to 1838. Students learn about the economics of the fur trade, as well as the culture of the traders.

Slave Auction

Grades: 7–12
Playing time: 1–2 hours
Participants: 25–41
Cost: $15.95
Publisher: Constitutional Rights Foundation
                  601 South Kingsley Drive
                  Los Angeles, CA 90005

Students take the roles of buyers, auctioneers, slave traders, and slaves, as they re-create a slave auction.

20 Short Plays for American History Classes

Grades: 6–9
Playing time: Variable
Participants: Variable
Cost: $15
Publisher: J. Weston Walch
                  P.O. Box 658
                  Portland, ME 04104

This resource contains 20 easy-to-use plays, 14 of which are brief plays that can be prepared for and read in one class period, and 6 of which can be staged for more formal presentation.

U.S. History Classroom Games

Grades: 7–12
Playing time: Variable
Participants: 2–35
Cost: $6 for each game

Publisher: Social Studies School Service
P.O. Box 802
Culver City, CA 90232
(developed by H.M.S. Historical Games)

This series of flexible games covers numerous topics in U.S. history, including explorers, the colonial era, the American Revolution, the Battles of Lexington and Concord, and the Civil War.

Womanspeak
Grades: 9–adult
Playing time: 1 hour
Participants: 12
Cost: $3.25
Publisher: National Women's History Project
P.O. Box 3716
Santa Rosa, CA 95402

This play shows a contemporary woman in search of her historical roots. Such women as Abigail Adams, Sojourner Truth, and Susan B. Anthony speak to her about the tradition of women in U.S. history.

Posters, Study Prints, and Other Visual Aids

American History Images on File
Grades: 7–12
Description: 3 books, each containing 300 reproducible images with annotations
Cost: $95 each
Publisher: Facts on File
460 Park Avenue South
New York, NY 10016

The first book in this series, *The Faces of America,* contains portraits and biographies of settlers, writers, politicians, artists, musicians, reformers, and sports figures. The second, *Key Issues in American Constitutional History,* contains annotated prints, drawings, paintings, photographs, and maps related to such topics as abolition, federalism vs. regionalism, women's rights, labor, and urbanization. Both of these volumes cover the full range of U.S. history; the third volume presents images related specifically to the *American Civil War and the Reconstruction.*

American History Transparency Books
Grades: 7–12
Description: 9 books, each containing 12 full-color transparencies, 28 duplicating masters, and a teacher's guide
Cost: $9.95 each
Publisher: Milliken Publishing
P.O. Box 21579
St. Louis, MO 63132

Each book in the series looks at a particular event or era in U.S. history, including the Revolutionary War, the growth of democracy in the Jacksonian era, and the Civil War. The full-color transparencies present maps, diagrams, and drawings.

American Studies Series
Grades: 5–12
Description: 10 full-color 50″ × 50″ wall maps
Cost: $288 with tripod; $348 with disc base or multi-roller
Publisher: Rand McNally
P.O. Box 7600
Chicago, IL 60680

Each of these full-color wall maps includes quotations, charts, and pictures, along with the maps. Topics include exploration, European settlement, the slave trade, westward expansion, and the Civil War.

American Timeline Series
Grades: 7–12
Description: 4 books, each containing a foldout timeline, 28 duplicating masters, and a teacher's guide
Cost: $5.95 each
Publisher: Milliken Publishing
P.O. Box 21579
St. Louis, MO 63132

These four books are titled *Settlement, Creating Federal America, Washington to Jackson,* and *America Divided.* The timelines presented can be removed for display in the classroom.

American West Wallcharts
Grades: 4–12
Description: 24 full-color 14½″ × 19″ wall charts

Cost: $29.75 for set
Publisher: Social Studies School Service
              P.O. Box 802
              Culver City, CA 90232

These 24 charts depict the history of the American West. They focus on pioneers, cowboys, gunfighters, Indians, and the Indian wars. Each chart is organized around a single concept and can be used to stimulate class discussion.

Americans Who Changed Our History

Grades: 9–12
Description: 100 black-and-white 8½″ × 11″ photographs with essays
                on reverse
Cost: $21.95 for set
Publisher: J. Weston Walch
                P.O. Box 658
                Portland, ME 04104

These 100 black-and-white study prints show photographs of Americans from various eras of history; those pictured contributed in the political, social, technological, economic, and reform fields. On the back of each photograph is a brief biography of the person pictured.

California Gold Rush

Grades: 7–adult
Description: 18 black-and-white 11″ × 14″ photographs
Cost: $17.00
Publisher: Documentary Photo Aids
                P.O. Box 956
                Mt. Dora, FL 32757

These 18 photographs show the many aspects of the rush to California in 1849, including both success and failure. A booklet discussing how historical photographs can be analyzed in the classroom is provided free with the set.

Chief Briefs

Grades: 5–12
Description: 2 sets of 12 full-color 11″ × 17″ posters
Cost: $17.95 for each set
Publisher: Perfection Form Company
                1000 North Second Avenue
                Logan, IA 51546

Each set of 12 posters depicts caricatures of 12 presidents, along with a humorous story or little-known fact about each president. The first set depicts presidents from Washington through Taylor; the second, Fillmore through McKinley. (A third set showing more recent presidents is also available.)

Civil War Generals
Grades: 5–12
Description: 2 sets of 15 three-color 10″ × 13″ posters
Cost: $9.95 for each set
Publisher: Perfection Form Company
               1000 North Second Avenue
               Logan, IA 51546

Each set of posters depicts generals from one side during the Civil War. The posters can be used to encourage research on the 30 generals shown, or on early photography.

Congressional Districts of the 100th Congress of the United States
Grades: 7–adult
Description: Wall map with guide
Cost: $4.75
Publisher: Government Printing Office
               Superintendent of Documents
               Washington, DC 20402
               (developed by the U.S. Bureau of the Census)

This wall map shows the congressional districts in the first, 25th, 50th, 75th, and 100th congresses, allowing students to examine population growth and distribution, as well as shifts in political power. A guide with background information and suggested activities is provided with the map.

Factory Study Prints and Farm Family Study Prints
Grades: 7–12
Description: 2 sets of black-and-white 11″ × 14″ study prints; 9 in factory print set, 11 in farm family set
Costs: $12.50 for factory prints, $15 for farm prints
Publisher: Old Sturbridge Village
               Sturbridge, MA 01566

These prints depict a family, a New England barnyard, views of a farm's interior, important steps of cotton production in a factory of the 1820s, and paintings of mill communities.

Famous Indians Posters
Grades: 5–12
Description: Set of 12 three-color 17″ × 22″ posters with 32-page
               booklet
Cost: $21.95
Publisher: Perfection Form Company
               1000 North Second Avenue
               Logan, IA 51546

Each poster in the series depicts a famous Native American leader.
The accompanying booklet provides biographies and additional
illustrations.

Freedom from Slavery Posters
Grades: 7–12
Description: Set of 10 three-color 11″ × 17″ posters
Cost: $13.95
Publisher: Perfection Form Company
               1000 North Second Avenue
               Logan, IA 51546

These 10 posters depict leaders in the fight against slavery, including
Harriet Tubman, Angelina Grimke, Sojourner Truth, and Frederick
Douglass. Each poster includes a quotation from the person pictured.

Indians of the Plains
Grades: 7–12
Description: 46 black-and-white 11″ × 14″ photographs
Cost: $43.50
Publisher: Documentary Photo Aids
               P.O. Box 956
               Mt. Dora, FL 32757

This collection depicts the history, culture, and society of the Plains
Indians, as well as their clashes with the U.S. government and white
settlers. A booklet on interpreting photographs in the classroom is
provided free.

Map History of the United States
Grades: 7–12
Description: 8 full-color 11″ × 17″ posters
Cost: $8.95

Publisher: Social Studies School Service
         P.O. Box 802
         Culver City, CA 90232
         (developed by Scholars Press)

This set of eight posters shows the expansion of the United States by presenting maps of the nation in 1790, 1803, 1821, 1848, 1863, 1896, 1917, and 1959.

Negro Experience in America
Grades: 7–12
Description: 49 black-and-white 11″ × 14″ photographs
Cost: $46.50
Publisher: Documentary Photo Aids
         P.O. Box 956
         Mt. Dora, FL 32757

This set includes 49 photographs depicting the black experience in America from the slave trade to the present. A booklet on interpreting photographs in the classroom is provided free with the set.

Newsmap of U.S. History
Grades: 7–12
Description: 4 sets of 6 double-sided full-color 22″ × 26″ charts, with 31-page guides
Cost: $59.95 for each set
Publisher: Curriculum Innovations
         60 Revere Drive
         Northbrook, IL 60062

The first set of charts covers America before 1783, the second the years from 1783 to 1815, the third 1815 to 1848, and the fourth 1848 to 1865. Graphics presented on the chart are simulated newspapers that describe events as though they had just happened. Many maps are featured.

North American Timeline
Grades: 4–12
Description: 7 full-color 31″ × 11½″ posters
Cost: $8.95
Publisher: Social Studies School Service
         P.O. Box 802
         Culver City, CA 90232
         (developed by *Instructor* magazine)

These seven posters can be attached to form an 18-foot timeline of American history from 1565 to the present. A detailed written time-line elaborates on the events pictured. Blank space is provided to allow students to add events.

Postcards of Old Sturbridge Village
Grades: 7–12
Description: 24 black-and-white postcards
Cost: $3
Publisher: Old Sturbridge Village
               Sturbridge, MA 01566

This set of 24 postcards depicts artifacts and living history scenes from Old Sturbridge Village. They can be used for bulletin boards, for writing activities, or to stimulate discussion.

Presidents of the United States, Vice Presidents of the United States, and Wives of Presidents
Grades: 5–12
Description: 3 black-and-white 20″ × 28″ posters
Cost: $4.95 each
Publisher: Social Studies School Service
               P.O. Box 802
               Culver City, CA 90232
               (developed by Waterwheel Press)

Each of these posters depicts the individuals indicated by its title—the 39 U.S. presidents, 43 vice presidents, and 44 first ladies.

Territorial Growth and History of the United States
Grades: 5–9
Description: 19 full-color transparencies with overlays
Cost: $150
Publisher: Eye Gate Media
               3333 Elston Avenue
               Chicago, IL 60618

This set of transparencies includes maps of territorial expansion, maps related to events that resulted in territorial expansion (such as the Mexican-American War), and maps showing geographical infor-mation about the United States to allow students to examine the type of land that was added during various periods of expansion.

War with Mexico: 1846–1849
Grades: 7–12
Description: 14 black-and-white 11″ × 14″ photographs
Cost: $13.50
Publisher: Documentary Photo Aids
               P.O. Box 956
               Mt. Dora, FL 32757

These photographs depict why the Mexican-American War started, how the American Army won despite a much larger Mexican opposition, and why the war's legacy has been so bitter. A booklet on interpreting photographs in the classroom is available free with the set.

Women and the Constitution Bulletin Board Kit
Grades: 8–12
Description: Packet including historical photographs and documents, suggestions for organizing a bulletin board, background information, mats for photos, and bunting
Cost: $10
Publisher: National Women's History Project
               P.O. Box 3716
               Santa Rosa, CA 95402

This kit provides all the materials and ideas needed to create a discussion-stimulating bulletin board on women and the Constitution. Numerous additional posters and visuals on women in U.S. history are available from this publisher.

Supplementary Print Materials

The materials listed in this section are varied in terms of their content, approach, and intent. Some materials were developed specifically for classroom use; others were written for general audiences but are also appropriate for secondary students. The listing is, of course, selective. All of the potential print resources on this period of U.S. history would fill several volumes themselves. Those selected are of high quality, address a range of subjects, and represent a wide sampling of publishers and authors. Note that no historical fiction is included, although that is another category of materials with utility in the history classroom.

Angle, Paul, and William C. Davis. **A Pictorial History of the Civil War Years.**
New York: Doubleday, 1985.
256 pp. Paperbound. $12.95. ISBN 0-385-18551-0.

This volume, suitable for grades 7 and up, uses photographs, drawings, political cartoons, maps, and documents to stimulate interest in and develop understanding of the Civil War and its impact on the nation. The materials are arranged in chronological order.

Arizzi, Mavis. **Thinking About American History Through Historical Fiction.**
Culver City, CA: Social Studies School Service (developed by Book Lures), 1985.
30 pp. Paperbound. $4.95.

This activity book presents exercises to help students in grades 5–9 use historical fiction to appreciate the American heritage. Some of the activities focus on particular works of fiction; others can be applied to any novel with a historical setting.

Billington, Roy A., and Martin Ridge. **American History Before 1877.**
Totowa, NJ: Littlefield, Adams, 1981.
278 pp. Paperbound. $5.95. ISBN 0-8226-0026-9.

This work provides an outline of U.S. history from colonial days through the end of Reconstruction. Key topics appear in bold type; important events, dates, and names are italicized and underlined. These design features make the book especially useful for review.

Binder, Frederick M., and David M. Reimers. **The Way We Lived: Essays and Documents in American Social History. Volume I: From 1607.**
Lexington, MA: D.C. Heath, 1988 (in press).
Paperbound. $12. ISBN 0-0669-09030-1C.

Suitable for advanced placement students, this resource provides essays on social history trends and topics. Each essay is followed by a collection of primary source materials that elaborate on the essay.

Breil, Ann, and others. **Basic Skills in United States History.**
Dubuque, IA: Wm. C. Brown Publishers, 1988.
294 pp. Spiralbound. $34.95. ISBN 0-697-02592-6.

This book of activities is designed to help middle school and high
school students develop reading, study, research, information acquisition, and social participation skills while learning U.S. history content. Approximately half of the 52 activities provided deal with the
pre–Civil War years.

Brown, Bernard E. **Great American Political Thinkers. Volume I:
Creating America/From Settlement to Mass Democracy.**
New York: Avon, 1983.
464 pp. Paperbound. $4.95. ISBN 0-380-83915-6.

Brown surveys American political thought from colonial times, using
the writings of such individuals as Thomas Paine, John Adams,
Thomas Jefferson, and Andrew Jackson to illuminate a range of topics, including religious freedom and democracy, women's rights, the
rise of democracy, and others.

Cababe, Louise, and others. **U.S. History, Book 1.**
Dubuque, IA: Wm. C. Brown Company, 1987.
285 pp. Spiralbound. $34.95. ISBN 0-697-02192-0.

This book contains 36 supplementary lessons and five unit tests expanding on topics covered in textbooks, providing more information
or helping students examine the topic from a different perspective.
Many lessons involve using source material and/or completing worksheets. The lessons cover the period to 1876.

Catton, Bruce. **The American Heritage Picture History of the Civil
War.**
New York: Outlet Books, 1985.
630 pp. Hardbound. $15.95. ISBN 0-517-38556-2.

This book, by the noted Civil War historian Bruce Catton, is suitable for students in grades 7 and up. It features more than 800
illustrations and a detailed narrative of events from 1860 to the
post–Civil War era.

Chapin, June, and Rosemary Messick. **You and the Constitution.**
Menlo Park, CA: Addison-Wesley, 1988.
*110 pp. Paperbound. $16.40 (includes 100-p. teacher's guide). ISBN 0-
201-22497-6.*

This program for students in grades 7–9 presents 23 lessons organized into four units: "Concepts of Government," "The History of the Constitution," "The Meaning of the Constitution," and "Constitutional Issues in Our Lives." The varied teaching strategies employed should keep students interested in the topics covered, which include power and authority, the Articles of Confederation, the Constitutional Convention of 1787, the Bill of Rights, and constitutional aspects of the Civil War, among others.

Combs, Eunice A., and Laurel R. Singleton. **Our Nation: Its Past and Present.**
Boulder, CO: Graphic Learning Corporation, 1986.
220-p. three-ring binder (ISBN 0-87746-033-7), 232-p. spiralbound teacher's guide (ISBN 0-87746-034-5), 30 laminated desk maps, and 30 marking pens. $325.00.

This activity-based program for students in grades 5–8 covers events from the earliest days of U.S. history to the present. Emphasis is placed on learning map and globe, social studies reading, thinking/ problem solving, research, and citizenship skills while learning about the history of the United States.

Community: People and Places.
Sturbridge, MA: Old Sturbridge Village, 1986.
Paperbound. $6.95.

This resource contains activities designed to help students examine "the physical aspects of communities and the relationships between people in a community." Students read diaries and use maps, illustrations, and the built environment to gather data and draw conclusions.

Cummins, D. Duane, and William Gee White, series editors. **Inquiries into American History.**
Mission Hills, CA: Glencoe, 1980.
6 books, 216–240 pp. each. Paperbound. $4.71 each. ISBN 0-020-652500-3, 652540-2, 652580-1, 652620-4, 652700-6, and 652740-5.

Each of these books looks in depth at a particular era, event, or region. Titles related to early American history are: *Our Colonial Heritage: Plymouth and Jamestown; The Middle Colonies: New York, New Jersey, Pennsylvania; The American Revolution; The Federal Period: 1790–1800; The American Frontier;* and *The Origins of the Civil War.*

Currie, David P., and Joyce L. Stevos. **The Constitution.**
Glenview, IL: Scott, Foresman, 1985.
*128 pp. Paperbound. $4.79. ISBN 0-673-13396-6. (Teacher's guide: 72
pp., paperbound, $2.49.) ISBN 0-673-13397-4.*

This program provides 16 lessons organized into three chapters:
"Background of American Government," "The United States Constitution," and "The Twenty-Six Amendments." The first chapter is
especially helpful to history teachers because it deals with the English legal heritage, colonial law, the Declaration of Independence, the
Articles of Confederation, and the Constitutional Convention.

Curti, Merle, Isadore Starr, and Lewis Paul Todd. **Living American
Documents.**
Orlando, FL: Harcourt Brace Jovanovich, 1971.
368 pp. Paperbound. $7.20. ISBN 0-15-371886-2.

This collection of primary source materials is organized chronologically, presenting documents related to the colonial period, the creation of the new nation, the conflict between the North and South,
reconstruction and expansion, and the modern era, in which the
United States has been a world leader.

Davidson, James West, and Mark H. Lytle. **After the Fact: The Art
of Historical Detection.**
Atlanta, GA: Random House, 1986 (2nd ed.).
400 pp. Paperbound. $15. ISBN 0-394-35475-3.

This unusual supplement uses 14 dramatic episodes in U.S. history
to demonstrate how historians go about their work—"historical detec-
tive work" as it were. Skills covered include selection of evidence,
document analysis, and oral interviews.

Dollar, Charles, and Gary Reichard. **American Issues: A Documentary Reader.**
Atlanta, GA: Random House, 1988.
*496 pp. Paperbound. $10.95. ISBN 0-676-35607-9. (Teacher's guide:
paperbound, $6.95, ISBN 0-676-35627-3.)*

This collection includes more than 200 sources, including primary
sources, secondary sources, and illustrations (maps, paintings, cartoons, etc.). The materials have been selected to focus on such recurring themes as race/ethnic relations and the evolution of democratic
institutions, as well as to develop students' ability to participate in
historical inquiry.

Evitts, William J. **Captive Bodies, Free Spirits: The Story of Southern Slavery.**
New York: Messner, 1985.
160 pp. Hardbound. $9.79. ISBN 0-671-54094-7.

This book uses an anecdotal approach to help students in grades 5–9 understand the effects of slavery on the slaves themselves, as well as on the larger society. Such well-known individuals as Frederick Douglass, Nat Turner, Harriet Tubman, and John Brown are discussed.

Family: Past and Present.
Sturbridge, MA: Old Sturbridge Village, 1986.
Paperbound. $6.95.

This sourcebook contains a range of activities that help students look at family composition, functions, and roles. Such documentary material as census records, journals, and vital records are used in the lessons, which focus on change over time.

Ferrero, Pat, Elaine Hedges, and Julie Silber. **Hearts and Hands: The Influence of Women and Quilts on American Society.**
Santa Rosa, CA: National Women's History Project, 1988.
112 pp. Paperbound. $19.95. ISBN 0-938625-8700-3.

This resource looks at the role of women and quilts in important events of the nineteenth century: abolition, the Civil War, westward expansion, temperance, and suffrage. The full-color photographs and unusual approach should capture the interest of high school students.

Forging the Nation: A Brief History of the United States to 1865.
Logan, IA: Perfection Form, 1985.
120 pp. Paperbound. $5.60 (includes free 28-p. paperbound teacher's guide).

This secondary-level workbook chronicles the history of the United States up to and including the Civil War. Illustrated with drawings, maps, and photographs, the book contains 12 units, each focusing on a particular period and providing narrative, a glossary, and exercises.

Frazier, Thomas R. **Voices of America: Readings in American History.**
Boston, MA: Houghton Mifflin, 1985.
304 pp. Paperbound. $11.76. ISBN 0-395-18608-2.

This collection of supplementary readings contains a variety of sources addressing salient issues in each time period. The readings are generally brief and are followed by questions to help students deepen their understanding of the document. Many readings focus on the experience of the "common people."

Giese, James R., and Lynn S. Parisi. **A Humanities Approach to Early National U.S. History: Activities and Resources for the Junior High School Teacher.**
Boulder, CO: Social Science Education Consortium, 1986.
211 pp. Unbound; 3-hole-punched. $12. ISBN 0-89994-308-X.

This volume provides 28 activities that integrate the study of the humanities—art, music, literature, architecture, and tasks of daily living—with the study of U.S. history. Although these teacher-developed lessons focus on the colonial and early national periods, the approach can be adapted to any era. Masters for student handouts are provided, as are extensive bibliographic listings.

Goldinger, Carolyn, ed. **Presidential Elections Since 1789.**
Washington, DC: Congressional Quarterly, 1987 (4th ed.).
245 pp. Paperbound. $11.95. ISBN 0-87187-431-8.

This book provides a wealth of statistical data on presidential elections, including information on the electoral college and electoral votes (1879–1984), the popular vote (1824–1984), party conventions (1831–1984), and primaries (1912–1984).

Gordon, Irving L. **American History.**
New York: Amsco, 1989 (2nd ed.).
770 pp. Paperbound. $9.25. ISBN 0-87720-852-2.

This review text in American history is presented in outline form, with important events or ideas in bold type and narrative generally brief. Each of the book's ten units ends with a series of questions to check for understanding.

Guide to the Study of Childhood, 1820–1920.
Rochester, NY: Margaret Woodbury Strong Museum, 1985.
Paperbound. $6.

This resource aims to give secondary students a better understanding of local, family, and cultural history in the nineteenth century. The book includes children's letters, photographs, advertisements, and other primary sources, as well as suggested activities.

Gurko, Miriam. **The Ladies of Seneca Falls: The Birth of the Women's Rights Movement.**
Santa Rosa, CA: National Women's History Project, 1988.
328 pp. Paperbound. $8.95. ISBN 0-938625-8606-4.

This book examines the origins, early years, and personalities of the women's movement, looking particularly at the role of the Seneca Falls convention in sparking the battle for suffrage. What is and what is not in the Constitution related to women is analyzed.

Heffner, Richard D. **A Documentary History of the United States.**
New York: New American Library, 1985 (4th ed.).
352 pp. Paperbound. $4.95. ISBN 0-451-62413-0.

This collection presents documents from the Declaration of Independence to recent Supreme Court decisions. The author provides annotations that explain the significance of the various documents to U.S. history.

Hilton, Suzanne. **We the People: The Way We Were 1783–1793.**
Philadelphia, PA: Westminster, 1981.
206 pp. Hardbound. $13.95. ISBN 0-664-32685-4.

This book, written for students in grades 6 and up, looks at social history in the period when the new nation was being formed. Journals are used to present information on home life, school, recreation, courtship and marriage, and business. A bibliography and list of places where the life of 1787 has been re-created are appended.

Hindle, Brooke, and Steven Lubar. **Engines of Change: The American Industrial Revolution, 1790–1860.**
Washington, DC: Smithsonian, 1986.
309 pp. Paperbound. $19.95. ISBN 0-87474-539-X.

This lavishly illustrated book examines developments in such areas as farming, mining, textiles, and transportation. The ways in which Americans adapted European inventions to suit their own environments are discussed. The book is suitable for use in grades 9 and up.

Hughes, Glenn E., Norman D. Miller, and Stephen L. Volkening. **Reading American History.**
Glenview, IL: Scott, Foresman, 1987 (rev. ed.).
148 pp. Paperbound. $6.28. ISBN 0-673-22237-5. (Teacher's edition: 148 pp., paperbound, $8.35, ISBN 0-673-22238-9.)

This workbook for students in grades 7 and 8 teaches reading skills in the context of content from the standard U.S. history curriculum. The 148 exercises, which focus on understanding the main idea, learning the vocabulary, and reading maps and graphs, are arranged chronologically, from "Reasons for Exploration" to "Baseball Attendance."

Hughes, Langston, Milton Meltzer, and C. Eric Lincoln. **A Pictorial History of Black Americans.**
New York: Crown, 1983 (5th ed.).
400 pp. Hardbound. $19.95. ISBN 0-517-55072-5.

This resource contains more than 1,200 illustrations depicting the economic, political, social, and cultural changes black Americans have undergone since arriving in North America in 1619.

Hymowitz, Carol, and Michaele Weissman. **A History of Women in America.**
New York: Bantam, 1978.
400 pp. Paperbound. $4.95. ISBN 0-553-24928-2.

This general history begins with European colonization and progresses to the women's movement of the 1970s. The book focuses on how women of all classes shaped the life and culture of America.

Jacobs, Wilbur R. **Dispossessing the American Indian: Indians and Whites on the Colonial Frontier.**
Norman, OK: University of Oklahoma Press, 1985.
246 pp. Paperbound. $9.95. ISBN 0-8061-1935-7.

This scholarly work focuses on how the conflicting needs and values of Native Americans and European settlers resulted in confrontations that finally destroyed the Native American way of life. Comparisons are drawn with the aboriginal peoples of Australia and New Guinea. The book is suitable for use by advanced secondary students.

Ketchum, Richard M. **The American Heritage History of the American Revolution.**
New York: Outlet Books, 1984.
384 pp. Hardbound. $14.98. ISBN 0-517-44736-3.

Illustrated with reproductions of artifacts and period prints, sketches, and engravings, this book covers the contributions of the farmers and shopkeepers who served in the Revolution, as well as the exploits of the better-known colonists. Many quotations of participants are included.

Klose, Nelson. **United States History: Volume 1.**
Santa Barbara, CA: Barrons, 1983 (4th ed.).
440 pp. Paperback. $7.95. ISBN 0-8120-2250-5.

This review text uses an outline format to present information on
U.S. history to 1877. Each chapter includes a chronology, a reading
list, and review questions, as well as the outline of events.

Kuzirian, Eugene, and Larry Madaras. **Taking Sides: Clashing Views
on Controversial Issues in American History, Volume I: The Colonial
Period to Reconstruction.**
Sluice Dock, CT: Dushkin, 1985.
276 pp. Paperbound. $8.95. ISBN 0-87967-562-4.

The authors look at opposing viewpoints on 16 issues, such as: Is
the American national character unique? What motivated the Salem
witchhunt? Was conflict between the Native Americans and colonists
unavoidable? Was slavery an economic necessity in the Old South?
Did women achieve greater autonomy in the new nation?

Lacour-Gayet, Robert. **Everyday Life in the United States Before the
Civil War: 1830–1860.**
New York: Ungar, 1983.
310 pp. Paperbound. $7.95. ISBN 0-8044-6376-X.

This work looks at public and private lifestyles in the 30 years be-
fore the Civil War. Sections of the book include "The Framework of
Life," "The Routine of Life," "Intellectual and Moral Life," and
"Civil Life."

Lake, Steven A. **The American Centuries.**
Glenview, IL: Decisionmakers, 1985.
2 books, 78–82 pp. each, drilled and bound with brads. $29.95 each.

Each volume in this set contains 20 lessons for one period of U.S.
history: the first volume covers the period to 1799, and the second,
1800–1899 (a third volume looks at the twentieth century). In each
lesson, the student assumes the role of a historical figure and makes
a decision about an issue or problem in U.S. history. A variety of
instructional activities are included.

Lang, H. Jack, ed. **Letters in American History: Words to
Remember.**
Culver City, CA: Social Studies School Service, 1982.
127 pp. Paperbound. $1.98.

This volume contains 122 historic letters, ranging from the standard to the unusual. Examples are Washington's rejection of the crown, Deborah Gannet's application for a Revolutionary army disability pension, and Mark Twain's birthday greeting to Walt Whitman. High school students should find the letters a fascinating supplement to their texts.

Lavender, David. **The Great West: American Heritage Library.**
Boston, MA: Houghton Mifflin, 1985.
468 pp. Paperbound. $8.95. ISBN 0-8281-0481-6.

Illustrated with numerous photographs, drawings, and maps, this text details the history of America's western frontier. Topics covered include pioneer life, gold rushes, railroads, land booms, and outlaws.

Lawrence, Bill. **Fascinating Facts from American History.**
Portland, ME: J. Weston Walch, 1982.
271 pp. Spiralbound. $9.95.

This book presents brief anecdotal articles providing human interest, debunking historical myths, and presenting other "sidelights" of history to stimulate the interest of students in grades 9–12.

Lawrence, Bill. **A Social History of America.**
Portland, ME: J. Weston Walch, 1986.
226 pp. Spiralbound. $8.95.

This resource provides an easy-to-read anecdotal account of the lives of everyday Americans. Topics covered include family life, social life, recreation, health and diet, fads, and jobs.

Lawson, Robert, ed. **Watchwords of Liberty: A Pageant of American Quotations.**
Boston, MA: Little, Brown, 1986 (rev. ed.).
115 pp. Paperbound. $7.95. ISBN 0-316-51754-2.

This collection of more than 50 quotations is presented in a unique story form and illustrated with entertaining drawings. The book is suitable for students in grades 5–12.

Lengel, James B., and Gerald Danzer. **Law in American History.**
Glenview, IL: Scott, Foresman, 1983.
263 pp. Paperbound. $8.54. ISBN 0-673-11690-1. (Teacher's guide: 72 pp., paperbound, $3.72, ISBN 0-673-11691-X.)

Important legal events from ten major periods of U.S. history have been chosen as the focal points of ten chapters in this text. For example, the first chapter examines sources of authority through a study of the origins of the Mayflower Compact. Many instructional activities are suggested to deepen and extend student understanding.

Levy, Tedd, and Donna Collins Krasnow. **A Guidebook for Teaching United States History: Earliest Times to the Civil War.**
Newton, MA: Allyn and Bacon, 1979.
478 pp. Paperbound. $29.95. ISBN 0-205-06503-1.

This comprehensive resource is designed "to provide practical ideas and resources for developing student understanding of significant historical events and processes." To that end, the authors present a general introduction to teaching U.S. history, along with numerous teaching activities for the following topics: exploration and colonization, the American Revolution, the U.S. Constitution, nationalism and sectionalism, and the Civil War and Reconstruction.

Lewin, Stephen, and Ted Silveira. **United States History: Volume I, 1620–1900.**
Belmont, CA: Fearon Education, 1986.
91 pp. Paperbound. $4.50. ISBN 0-8224-7681-9.

This volume presents basic concepts from junior and senior high school history courses in a grade 5 reading level. Illustrated with historic black-and-white photographs and artworks, the book covers the landing of the Pilgrims, the American Revolution, creation of the new government, westward expansion, the Civil War, and industrialization.

Lockwood, Alan L., and David E. Harris. **Reasoning with Democratic Values: Ethical Problems in United States History.**
New York: Teachers College Press, 1985.
224 pp. Paperbound. $8.95. ISBN 0-8077-6094-3. (Teacher's guide: 176 pp., paperbound, $11.95, ISBN 0-8077-6101-X.)

This unique teaching resource includes 21 historical episodes that presented ethical dilemmas for individual citizens or decision makers, beginning with the colonial era and ending with Reconstruction (a companion volume presents episodes from the past century). The teacher's guide presents detailed instructions for using the episodes to develop students' reasoning skills and commitment to democratic values.

Maddox, Robert James. **Annual Editions: American History, Volume I: Pre-Colonial Through Reconstruction.**
Sluice Dock, CT: Dushkin, annual.
224 pp. Paperbound. $8.95.

These resources, published annually, contain articles from such sources as *American History Illustrated, Saturday Review, Smithsonian, Early American Life,* and other periodicals. Topics are varied, covering all periods within the scope of the volume.

Maher, C. **American History Project File.**
Portland, ME: J. Weston Walch, 1982.
156 cards. $12.

This set of cards presents 156 creative projects to help students explore U.S. history. Projects involve reading, writing, research, and self-expression.

Meltzer, Milton. **The Black Americans: A History in Their Own Words.**
New York: Crowell, 1984 (rev. ed.).
306 pp. Hardbound. $13.50. ISBN 0-690-04419-4.

This condensed version of the original three-volume work contains letters, speeches, memoirs, and testimonies regarding the black experience in the United States. Both individual lives and the struggle for political and economic equity are chronicled. The book is suitable for grades 7 and up.

Nurse, Ronald J. **The Development of American Foreign Policy.**
Orlando, FL: Harcourt Brace Jovanovich, 1980.
192 pp. Paperbound. $10.45. ISBN 0-15-379-206-X. (Teacher's guide: 96 pp., paperbound, $2.25, ISBN 0-15-379-232-9.)

This readable supplementary text presents a lively survey of the development of American foreign policy from 1776 to 1980. A section of primary sources concludes the volume. The teacher's guide suggests a range of instructional strategies for use with the text.

O'Reilly, Kevin. **Critical Thinking in History.**
South Hamilton, MA: Critical Thinking Press, 1983–1984.
2 books, each containing 86 pp. Paperbound. $2.95 each. (Teacher's guides, each containing 156 pp., paperbound, $12.95 each.)

These units, *Colonies/Revolution/Constitution* and *New Republic/ Jackson/Civil War,* are designed to help students evaluate historical evidence, recognize assumptions, analyze interpretations, and use data to assess hypotheses. The teacher's guides present detailed plans for presenting the material. Teacher training in use of the materials is available.

Patrick, John J., and Richard C. Remy. **Lessons on the Constitution: Supplements to High School Courses in American History, Government, and Civics.**
Boulder, CO: Social Science Education Consortium, 1985.
302 pp. Spiralbound. $19.50. ISBN 0-89994-302-0.

This collection presents 60 original lessons. The first chapter contains copies of the Constitution, amendments to the Constitution, amendments proposed but not ratified, and selected Federalist Papers. The four chapters that follow focus on the origin and purposes of the Constitution, principles of constitutional government, amending and interpreting the Constitution, and landmark Supreme Court cases.

Patrick, John J., and Clair W. Keller. **Lessons on the Federalist Papers: Supplements to High School Courses in American History, Government, and Civics.**
Bloomington, IN: Social Studies Development Center, 1987.
97 pp. Paperbound. $10. ISBN 0-941339-00-9.

This volume contains ten lessons, looking at such concepts as limited government, the rule of law, republicanism, checks and balances, judicial review, rights of individuals, and national security. Each lesson involves students in defining core ideas to establish a context for examining excerpts from *The Federalist*. Reading, discussion, and writing are the instructional strategies employed in the lessons.

Patrick, John J. **Lessons on the Northwest Ordinance of 1787: Learning Materials for Secondary School Courses in American History, Government, and Civics.**
Bloomington, IN: Social Studies Development Center, 1987.
100 pp. Paperbound. $10. ISBN 0-941339-02-5.

Following the pattern of Patrick's two publications listed above, this volume provides a series of lessons that help students better understand a key document in U.S. history—the Northwest Ordinance of 1787, perhaps the most important piece of legislation passed under the Articles of Confederation. This is one of the very few pieces of teaching material on the topic and is thus a valuable aid to teachers.

Perspectives: Readings on Contemporary American Government.
Arlington, VA: Close Up Foundation, 1987 (8th ed.).
258 pp. Paperbound. $14. ISBN 0-932765-04-1.

This anthology, designed for use in government classes, also provides material of interest to history teachers and students, particularly in the section on the Constitution. Other topics covered are the presidency, the Congress, the judiciary, the media, the bureaucracy, interest groups, and the people.

The Public Issues Series: American Revolution: Crisis of Law and Change.
Boulder, CO: Social Science Education Consortium, 1988.
68 pp. Paperbound. $2.50. ISBN 0-89994-331-4 (with teacher's guide).

Originally developed by the Harvard Social Studies Project in the 1960s, the *Public Issues Series* focuses on enduring public issues and the development of analysis and discussion skills. In this unit, the first in the revision of the series, students examine when and how authority should be challenged, reading primary and secondary source materials on the escalating disagreements between the colonists and their British rulers. Analogies are drawn with the civil rights movement and various protest movements of the 1980s.

Reid, William, Jr. **American Crafts: A Reproducible Guide for 100 Projects.**
Portland, ME: J. Weston Walch, 1986.
265 pp. Spiralbound. $18.

The projects described in this resource give students a feeling for the everyday lives of Americans in various periods of history. The projects are organized into five sections: "Folk Art and Crafts of the American Indians," "Folk Art and Crafts of the Colonial Era," "Folk Art and Crafts of the Young Republic," "Folk Art and Crafts of the Victorian Period," and "Folk Art and Crafts of the Modern Era."

Reid, William, Jr. **Popular Music in American History.**
Portland, ME: J. Weston Walch, 1981.
221 pp. Spiralbound. $8.95.

This resource provides activities to help students "understand American history through their knowledge of song" and vice versa. Music and activities are provided throughout the book.

Resource Packets: Meeting the People of the Past.
Sturbridge, MA: Old Sturbridge Village, n.d.
8 packets, each containing 10 to 15 documents. $9.50 each.

These resource packets examine life in the early 1800s through the eyes of children and young people. Topics of the eight packets are childhood, youth, work, factory work, trades and trading, recreation, farming, and housework.

Riley, Glenda. **Inventing the American Woman: A Perspective on Women's History, Volume I, 1607–1877.**
Arlington Heights, IL: Harlan Davidson, 1987.
176 pp. Paperbound. $8.95. ISBN 0-88295-837-2.

This book combines recent scholarship on women's history, biographical data, statistics, and narrative on social history to describe the role of women in American life from 1607 to 1877. The text is suitable for students in grades 9 and up, as well as adults.

Rosenzwieg, Linda W., and Peter N. Stearns. **Themes in Modern Social History.**
Pittsburgh, PA: Carnegie-Mellon University Press, 1985.
225 pp. Softbound. $8.95. ISBN 0-88748-059-4 (with 13-p. teacher's guide).

This supplementary text is organized around themes reflecting the everyday lives of ordinary people who lived in four different time periods: preindustrial society (1600–1780), early industrial society (1780–1870), mature industrial society (1870–1950), and advanced industrial society (1950–present). The themes covered are work and leisure, family and childhood, health and medicine, and crime and law enforcement. Source material is provided in each section.

Schlesinger, Arthur M., ed. **The Almanac of American History.**
New York: Putnam, 1983.
623 pp. Hardbound. $10.25. ISBN 0-399-51082-6.

An excellent research resource for students, this volume is divided into five sections, each introduced by a prominent U.S. historian. The sections cover founding the nation, testing the union, forging the nation, expanding resources, and emerging as a world power. Many biographies and short essays on special topics are included.

Scott, John Andrew. **The Ballad of America: The History of the United States in Song and Story.**
Carbondale, IL: Southern Illinois University Press, 1983 (rev. ed.).
439 pp. Paperbound. $14.95. ISBN 0-8093-1061-9.

This text attempts to "show how the story of the American people is revealed in their song." Popular songs of various eras are presented, along with narrative that places the songs in their historical and geographic contexts.

Shaping American Democracy: U.S. Supreme Court Decisions.
Albany, NY: New York State Bar Association, 1985.
89 pp. Paperbound. $8.95.

This resource booklet briefly examines a number of Supreme Court cases dealing with issues of capital punishment, civil rights, freedom of assembly, free speech, freedom of the press, religious freedom, separation of powers, search and seizure, and voting rights. The cases range from *Chisholm* v. *Georgia* in 1793 to *New York* v. *Quarles* in 1984.

SIRS/National Archives Supplementary Teaching Units.
Boca Raton, FL: Social Issues Resource Series, 1985.
2 kits, each containing a teacher's guide, activities, and documents. $35 each.

Prepared in cooperation with the National Archives, these teaching kits provide about 50 reproductions of historical documents, along with activities for developing student understanding. Topics of the kits are *The Constitution: Evolution of a Government* and *The Civil War—Soldiers and Civilians.* (Six additional kits focus on events in later years of U.S. history.)

Slosson, Preston W. **Pictorial History of the American People.**
Essex, CT: Gallery Press, 1985 (rev. ed.).
328 pp. Hardbound. $14.98.

This well-illustrated text focuses on the social history of the United States from pre-colonial days to 1984. Titles of some of the sections of the book include "Utopias in the Backwoods," "The Day of the Cowboy," "Abraham Lincoln: The New Man from the West," and "American Science and Invention."

Smith, Gary, John Zola, and Jaye Zola. **Teaching About U.S. History: A Comparative Approach.**
Denver, CO: Center for Teaching International Relations, 1988 (rev. ed.).
Paperbound. $21.95.

This book presents more than 30 activities employing a comparative approach to the study of U.S. history. The activities use a broad range of strategies, including data collection, interviews, decision-making games, and use of community resources. Activities are suitable for students in grades 6–12.

Smith, Melinda R., ed. **Law in U.S. History: A Teacher Resource Manual.**
Boulder, CO: Social Science Education Consortium, 1983.
335 pp. Spiralbound. $19.95. ISBN 0-89994-281-4.

This collection contains more than 35 activities designed to develop legal issues and themes in secondary U.S. history courses. Especially timely are the numerous activities that focus on development of vital constitutional issues over time.

Stallone, Carol N., ed. **Faces and Phases of Women.**
Seneca Falls, NY: National Women's Hall of Fame, 1983.
76 pp. Paperbound. $6.95. ISBN 9610622-0-7.

This resource for students in grades 5–9 includes biographies and sketches of 31 women who have been inducted into the National Women's Hall of Fame. Among these are Abigail Adams, Jane Addams, Carrie Chapman Catt, Sojourner Truth, and Harriet Tubman. A set of posters is also available from the publisher.

Stampp, Kenneth M., ed. **The Causes of the Civil War.**
Magnolia, MA: Peter Smith, 1986 (rev. ed.).
182 pp. Hardbound. $12.75. ISBN 0-8446-2993-6.

This volume contains primary sources written by people who participated in the events leading up to the Civil War (e.g., John C. Calhoun, Horace Greeley, Jefferson Davis). The conclusions of postwar historians such as Eugene Genovese are also included.

Stoler, Mark, and Marshall True. **Explorations in American History, Volume I: To 1865.**
Atlanta, GA: Random House, 1987.
160 pp. Paperbound. $8.00. ISBN 0-394-35281-5 (with teacher's guide).

This book introduces research and writing skills in the context of American history. Such skills as analysis of sources, using the library, and forming hypotheses are developed.

Strasser, Susan. **Never Done: History of American Housework.**
New York: Pantheon, 1982.
365 pp. Paperbound. $11.95. ISBN 0-394-51024-0.

This history covers American household technology and ideas about housework in a style that makes it suitable for students in grades 9 and up. The author analyzes the relationship of housework and the housewife's role to economic and demographic changes in the United States. The influence of advertising and commercial interests is covered.

Suter, Coral, and Marshall Croddy. **American Album: 200 Years of Constitutional Democracy.**
Los Angeles, CA: Constitutional Rights Foundation, 1986.
139 pp. Paperbound. $12.50 (with teacher's guide).

This publication contains eight units arranged chronologically from the Constitution's first implementation in the late eighteenth century to the civil rights movement of the 1960s. The material, designed specifically for infusion in secondary U.S. history courses, is presented through a wide array of teaching strategies.

Ver Steeg, Clarence L., and Richard Hofstadter, eds. **Great Issues in American History, Volume I: From Settlement to Revolution; Volume II: From the Revolution to the Civil War.**
New York: Vintage, 1969.
Volume I: 480 pp. Paperbound. $7.95. ISBN 0-394-70540-8.
Volume II: 448 pp. Paperbound. $6.95. ISBN 0-394-70541-X.

The editors have presented a variety of primary source materials related to major political controversies in U.S. history. Included are speeches, debates in Congress, letters, political pamphlets, and other materials presenting both sides of the controversies covered.

Voices of Freedom: Sources in American History.
Englewood Cliffs, NJ: Prentice Hall, 1987.
176 pp. Paperbound. $10.94. ISBN 0-139-43655-3.

This collection of primary source materials focuses on real-life experiences of Americans. Included are letters, poetry, diaries, songs, drawings, and other types of source materials, each with background information and reading review questions to help students interpret and analyze the source.

Walvin, John. **Slavery and the Slave Trade: A Short Illustrated History.**
Jackson, MS: University of Mississippi Press, 1983.
168 pp. Paperbound. $8.95. ISBN 0-87805-180-5.

This resource looks not only at slavery in the United States, but also includes slavery in ancient Greece and Rome and serfdom in Europe, providing a broader historical perspective. The social and work lives of slaves, slave revolts, and the events leading to abolition are examined.

Water: A Powerful Resource for New England.
Sturbridge, MA: Old Sturbridge Village, 1986.
Paperbound. $5.95 (with teacher's guide).

This sourcebook looks at the importance of water as an energy source in the early nineteenth century. Students examine the technology of New England in the time period, as well as the impact of that technology on people's lives.

We the People . . . Do Ordain and Establish This Constitution for the United States of America.
Calabasas, CA: Center for Civic Education, 1987.
171 pp. Paperbound. $5. ISBN 0-89818-126-7. (Teacher's guide: 125 pp., paperbound, $5, ISBN 0-89818-129-1.)

This material, developed as part of the U.S. bicentennial competition program, is intended to provide students with a grasp of fundamental principles of the U.S. Constitution, the evolution of those principles, and the operation of U.S. constitutional government. Special emphasis is placed on the political theory underpinning the Constitution, as well as the events prior to the Revolution that shaped the thinking of the framers.

Weiner, Lynn Y. **From Working Girl to Working Mother: The Female Labor Force in the United States, 1820–1980.**
Chapel Hill, NC: University of North Carolina Press, 1986.
187 pp. Paperbound. $8.95. ISBN 0-8078-1612-4.

This text focuses on changes in social attitudes, women's self-image, and economic necessity and how they have impacted women's participation in the work force. Beginning with entry of single women into the labor force in the 1820s and proceeding to the post–World War

II era of working mothers, the text provides a readable narrative suitable for students in grades 9 and up.

Whiteaker, Larry. **The Individual and Society in America.**
Orlando, FL: Harcourt Brace Jovanovich, 1979.
176 pp. Paperbound. $9.45. ISBN 0-15-379208-6. (Teacher's guide: 96 pp., paperbound, $2.25, ISBN 0-15-379234-5.)

This supplementary text for grades 9–12 looks at four periods of change in American history, examining the goals, beliefs, and government of Puritan New England; growth of individualism in the 1800s; urban life in the early 1900s; and the post–World War II society.

Zinn, Howard. **A People's History of the United States.**
New York: Harper and Row, 1980.
614 pp. Paperbound. $8.95. ISBN 0-06-090792-4.

This resource focuses on the role of the powerless in American history. Coverage of the views and experiences of indentured servants, women, Native Americans, blacks, and the poor provides a unique view of U.S. history.

Textbooks

This section includes basal textbooks specifically designed for the secondary market. Texts written for the college market and marketed to secondary teachers are not included, although teachers in advanced placement courses may find such texts suitable for their students. The texts in this section include both those that cover only the period emphasized in this volume and those that provide a general survey of U.S. history. In examining texts that cover only the early years of U.S. history, teachers should be cautious in that many such texts are mildly revised versions of the first half of another text expanded with primary sources or other features. This is not to suggest that packaging a text in this matter is not a legitimate marketing strategy; it merely indicates that teachers should be fully aware of what they are buying.

Berkin, Carol, and Leonard Wood. **Land of Promise: A History of the United States, Volume I: To 1877.**
Glenview, IL: Scott, Foresman, 1986.
592 pp. Hardbound. $22.90. (A teacher's annotated edition, teacher's resource book, and test generator package are available to supplement the text.) ISBN 0-63-02214-7.

Land of Promise surveys U.S. history from the days of exploration to the end of Reconstruction. Although the primary focus is on political, economic, and military developments, social history and such subjects as women and minorities are given adequate treatment. Special features on "The Geographic Setting" link history and the environment. A lengthy section entitled "Documents, Artifacts, Exhibits, and Other National Treasures" concludes the text. *Land of Promise* is also available as a single-volume survey of U.S. history from the earliest times to the present; that volume does not have the extensive document section at the end.

Bidna, David B., Morris S. Greenberg, and Jerold H. Spitz. **We the People: A History of the United States.**
Lexington, MA: D.C. Heath, 1982.
639 pp. Hardbound. $23.61. (An annotated teacher's edition, activities book, and evaluation program are available to supplement the text.) ISBN 0-669-04484-9.

We The People is designed for average and below-average junior high school students and thus has a controlled reading level and uses stories and graphics to stimulate interest. The text covers events from pre-Columbian times through the election of President Reagan. Social and cultural aspects of history receive ample attention.

Boorstin, Daniel, and Brooks Mather Kelley. **A History of the United States.**
Englewood Cliffs, NJ: Prentice Hall, 1986 (rev. ed.).
752 pp. Hardbound. $24.48. (A teacher's resource book, computer test bank, and critical thinking skill transparencies are available to supplement the text.) ISBN 0-663-37997-0.

This high school text provides comprehensive coverage of events in U.S. history. The text focuses most heavily on a chronological presentation of political and military history, but also examines economic, social, and cultural developments. The authors of this text are probably the most distinguished historians currently writing for the school market.

Branson, Margaret Stimman. **America's Heritage.**
Englewood Cliffs, NJ: Prentice Hall, 1986.
658 pp. Hardbound. $23.91. (A teacher's resource book, student work-book, and critical thinking skill transparencies are available to sup-plement the text.) ISBN 0-663-40907-1.

This junior high school text provides a chronological presentation emphasizing ideas, issues, and confrontations that have shaped the United States. The treatment of ethnic groups and women is bal-anced throughout the narrative, which is written in a question-and-answer format designed to help students focus on significant points of history.

Brown, Richard C. and Herbert J. Bass. **One Flag, One Land.**
Morristown, NJ: Silver Burdett and Ginn, 1988.
818 pp. Hardbound. $22.95. (An annotated teacher's edition and teacher resource files including a planning guide, masters for work-sheets and tests, outline maps, wall maps, and a workbook are avail-able to supplement the text.) ISBN 0-382-08414-4.

One Flag, One Land is designed for use in eighth-grade survey courses. It presents a chronological narrative of U.S. history, empha-sizing political and economic history. Because the text is essentially the final book in the publisher's elementary series, a vast array of support material is provided the teacher.

Buggey, L. Joanne and others. **America! America!**
Glenview, IL: Scott, Foresman, 1987.
768 pp. Hardbound. $22.65. (A teacher's annotated edition, teacher's resource book, workbook, and testing program are available to supple-ment the text.) ISBN 0-673-03501-9.

This junior high school text presents a chronological treatment of U.S. history, emphasizing the people who contributed to the history of our country. Primary source materials and a variety of illustra-tions enliven the text, which is written at the fifth- to seventh-grade reading level.

Conlin, Joseph R. **Our Land, Our Time: A History of the United States.**
Austin, TX: Holt, Rinehart and Winston, 1986.
850 pp. Hardbound. $22.54. (A teacher's annotated edition, teacher's resource book, workbook, test book, and test generator are available to supplement the text.) ISBN 0-15-772000-4.

This senior high text is weighted heavily toward political, economic, and diplomatic history; it deemphasizes social and cultural history, but contains more law-related content than most history texts. The use of maps, graphics, and other kinds of artwork is particularly strong.

Davidson, James West, and John E. Batchelor. **The American Nation.**
Englewood Cliffs, NJ: Prentice Hall, 1986.
816 pp. Hardbound. $24.48. (An annotated teacher's edition, teacher's resource manual, computer test bank, and critical thinking skill transparencies are available to supplement the text.) ISBN 0-13-027599-9.

This junior high school text provides a chronological treatment of U.S. history, with emphasis on the following themes: forging a national identity from a diverse population, strengthening our democratic institutions, and improving our economic and technological capacity. The text is easy to read, with such special features as "Americans in History," "Where History Happened," and "Arts in America" provided to stimulate interest.

Davidson, James West, and John E. Batchelor. **A History of the Republic, Volume 1: The United States to 1877.**
Englewood Cliffs, NJ: Prentice Hall, 1986.
640 pp. Hardbound. $23.97. (An annotated teacher's edition, teacher's resource manual, and computer test bank are available to supplement the text.) ISBN 0-13-391970-6.

This text essentially repeats the first six units of *The American Nation,* providing chronological coverage of events up to 1877. A lengthy section of primary source documents has been added to the end of the book.

Davidson, James West, and Mark H. Lytle. **The United States: A History of the Republic.**
Englewood Cliffs, NJ: Prentice Hall, 1986 (rev. ed.).
832 pp. Hardbound. $24.48. (An annotated teacher's edition, teacher's resource book, student study guide, computer test bank, and critical thinking skills transparencies are available to supplement the text.) ISBN 0-13-937301-2.

This high school text contains a chronological narrative that the authors believe will acquaint students with our nation's past experiences and prepare them to face the future. Special coverage is given to geography in history, primary sources, connections between past and present, and ties between U.S. and world events. The latter chapters in this book make up the second volume of *A History of the Republic.*

Drewry, Henry N., and Thomas H. O'Connor. **America Is.**
Columbus, OH: Merrill, 1987 (rev. ed.).
798 pp. Hardbound. $21.90. (A teacher's annotated edition, teacher resource book, activity book, transparency package, and set of classroom posters are available to supplement the text.) ISBN 0-675-1013-6.

America Is presents a chronological treatment of U.S. history and, like other U.S. history texts for junior high students, the text also develops such themes as opportunity, independence, democracy, and power. An unusual feature of this readable text is "City Sketches," which provides insight into urban life at various periods in U.S. history.

Drewry, Henry N., and others. **United States History, Volume I: Beginnings Through Reconstruction.**
Columbus, OH: Merrill, 1986.
568 pp. Hardbound. $19.80. (A teacher's annotated edition, teacher's resource book, citizenship activities, and testing program are available to supplement the text.) ISBN 0-675-02040-9.

This volume, designed for middle and junior high students, is comprised of the first five units of the 1984 edition of *America Is,* supplemented with a section of primary sources at the end of the text.

Garraty, John A. **American History.**
Orlando, FL: Harcourt Brace Jovanovich, 1986 (rev. ed.).
960 pp. Hardbound. $23.25. (A teacher's edition, teacher's resource book, workbook, and tests are available to supplement the text.) ISBN 0-15-370680-0.

Written by an eminent historian, this junior high text provides approximately equal coverage to the various periods of U.S. history, not stressing early history at the expense of more recent events. Special features of the text include numerous skill development activities and an emphasis on the use of "historical imagination." The narrative is written in an engaging style that would also appeal to high school students.

Graff, Henry F. **America: The Glorious Republic, Volume 1: Beginnings to 1877.**
Boston, MA: Houghton Mifflin, 1986.
672 pp. Hardbound. $21.60. (A teacher's manual, teacher's resource book, workbook, and test generator are available to supplement the text.) ISBN 0-395-38153-3.

This text uses the traditional chronological approach to U.S. history, beginning with European exploration and ending with the end of Reconstruction. Special features of note are primary source readings, "How to Study American History" lessons, and geography lessons. This text is also available as a single-volume history of the full span of U.S. history.

Green, Robert P., Jr., Laura L. Becker, and Robert E. Coviello. **The American Tradition: A History of the United States.**
Columbus, OH: Merrill, 1986 (rev. ed.).
816 pp. Hardbound. $21.90. (A teacher's annotated edition, teacher resource book, activity book, transparency package, and set of classroom posters are available to supplement the text.) ISBN 0-675-00960-X.

The major portion of the chronological narrative in this text stresses the development of America's government, economy, society, and role in world affairs. Basic values of the American political system are also stressed. The text emphasizes the work of historians more than do most other texts, a feature that is appropriate for the high school audience. The latter units in this text make up the second volume of this publisher's two-volume program, *United States History.*

Hart, Diane, and David Baker. **Spirit of Liberty: An American History.**
Menlo Park, CA: Addison Wesley, 1987.
Hardbound. $23.70. (A teacher's edition, teacher's resource manual, and test generator are available to supplement the text.) ISBN 0-201-20921-4.

This junior high school text provides coverage of political, economic, and social events from the time of the first Americans through predictions about the twenty-first century. Special features stress reading skills, the importance of geography, and the influence of values in history.

Hart, Diane, and David Baker. **United States History to 1877.**
Menlo Park, CA: Addison Wesley, 1986.
592 pp. Hardbound. $21.83. (A teacher's edition and teacher's resource manual are available to supplement the text.) ISBN 0-201-20906-3.

This text is based on the first five units of *Spirit of Liberty,* supplemented by special exercises on "Using the Tools of History" and a section of primary source materials entitled "American Voices."

Jordan, Winthrop D., Miriam Greenblatt, and John S. Bowes. **The Americans: The History of a People and a Nation.**
Evanston, IL: McDougal, Littell, 1985.
864 pp. Hardbound. $21.60. (A teacher's edition, teacher's manual, reinforcement activities, enrichment activities, and tests are available to supplement the text.) ISBN 0-86609-291-9.

This high school text presents a traditional chronological narrative. Emphasis is placed on the global aspects of various events, as well as relevant themes from American literature. The history of women and ethnic groups is well integrated into the text.

King, David, and others. **United States History.**
Menlo Park, CA: 1986.
848 pp. Hardbound. $24.30. (A teacher's edition, teacher's resource manual, book of readings, and test generating program are available to supplement the text.) ISBN 0-201-20916-0.

This ten-unit high school text focuses on politics, geography, and economics within a chronological framework. Emphasis is placed on recurring issues in American history, contemporary observers in each period, and skill development in social studies.

Linden, Glenn M., Dean C. Brink, and Richard H. Huntington. **Legacy of Freedom, Volume 1: United States History Through Reconstruction.**
Mission Hills, CA: Glencoe, 1986 (rev. ed.).
608 pp. Hardbound. $22.65. (A teacher's edition, teacher's resource binder, and study guide are available to supplement the text.) ISBN 0-8445-6921-6.

This junior high text provides a traditional chronological narrative of events in U.S. history, supplemented with special features on the historian's skills, conflicting opinions on historical events, and the future. A lengthy section of primary source documents concludes the text. The text is also available as a one-volume comprehensive survey of U.S. history to the present; the publisher recommends the use of the one-volume text in high school classes, although the reading level does not appear to be appreciably different.

Maier, Pauline. **The American People: A History.**
Lexington, MA: D.C. Heath, 1986.
800 pp. Hardbound. $22.95. (A teacher's edition, teacher's resource binder, workbook, testing program, posters, and transparencies are available to supplement the text.) ISBN 0-669-04883-6.

This chronological treatment of U.S. history for junior high school students emphasizes the Constitution, government, and citizenship. Special features focus on biographies, skills, and global connections throughout U.S. history.

May, Ernest R., and Winthrop D. Jordan. **The American People: A History to 1877.**
Evanston, IL: McDougall, Littell, 1986.
626 pp. Hardbound. $21.60. (A teacher's edition, teacher's manual, reinforcement activities, enrichment activities, and mastery tests are available to supplement the text.) ISBN 0-86609-639-6.

This junior high text is based on the first several units of May's *A Proud Nation,* with the addition of a "Perspectives" page in each chapter to draw connections between past and present and the addition of several brief excerpts from primary sources in each unit.

May, Ernest R. **A Proud Nation.**
Evanston, IL: McDougall, Littell, 1984 (rev. ed.).
784 pp. Hardbound. $21.96. (A teacher's edition, teacher's manual, enrichment activities, reinforcement activities, and mastery tests are available to supplement the text.) ISBN 0-86609-285-4.

This chronological presentation covers historical periods from before Columbus through Ronald Reagan, encouraging historical analysis and comparison through the use of social studies skills. American families—both famous and not-so-famous—are featured in each unit. The text is suitable for middle school and junior high students.

O'Connor, John R., Sidney Schwartz, and Leslie A. Wheeler. **Exploring United States History.**
New York: Globe Book, 1986 (rev. ed.).
824 pp. Hardbound. $23.98. (A teacher's resource manual, workbook, and testing program are available to supplement the text.) ISBN 0-87065-558-2.

This high school history text is aimed at average students with below-average reading skills. Emphasis is placed on domestic politics and social history from pre-Columbian days through the 1984 presidential election. The text is structured with short reading segments, organizing questions, and frequent reviews.

Patrick, John, and Carol Berkin. **History of the American Nation.** New York: Macmillan, 1987 (rev. ed.). *802 pp. Hardbound. $21.96. (A teacher's manual, skills workbook, overhead transparencies, and tests are available to supplement the text.) ISBN 0-02-151200-0.*

This chronological presentation incorporates both political and social history, with an emphasis on citizenship analysis and the role of individual's values on history. The text is well illustrated, with timelines that are particularly noteworthy.

Peck, Ira, Steven Jantzen, and Daniel Rosen. **American Adventures.** Jefferson City, MO: Scholastic, 1987 (rev. ed.). *759 pp. Hardbound. $22.50. (A teacher's edition, print masters, and teacher's resource binder are available to supplement the text.) ISBN 0-8114-1638-0.*

American Adventures is a basal U.S. history text for junior high students of average or mixed abilities or for high school students who are below-average readers. The materials emphasize short, easy-to-read chapters of high interest to the intended audience. Each chapter focuses on an important personality, event, or idea in U.S. history from the arrival of the first Native Americans to the Reagan years. Although the overall content coverage is not as extensive as in most typical texts, the coverage of social history is quite good.

Rawls, James J., and Philip Weeks. **Land of Liberty: A United States History.** Austin, TX: Holt, Rinehart and Winston, 1985. *768 pp. Hardbound. $23.52. (A teacher's annotated edition, teacher's resource book, and study disk are available to supplement the text.) ISBN 0-03-064226-4.*

This chronological survey of U.S. history is designed for junior high school courses. Focus is on economic and political history, with comprehensive coverage of events, dates, and facts. Skills, particularly those related to geography, chronology, critical thinking, and reading, are emphasized. Special features focus on American contributions to technology.

Reich, Jerome R., and Edward L. Biller. **United States History.**
Austin, TX: Holt, Rinehart and Winston, 1988.
878 pp. Hardbound. $23.13. (A teacher's edition and teacher's re-
source book are available to supplement the text.) ISBN 0-03-14808-1.

This new text provides a traditional chronological survey of U.S. history. It is exceptionally well illustrated and includes questions with
every illustration to ensure that students attend to and think about
the visual material. Skills, especially map skills, are emphasized. Advance organizers are used for every text section, which should help
students understand the material presented.

Ritchie, Donald A. **Heritage of Freedom: History of the United
States to 1877.**
Riverside, NJ: Scribner-Laidlaw, 1986.
640 pp. Hardbound. $24.57. (A teacher's resource book, workbook,
and testing program are available to supplement the text.) ISBN 0-
02-115500-3.

This high school text presents a chronological treatment of U.S. history that aims to cover both political and social history, as well as
examining democratic values and their role in shaping our heritage.
A lengthy section of primary source readings and a very brief treatment of the past 100 years in U.S. history conclude the text. These
two elements are deleted from the one-volume survey by the same
title, which covers U.S. history from the earliest times to the present.

Roden, Philip and others. **Life and Liberty: An American History.**
Glenview, IL: Scott, Foresman, 1987 (rev. ed.).
752 pp. Hardbound. $23.95. (A teacher's handbook, workbook, and
testing program are available to supplement the text.) ISBN 0-673-
22240-3.

This text provides secondary students who have difficulty using standard texts with a chronological introduction to U.S. history and the
opportunity to strengthen communication, social studies, and critical
thinking skills. Information about the culture and people of an era
supplements the basic account of political and military events. Tables
and graphs are particularly well employed.

Schwartz, Melvin, and John R. O'Connor. **Exploring American
History.**
New York: Globe Books, 1986 (rev. ed.).

570 pp. Hardbound. $19.47. (A teacher's resource manual, workbook, and testing program are available to supplement the text.) ISBN 0-87065-4497-7.

This text is aimed at junior high school students with reading and work-study difficulties. Arranged chronologically, the text contains eight units based on the following themes: discovery and settlement, the growth of freedom, the law of the land, the Civil War, expansion, technology, the United States and the world, and the United States today. Each chapter begins with a question to be considered while reading, a feature that should aid less-able readers.

Smith, Lew. **The American Dream: A United States History.**
Glenview, IL: Scott, Foresman, 1983 (rev. ed.).
729 pp. Hardbound. $24.45. (A teacher's handbook, worksheets, and tests are available to supplement the text.) ISBN 0-673-13347-8.

The American Dream offers a survey of U.S. history that emphasizes the values and ideals to which Americans have paid homage. Political and economic history are not overlooked, but social and cultural history are the principal focus. This emphasis is borne out in such special features as "Who's Who," sections of primary source readings, and a section titled "Americanistic."

Sobel, Robert, and others. **The Challenge of Freedom.**
Mission Hills, CA: Glencoe, 1986.
768 pp. Hardbound. $23.55. (A teacher's edition, teacher's resource binder, study guide, workbook, tests, and enrichment activities are available to supplement the text.) ISBN 0-8445-6560-1.

This junior high school text presents a traditional chronological treatment of U.S. history. Two interesting content features are a case study in each chapter that helps students look at one event in an era in depth and an investigation of the social sciences at the end of each unit. Skills are also emphasized.

Todd, Lewis Paul, and Merle Curti. **Triumph of the American Nation.**
Orlando, FL: Harcourt Brace Jovanovich, 1986 (rev. ed.).
1,060 pp. Hardbound. $24.30. (An annotated teacher's edition, teacher's manual, test booklet, workbook, and posters are available to supplement the text.) ISBN 0-15-375950-X.

This best-selling—and longest—of U.S. history texts provides comprehensive chronological coverage of the entire span of American history. The new edition contains features that help students understand the importance of the individual, the humanities, and geography. History study skills are emphasized in skill-development sections.

Weisberger, Bernard A. **From Sea to Shining Sea: A History of the United States.**
New York: McGraw-Hill, 1982.
800 pp. Hardbound. $21.99. (A teacher's resource guide is available to supplement the text.) ISBN 0-07-069099-5.

This junior high school text is designed to teach average students about social, cultural, political, and economic history. Skills in reading, using maps, researching and writing, and critical thinking are developed.

Wilder, Howard B., Robert P. Ludlum, and Harriet McCune Brown. **This Is America's Story.**
Boston, MA: Houghton Mifflin, 1983 (rev. ed.).
792 pp. Hardbound. $23.76. (A teacher's edition, workbook, and tests are available to supplement the text.) ISBN 0-395-31145-4.

This Is America's Story is designed for use with average junior high students. The authors present a blend of political and social history in their chronological treatment. Although adequate material is presented for a year-long course, this text does allow for incorporation of current events or special topics.

Wood, Leonard C., Ralph H. Gabriel, and Edward L. Biller. **America: Its People and Values.**
Orlando, FL: Harcourt Brace Jovanovich, 1985 (rev. ed.).
864 pp. Hardbound. $23.25. (An annotated teacher's edition, teacher's resource book, workbook, and tests are available to supplement the text.) ISBN 0-15-377785-0.

Like other texts annotated in this section, *America: Its People and Values* provides chronological coverage of events in U.S. history. Special features focus on people and the humanities. Emphasis is also given to development of map and chart skills.

Videocassettes and Films

The following listing does not include movies produced for theatrical release, although many such films could be used in secondary U.S. history classes as motivational tools. Teachers are cautioned, however, to preview all such films before showing them to students, making note of any historical inaccuracies for later discussion with the class.

America Past
Type: 16 color videocassettes: VHS, Beta, or ¾″ U-Matic
Grades: 10–12
Length: 15 min. each
Buy/rent: $125/$25 per program; $1499 for purchase of series
            (includes teacher's guide)
Source: Agency for Instructional Technology
            Box A
            Bloomington, IN 47402
Date: 1987

These programs focus on social history, with topics selected to coordinate with chapters in widely used U.S. history textbooks. These topics are: New Spain, New France, Southern colonies, New England colonies, canals and steamboats, roads and railroads, the American tradition of painting, the American literary tradition, abolitionists, the role of women, utopias, religion, social life in the nineteenth century, westward expansion, the industrial North, and the antebellum South.

America at War: The Revolutionary and Civil Wars
Type: Color videocassette: VHS or ¾″ U-Matic
Grades: 7–12
Length: 40 min.
Buy/rent: VHS: $99/no rental
            ¾″ U-Matic: $134/no rental
            (includes teacher's guide and 12 worksheets)
Source: Society for Visual Education
            1345 Diversey Parkway
            Chicago, IL 60614
Date: 1986

This program examines the causes, courses, leaders, and effects of two of America's early wars. The program is divided into two 20-minute segments that can be used separately.

American Heritage Media Collection
Type: 6 color videocassettes: VHS
Grades: 7–12

Length: 35 min. each
Buy/rent: $180 each/no rental
(includes teacher's guides)
Source: Zenger Video
P.O. Box 802
Culver City, CA 90232
(produced by Westport Media)
Date: 1985–1986

Each program presents the reenactment of a major event in U.S. history; the reenactments were supervised by *American Heritage* to ensure historical accuracy. Topics covered are discovery and exploration, colonial America, the Revolution, the early national period, the West, and the Civil War.

American Revolution: The Cause of Liberty and **American Revolution: The Impossible War**
Type: 2 color videocassettes: VHS, Beta, or ¾″ U-Matic; or 16mm films (also available in Spanish)
Grades: 7–adult
Length: 24 min.
Buy/rent: Videocassettes: $300/$40 each
16mm films: $445/$40 each
Source: Learning Corporation of America
108 Wilmot Road
Deerfield, IL 60015
Date: 1972

The Cause of Liberty is based on actual correspondence between an American law student in London and his father, who was president of the First Continental Congress. The sequel, *The Impossible War,* deals with the son's service in the Continental Army.

American Revolution: Two Views
Type: Color videocassette: VHS, Beta
Grades: 7–12
Length: 65 min.
Buy/rent: $189/no rental
(includes teacher's guide)
Source: Educational Audio Visual
Pleasantville, NY 10570
Date: 1986

This program examines the American Revolution from the American and British perspectives. The program is divided into four segments that can be used separately.

American West: Myth and Reality

Type: Color videocassette: VHS or Beta
Grades: 7–12
Length: 52 min.
Buy/rent: $149/no rental
             (includes teacher's guide)
Source: Educational Audio Visual
             Pleasantville, NY 10570
Date: 1986

This program looks at the myths of the west from James Fenimore Cooper to John Wayne, contrasting these with the reality of westward expansion. The difficulty of distinguishing between fantasy and reality is examined. The three-segment program includes daguerrotypes, tintypes, photographs, paintings, and movie stills.

Americans, 1776

Type: Color videocassette: VHS
Grades: 7–12
Length: 28 min.
Buy/rent: $65/no rental
Source: Zenger Video
             P.O. Box 802
             Culver City, CA 90232
Date: 1974

This program looks at lifestyles and attitudes on the eve of the Revolution. Of particular note is the inclusion of slaves, who were offered freedom if they would fight for the British.

America's Railroads: How the Iron Horse Shaped Our Nation

Type: Color videocassette: VHS, Beta, or ¾″ U-Matic; or
             16mm film
Grades: 4–12
Length: 22 min.
Buy/rent: Videocassette: $310/$40
             16mm film: $440/$40
             (includes teacher's guide)

Source: Churchill Films
              662 North Robertson Boulevard
              Los Angeles, CA 90069
              (produced by Cypress Films)
Date: 1985

This film traces the history of railroads in the United States, looking at their impact on growth, settlement, and the economy.

Antietam Visit
Type: Color videocassette: VHS
Grades: 7–12
Length: 27 min.
Buy/rent: $60/no rental
Source: Zenger Videos
              P.O. Box 802
              Culver City, CA 90232
              (produced by National Park Service)
Date: 1982

This program presents a reenactment of the battle at Antietam and the subsequent meeting between President Lincoln and General Mc-Clellan. Quotations from contemporary diaries and letters are used to lend a personal view to the program.

Appomattox Court House
Type: Sepia-tone 16mm film
Grades: 7–12
Length: 30 min.
Buy/rent: $400/$55
Source: Films Incorporated
              5547 North Ravenswood Avenue
              Chicago, IL 60640
Date: 1974

This program focuses on the meeting between Robert E. Lee and Ulysses S. Grant that ended the Civil War.

The Background of the Civil War
Type: Color videocassette: VHS, Beta, or ¾″ U-Matic; or
              16mm film
Grades: 5–12
Length: 20 min.
Buy/rent: Videocassette: $275/$63
              16mm film: $425/$63

Source: BFA Educational Media
468 Park Avenue South
New York, NY 10016
Date: 1981

This program looks at the differences between the North and South that resulted in the Civil War. The program focuses not only on differing attitudes toward slavery, but also variations in economies, differences in lifestyles, and how the two sides attempted to control the federal government.

The Background of the United States Constitution
Type: Black-and-white videocassette: VHS, Beta, or ¾″ U-Matic; or 16mm film
Grades: 5–12
Length: 20 min.
Buy/rent: Videocassette: $250/$63
16mm film: $420/$63
Source: BFA Educational Media
468 Park Avenue South
New York, NY 10016
Date: 1982

This film examines the problems under the Articles of Confederation that led to the Constitutional Convention, the series of compromises that made the final document possible, and the necessity for the *Federalist Papers* and the agreement to adopt a Bill of Rights. The film uses art and graphics of the period.

Battle of Yorktown
Type: Color videocassette: VHS, Beta, or ¾″ U-Matic; or 16mm film
Grades: 7–adult
Length: 30 min.
Buy/rent: Videocassette: $315/$79
16mm film: $525/$79
Source: BFA Educational Media
468 Park Avenue South
New York, NY 10016
Date: 1983

Produced in association with the Smithsonian, this film presents a reenactment of the final battle of the Revolutionary War. Used with film of the reenactment are paintings and illustrations of the period and readings from writers of the time.

Benjamin Franklin: Citizen-Sage of a New Age

Type: Color videocassette: VHS
Grades: 7–12
Length: 24 min.
Buy/rent: $69.95/no rental
Source: Zenger Video
P.O. Box 802
Culver City, CA 90232
Date: 1986

This profile of Benjamin Franklin examines both the private and public sides of this famous American. The film mixes reproductions of paintings from the Franklin era with shots of historic Philadelphia (Independence Hall, the first hospital in the United States, and the University of Pennsylvania).

Civil War: The Anguish of Emancipation

Type: Color videocassette: VHS, Beta, or ¾" U-Matic; or 16mm film (also available in Spanish)
Grades: 7–adult
Length: 27 min.
Buy/rent: Videocassette: $300/$40
16mm film: $440/$40
Source: Learning Corporation of America
108 Wilmot Road
Deerfield, IL 60015
Date: 1972

This film presents a reenactment of the issuance of the Emancipation Proclamation, focusing on the difficulty Lincoln faced in making the decision. The dialogue is based on diaries, journals, and letters of the period.

Civil War Series

Type: 4 color videocassettes: VHS or ¾" U-Matic; or 16mm films
Grades: 7–12
Length: 20 min. each
Buy/rent: Videocassettes: $250/$75 each
16mm film: $465/$75 each
Source: Coronet Films
108 Wilmot Road
Deerfield, IL 60015
Date: 1983

This series of four films traces the Civil War from background issues (one film), through the war itself (two films), to the postwar period (one film).

The Civil War: Two Views
Type: Color videocassette: VHS or Beta
Grades: 7–12
Length: 75 min.
Buy/rent: $189/no rental
(includes teacher's guide)
Source: Educational Audio Visual
Pleasantville, NY 10570
Date: 1986

This video is divided into four segments, looking at the North before the war, the South before the war, the war itself, and the aftermath. The film uses not only writings, photographs, and paintings from the time, but songs as well. The teacher's guide includes a pre/posttest, a simulation and other activities, and a bibliography.

Colonial Life Series
Type: 4 color videocassettes: VHS or ¾" U-Matic; or 16mm
films
Grades: 5–9
Length: 10–16 min. each
Buy/rent: Videocassette: $185–$250/$75 each
16mm film: $280–$375/$75 each
Source: Coronet Films
108 Wilmot Road
Deerfield, IL 60015
Date: 1975

The first film in the series looks generally at colonial life and crafts; the other three films look specifically at colonial life in the various colonial regions (New England, middle colonies, South).

The Constitution: The Compromise That Made a Nation
Type: Color videocassette: VHS, Beta, or ¾" U-Matic; or
16mm film (also available in Spanish)
Grades: 7–adult
Length: 27 min.
Buy/rent: Videocassette: $300/$40
16mm film: $445/$40

Source: Learning Corporation of America
             108 Wilmot Road
             Deerfield, IL 60015
Date: 1975

This film presents a re-creation of debates among the delegates to the Constitutional Convention. Special emphasis is given to the forming of the Great (or Connecticut) Compromise.

Deborah Sampson: A Woman in the Revolution
Type: Color videocassette: VHS, Beta, or ¾" U-Matic; or
             16mm film
Grades: 5–adult
Length: 15 min.
Buy/rent: Videocassette: $195/$46
             16mm film: $305/$46
Source: BFA Educational Media
             468 Park Avenue South
             New York, NY 10016
             (produced by Greenhouse Films)
Date: 1976

This film tells the story of Deborah Sampson, who enlisted in the Continental Army under the assumed name of Robert Shurtlieff. Sampson fought in such battles as Tarrytown and Yorktown.

The Defense of Fort McHenry
Type: Color videocassette: VHS
Grades: 7–12
Length: 17 min.
Buy/rent: $95/no rental
Source: Zenger Video
             P.O. Box 802
             Culver City, CA 90232
             (produced by the National Park Service)
Date: 1985

This film focuses on the battle that inspired Francis Scott Key to write the national anthem but also provides background on the War of 1812. The U.S. Naval Academy choir sings the anthem to conclude the film.

Down to the *Monitor*
Type: Color videocassette: VHS
Grades: 7–12

Length: 24 min.
Buy/rent: $80/no rental
Source: Zenger Videos
              P.O. Box 802
              Culver City, CA 90232
              (produced by the National Oceanic and Atmospheric
              Administration)
Date: 1980

This film examines the uses of ironclad warships in the Civil War. Footage taken during an archaeological diving expedition to the *USS Monitor* is featured, as is a re-creation of the battle between the *Monitor* and the *Merrimac.*

Dwellings of the West
Type: Color videocassette: VHS
Grades: 4–12
Length: 12 min.
Buy/rent: $49/no rental
Source: Centre Productions
              1800 30th Street, Suite 207
              Boulder, CO 80301
Date: 1981

This brief video focuses on the dwellings people have built throughout history on the Great Plains and in the Rocky Mountains. Dwellings include tents, cliff dwellings, tipis, adobe, log cabins, and others.

Equal Justice Under Law
Type: 4 color videocassettes: VHS
Grades: 7–12
Length: 36 min. each
Buy/rent: $535 for series, $125 each/no rental
              (includes teacher's guide)
Source: Zenger Videos
              P.O. Box 802
              Culver City, CA 90232
              (produced by Metropolitan Pittsburgh Public
              Broadcasting)
Date: 1977

This series, commissioned by the U.S. Supreme Court, focuses on four critical Supreme Court decisions in the early 1800s: *Marbury* v. *Madison, United States* v. *Aaron Burr, McCulloch* v. *Maryland,* and *Gibbons* v. *Ogden.* These decisions by the Marshall Court established some of the fundamental tenets of U.S. constitutional law and, as such, are critical to understanding the development of our country. The teacher's guide contains background information, discussion questions, instructional activities, and a bibliography.

The Fall of Fort Sumter
Type: Color videocassette: VHS, Beta, or ¾" U-Matic
Grades: 7–12
Length: 30 min.
Buy/rent: VHS and Beta: $97/no rental
            ¾" U-Matic: $117/no rental
Source: Guidance Associates
            Communications Park
            P.O. Box 3000
            Mount Kisco, NY 10549
            (produced by Prentice-Hall Media)
Date: 1987

This program focuses on the attack on Fort Sumter, Lincoln's decision to defend the fort, the battle itself, and the results.

The First Americans
Type: Color videocassette: VHS
Grades: 7–12
Length: 54 min.
Buy/rent: $85/no rental
Source: Zenger Video
            P.O. Box 802
            Culver City, CA 90232
Date: 1969

This program looks at the prehistoric peoples who are believed to have migrated across the Bering land bridge from Asia to North America. An unusual feature of the film is interviews with scientists—anthropologists, archaeologists, paleontologists, and geologists—regarding how they go about trying to reconstruct the prehistoric past.

Forged in Wood
Type: Color videocassette: VHS or Beta
Grades: 7–college
Length: 23 min.
Buy/rent: $26.95/no rental

Source: Colonial Williamsburg
             P.O. Box C
             Williamsburg, VA 23187
Date: 1987

This film shows the reconstruction of a colonial blacksmith shop, combining scenes of the building with comments from people who worked on the project.

Fredericksburg and Chancellorsville: The Bloody Road to Richmond

Type: Color videocassette: VHS
Grades: 7–12
Length: 12 min.
Buy/rent: $110/no rental
Source: Zenger Videos
             P.O. Box 802
             Culver City, CA 90232
             (produced by the National Park Service)
Date: 1982

This program looks at the path the Union Army took to get to the Confederate capital in Richmond, Virginia. Artwork, maps, and photographs of the period are used to inform students of the high cost—particularly in human life—of the battles fought en route.

From These Honored Dead

Type: Color videocassette: VHS
Grades: 7–12
Length: 13 min.
Buy/rent: $55/no rental
Source: Zenger Videos
             P.O. Box 802
             Culver City, CA 90232
Date: 1969

This program focuses on Gettysburg—both the battle and Lincoln's famous address. The program focuses more on human emotions about the battle than on military tactics or outcomes.

George Washington and the Whiskey Rebellion: Testing the Constitution

Type: Color videocassette: VHS, Beta, or ¾" U-Matic; or
             16mm film (also available in Spanish)
Grades: 7–adult
Length: 27 min.

Buy/rent: Videocassette: $300/$40
16mm film: $445/$40
Source: Learning Corporation of America
108 Wilmot Road
Deerfield, IL 60015
Date: 1975

This film portrays the new nation as having a "backwoods flavor."
The central event in the film is the first challenge to the new nation
under President Washington; the challenge involved a protest against
a tax on distilled liquor.

Gettysburg: The Video History of the Civil War
Type: Color videocassette: VHS
Grades: 7–12
Length: 27 min.
Buy/rent: $29.95/no rental
Source: Zenger Video
P.O. Box 802
Culver City, CA 90232
Date: 1987

A reenactment of the battle at Gettysburg is presented, along with
scenes of Gettysburg today and paintings and photographs from the
period. The narration focuses on the tactics of the two sides.

The Growth of America's West Series
Type: 4 color videocassettes: VHS, Beta, or ¾″ U-Matic; or
16mm film
Grades: 5–12
Length: 14–22 min. each
Buy/rent: Videocassettes: $180–$275/$43–$62 each
16mm films: $295–$450/$43–$62 each
Source: BFA Educational Media
468 Park Avenue South
New York, NY 10016
(produced by Capricorn Films and Allied Film Artists)
Date: 1978–1979

This four-part series looks at the American cowboy, contrasting the
reality of that life in the nineteenth century with our romanticized
version today; the mountain men and their role in westward expansion; the settlers who ventured west after the Louisiana Purchase;
and the Spanish in the Southwest, from the earliest times to the
present.

Homeland

Type:	Color videocassette: VHS or ¾″ U-Matic; or 16mm film
Grades:	10–adult
Length:	25 min.
Buy/rent:	VHS videocassette: $279/$50
	¾″ U-Matic videocassette: $299/$50
	16mm film: $470/$50
Source:	Centre Productions
	1800 30th Street, Suite 207
	Boulder, CO 80301
Date:	1986

This film provides a history of American farming on the Great Plains, looking at the technology of farming, its successes and problems, and the people who farm.

Hopi: Songs of the Fourth World

Type:	Color videocassette: VHS, Beta, or ¾″ U-Matic; or 16mm film
Grades:	9–12
Length:	58 min.
Buy/rent:	Videocassette: $600/no rental
	16mm film: $850/$100
Source:	New Day Film Co-op
	22 Riverview Drive
	Wayne, NJ 07470
Date:	1984

This award-winning film focuses on how the Hopi have preserved the ways of life that have been handed down from generation to generation. Of special interest is the integration of art and daily life, both now and in the past.

Independence

Type:	Color videocassette: VHS
Grades:	7–12
Length:	30 min.
Buy/rent:	$19.95/no rental
Source:	Zenger Video
	P.O. Box 802
	Culver City, CA 90232
	(produced by the National Park Service)
Date:	1975

Directed by John Huston, this film presents reenactments of such events as naming Washington as commander of the Continental Army and approving the Declaration of Independence. Actors representing such historical figures as Benjamin Franklin and Abigail Adams present their opinions on topics of the day.

Indian Crafts: Hopi, Navajo and Iroquois
Type: Color videocassette: VHS, Beta, or ¾″ U-Matic; or
            16mm film
Grades: 5–9
Length: 11 min.
Buy/rent: Videocassette: $150/$35
            16mm film: $255/$35
Source: BFA Educational Media
            468 Park Avenue South
            New York, NY 10016
Date: 1980

Covering basket making, pottery making, kachina carving, weaving, jewelry making, and mask carving, this movie illustrates the historical crafts of the Hopi, Navajo, and Iroquois.

Is There an American Stonehenge?
Type: Color videocassette: VHS
Grades: 7–adult
Length: 29 min.
Buy/rent: $75/no rental
Source: Zenger Video
            P.O. Box 802
            Culver City, CA 90232
            (produced by Harold Mayer Productions)
Date: 1978

Scientist John Eddy explains his theories regarding the ancient rock formation found in the Bighorn Mountains of Wyoming. Eddy believes that the Plains Indians constructed the wheel-shaped formation as a primitive means of pinpointing dates for important ceremonies.

The Jackson Years
Type: 2 color videocassettes: VHS, Beta, or ¾″ U-Matic; or
            16mm films (also available in Spanish)
Grades: 7–adult
Length: 27 min. each
Buy/rent: Videocassettes: $300/$40 each
            16mm films: $445/$40 each

Source:　Learning Corporation of America
　　　　　108 Wilmot Road
　　　　　Deerfield, IL 60015
Date:　1971

The first of these two films, subtitled *The New Americans,* looks at the life of Andrew Jackson and how it exemplified the new "frontier man." The second film, *Toward Civil War,* looks at major events in Jackson's administration.

Jacksonian Democracy
Type:　Color videocassette: VHS or Beta
Grades:　7–12
Length:　39 min.
Buy/rent:　$104/no rental
　　　　　(includes teacher's guide)
Source:　Educational Audio Visual
　　　　　Pleasantville, NY 10570
Date:　1976

This exploration of the political and social changes that occurred during the age of Jackson uses documentary visuals and narration to draw a "vivid portrait of the first 'common man' president." The accompanying teacher's guide provides questions for discussion.

Jamestown
Type:　Color videocassette: VHS
Grades:　7–12
Length:　14 min.
Buy/rent:　$70/no rental
Source:　Zenger Video
　　　　　P.O. Box 802
　　　　　Culver City, CA 90232
　　　　　(produced by the National Park Service)
Date:　Not available

This film tells the story of the first permanent English settlement in North America. The government and attempts to establish trade are both covered.

Lincoln's Gettysburg Address
Type:　Color videocassette: VHS
Grades:　5–12
Length:　15 min.
Buy/rent:　$69.95/no rental

Source: Zenger Video
         P.O. Box 802
         Culver City, CA 90232
         (produced by Oxford Films)
Date: Not available

This film presents background leading up to the Battle of Gettysburg and Lincoln's renowned address. Unusual features are the use of battle scenes from the movie *Red Badge of Courage* and delivery of the address by actor Charlton Heston.

"A Little Rebellion Now and Then": Prologue to the Constitution
Type: Color videocassette: VHS or ¾″ U-Matic; or 16mm film
Grades: 7–adult
Length: 30 min.
Buy/rent: Videocassette: $365/$50
         16mm film: $540/$50
Source: Churchill Films
         662 North Robertson Boulevard
         Los Angeles, CA 90069
Date: 1986

This dramatization of the events leading up to Shays' Rebellion and the calling of the Constitutional Convention presents the viewpoints of such individuals as James Madison, Noah Webster, and Daniel Shays.

Manassas
Type: Black-and-white videocassette: VHS
Grades: 7–adult
Length: 14 min.
Buy/rent: $95/no rental
Source: Zenger Video
         P.O. Box 802
         Culver City, CA 90232
         (produced by the National Park Service)
Date: 1983

This video presents an eyewitness account, from the diary of a Confederate soldier, of the two Civil War battles at Manassas. The visuals are drawn from portraits, photographs, and maps of the day.

Mastervision History of America Series
Type: 10 color videocassettes: VHS
Grades: 7–12

Length: 60 min. each
Buy/rent: $64.95 each/no rental; $649.95 for series
Source: Perfection Form Company
             1000 North Second Avenue
             Logan, IA 51546
             (produced by McGraw-Hill)
Date: 1982

This comprehensive series covers U.S. history through World War II. Topics related to the early years are colonial life, the Revolution, drafting of the Constitution, and the Civil War.

Meet George Washington

Type: Color videocassette: VHS
Grades: 7–12
Length: 54 min.
Buy/rent: $85/no rental
Source: Zenger Video
             P.O. Box 802
             Culver City, CA 90232
             (produced by NBC)
Date: 1969

This biographical film looks at Washington's early life and retirement as well as his better-known years as commander of the Continental Army and the nation's first president.

The Missions: Mission Life and Missions of the Southwest

Type: Color videocassette: VHS
Grades: 7–12
Length: 35 min.
Buy/rent: $14.99/no rental
Source: Zenger Video
             P.O. Box 802
             Culver City, CA 90232
             (produced by Arthur Barr Productions)
Date: Not available

Focusing on Spanish missions in the Southwest, this program presents reenactments of such activities as molding mud bricks for adobe buildings, constructing a mission, making candles, grinding corn, and tanning hides. How the missions spread Spanish culture is also discussed.

Opposites in Harmony

Type:	Color videocassette: VHS
Grades:	7–12
Length:	17 min.
Buy/rent:	$95/no rental
Source:	Zenger Video
	P.O. Box 802
	Culver City, CA 90232
	(produced by the National Park Service)
Date:	1975

This film presents an early meeting between President George Washington and his cabinet, which debates such issues as the separation of powers and establishing foreign relations. The issues are not resolved, so students have the opportunity to recommend actions they believe are justified.

Profiles in Courage

Type:	26 color videocassettes: VHS, Beta, or ¾″ U-Matic
Grades:	7–adult
Length:	50 min. each
Buy/rent:	VHS and Beta: $49.95 each, $1,250 for series/no rental
	¾″ U-Matic: $59.95 each, $1495 for series/no rental
Source:	Zenger Videos
	P.O. Box 802
	Culver City, CA 90232
Date:	1964

This series, inspired by John F. Kennedy's book, covers the lives of the following early Americans: Anne Hutchinson, John Adams, Alexander Doniphan, John Quincy Adams, Thomas Corwin, John Marshall, George Mason, Frederick Douglass, Thomas Hart Benton, Daniel Webster, Prudence Crandall, and Sam Houston.

The Puritan Experience

Type:	2 color videocassettes: VHS, Beta, or ¾″ U-Matic; or
	16mm film (also available in Spanish)
Grades:	7–adult
Length:	28–31 minutes each
Buy/rent:	Videocassettes: $300/$40 each
	16mm film: $445/$40 each
Source:	Learning Corporation of America
	108 Wilmot Road
	Deerfield, IL 60015
Date:	1975

These two films look at the reasons why the Puritans left England and how they established a new community in North America. The information is provided through the story of one Puritan family.

Queen Victoria and the Indians

Type:	Color videocassette: VHS, Beta, or ¾″ U-Matic; or 16mm film
Grades:	3–9
Length:	11 min.
Buy/rent:	VHS or Beta: $139/$30
	¾″ U-Matic: $199/$30
	16mm film: $240/$30
Source:	Centre Productions
	1800 30th Street, Suite 207
	Boulder, CO 80301
Date:	1985

The subject of this film is a little-known event in history. In the late 1840s, a group of Ojibwe Indians traveled to London to dance at the opening of the Indian Gallery. While there, they met with Queen Victoria. The film's recounting of this event will direct student attention to issues of history, cultural values, and art.

The 1780's

Type:	Color videocassette: VHS, Beta, or ¾″ U-Matic; or 16mm film
Grades:	5–12
Length:	27 min.
Buy/rent:	Videocassette: $250/$75
	16mm film: $540/$75
Source:	Coronet Film and Video
	108 Wilmot Road
	Deerfield, IL 60015
Date:	1986

This film examines the major changes the United States underwent during the decade named in the title. Specific topics covered are the end of the American Revolution, the differing economic development in North and South, and the framing of the Constitution.

A Slave's Story: Running a Thousand Miles to Freedom

Type:	Color videocassette: VHS, Beta, or ¾″ U-Matic; or 16mm film (also available in Spanish and captioned)
Grades:	7–adult
Length:	29 min.

Buy/rent: Videocassette: $300/$40
          16mm film: $445/$40
Source: Learning Corporation of America
          108 Wilmot Road
          Deerfield, IL 60015
Date: 1972

This film, based on a slave narrative, dramatizes a couple's escape from the South to Philadephia in 1848. Discrimination in the North is also depicted.

Spirit of the Hunt

Type: Color videocassette: VHS, Beta, or ¾″ U-Matic; or
          16mm film
Grades: 10–adult
Length: 29 min.
Buy/rent: VHS or Beta: $279/$50
          ¾″ U-Matic: $299/$50
          16mm film: $525/$50
Source: Centre Productions
          1800 30th Street, Suite 207
          Boulder, CO 80301
Date: 1982

The focus of this film is the importance of the buffalo to the culture of the Plains Indians. The film provides a historical perspective, as well as a contemporary view, of the Chippewa, Cree, and Dogrib peoples.

Surrender at Fort Donelson

Type: Color videocassette: VHS, Beta, or ¾″ U-Matic; or
          16mm film
Grades: 7–12
Length: 6 min.
Buy/rent: VHS or Beta: $80/no rental
          ¾″ U-Matic: no purchase/$25
          16mm film: $55/$45
Source: National Audio Visual Center
          National Archives Trust Fund Board
          8700 Edgeworth Drive
          Capital Heights, MD 20743
Date: 1980

This brief film presents the dilemma that faced the Confederate military leaders on the eve of the fall of Fort Donelson, Tennessee.

To Do Battle in the Land

Type: Color videocassette: VHS
Grades: 7–12
Length: 27 min.
Buy/rent: $110/no rental
Source: Zenger Video
P.O. Box 802
Culver City, CA 90232
(produced by the National Park Service)
Date: Not available

John Brown is the focus of this film, which uses paintings and drawings from the period and dramatic reenactments to examine the raid on Harper's Ferry. Connections are made with contemporary issues related to terrorism.

To Keep Our Liberty

Type: Color videocassette: VHS
Grades: 7–12
Length: 23 min.
Buy/rent: $65/no rental
Source: Zenger Video
P.O. Box 802
Culver City, CA 90232
(produced by the National Park Service)
Date: 1974

This award-winning film presents a reenactment of several events that occurred between 1763 and 1775 and led to the conflict at Concord and Lexington.

Too Much, Too Little

Type: Color videocassette: VHS, Beta, or ¾" U-Matic
Grades: 10–college
Length: 25 min.
Buy/rent: $105/$35
(includes teacher's guide)
Source: Agency for Instructional Technology
P.O. Box A
Bloomington, IN 47402
(produced by the Federal Reserve Bank of New York)
Date: 1985

This program traces development of the nation's monetary system from the colonial era to the present. Highlights from the early years of U.S. history include the issuing of paper money by the Continental Congress, the constitutional provision for minting of coins, the chartering of banks authorized to issue paper money backed by gold and silver, and the economic demands of the Civil War.

Transportation in America . . . A History
Type: Color videocassette: VHS or ¾″ U-Matic; or 16mm film
Grades: 5–9
Length: 17 min.
Buy/rent: Videocassette: $230/$40
             16mm film: $325/$40
Source: Churchill Films
             662 North Robertson Boulevard
             Los Angeles, CA 90069
Date: 1983

This film provides a history of U.S. transportation focusing on economic and social pressures and the changes brought about by steam and internal combustion engines. Animation enlivens the film.

United States Constitution
Type: 6 color videocassettes: VHS, Beta, and ¾″ U-Matic; or
             16mm film
Grades: 7–12
Length: 30 min. each
Buy/rent: Videocassettes: $180/$35 each
             16mm films: $400/$35 each
             (includes teacher's guide)
Source: Agency for Instructional Technology
             P.O. Box A
             Bloomington, IN 47402
             (produced by Project '87)
Date: 1987

This series presents episodes in which teenagers are affected by constitutional law. These episodes are then explained in terms of how various principles of law have evolved since the Constitution was written. The principles covered are the rule of law, checks and balances, federalism, freedom of speech, equal protection of the laws, and property rights.

The United States Constitution: Document for Democracy
Type: Color videocassette: VHS
Grades: 5–9
Length: 25 min.

Buy/rent: $59/no rental
                (includes teacher's guide)
Source: Society for Visual Education
                1345 Diversey Parkway
                Chicago, IL 60614
Date: 1986

This program examines the Constitutional Convention, looking at the debates and compromises that occurred in Philadelphia. Also covered is the role of the Constitution in our lives today.

Unknown Soldiers

Type: Color videocassette: VHS, Beta, or ¾″ U-Matic
Grades: 10–adult
Length: 58 min.
Buy/rent: $495/$90
Source: Films Incorporated
                5547 North Ravenswood Avenue
                Chicago, IL 60640
                (produced by WNET)
Date: 1984

This program covers the role of black soldiers in the military, beginning with the Civil War and continuing to the Indian wars and the Spanish-American War. Accomplishments of black soldiers, discrimination faced by blacks, and changes over time are examined.

Walt Whitman's Civil War

Type: Color videocassette: VHS, Beta, or ¾″ U-Matic; or
                16mm film
Grades: 7–college
Length: 15 min.
Buy/rent: Videocassette: $79/no rental
                16mm film: $235/no rental
Source: Churchill Films
                662 North Robertson Boulevard
                Los Angeles, CA 90069
Date: 1972

This unusual film uses the poems and prose of Whitman to provide a unique perspective on the Civil War. Visuals include photographs of the period and reenactments.

Why the New World Was Explored
Type: Color videocassette: VHS, Beta, ¾″ U-Matic; or 16mm
            film
Grades: 5–12
Length: 11 min.
Buy/rent: Videocassette: $135/$31
            16mm film: $225/$31
Source: BFA Educational Media
            468 Park Avenue South
            New York, NY 10016
            (produced by Film Associates)
Date: 1968

This film examines the changing reasons for exploring the Americas, beginning with the search for a shorter route to Asia and ending with the search for such resources as land.

Wilson's Creek
Type: Color videocassette: VHS or Beta; or 16mm film
Grades: 7–college
Length: 15 min.
Buy/rent: Videocassette: $95/no rental
            16mm film: $150/$45
Source: National Audio Visual Center
            National Archives Trust Fund Board
            8700 Edgeworth Drive
            Capital Heights, MD 20743
Date: 1985

This film focuses on the Civil War in Missouri. Its narrator is George Caleb Bingham, an artist and legislator who opposed secession.

The Witches of Salem: The Horror and the Hope
Type: Color videocassette: VHS, Beta, or ¾″ U-Matic; or
            16mm film (also available in Spanish and captioned)
Grades: 7–adult
Length: 34 min.
Buy/rent: Videocassette: $300/$40
            16mm film: $445/$40
Source: Learning Corporation of America
            108 Wilmot Road
            Deerfield, IL 60015
Date: 1972

This dramatization of the Salem witchcraft trials is based on actual historical records.

You Are There Series

Type: 15 color videocassettes: VHS, Beta, or ¾″ U-Matic; or 16mm films

Grades: 5–9

Length: 22 min. each

Buy/rent: Videocassettes: $285/$72 each
16mm films: $480/$72 each

Source: BFA Educational Media
468 Park Avenue South
New York, NY 10016
(produced by CBS)

Date: 1972

Narrated by Walter Cronkite, this series presents "eyewitness enactments." Events in early U.S. history covered in the series include Columbus's efforts to get Spain to support his voyage, Paul Revere's ride, the trial of Benedict Arnold, the Lewis and Clark expedition, the siege at the Alamo, the underground railroad, and the nomination of Abraham Lincoln.

Glossary

abolitionist   One who wanted to end (abolish) slavery in the United States.

adobe   Claylike material often used in building construction in the American southwest.

Alien and Sedition Acts   The four laws passed in 1798 to reduce criticism of government and the influence of foreign persons in American politics.

almanac   A book or booklet that contains yearly calendars and information of general interest.

amendment   A change in or addition to a legal document, a law, or a constitution.

American system of manufacturing   The method of producing manufactured goods through mass production and interchangeable parts.

annex   To attach new territory to an already existing area, usually a political entity like a nation or city.

antebellum   The period before a war; used in U. S. history to describe the period before the Civil War.

antifederalist   One who opposed the adoption of the U.S. Constitution in 1787–88.

apportion   To distribute among; usually refers to distributing taxes or representatives among election districts.

archives   Places where documents and other historical sources are deposited and preserved.

arsenal   A government building (or buildings) where arms and other war supplies are manufactured or stored.

Articles of Confederation   The agreement under which the original thirteen states established a government among themselves in 1781.

astrolabe   Navigation instrument used to measure the position of the stars and thereby help sailors find their location at sea.

balance of power   A condition of relatively equal power (military and economic) between two countries or two alliances in which neither side is dominant.

balance of trade   The relationship of the amount of a country's imported goods compared to its exported goods. If imports are greater than exports, a negative balance occurs and vice versa.

barter   System of trade in which goods are exchanged for other goods rather than through the medium of money.

Bill of Rights   The first ten amendments to the United States Constitution; promise of their inclusion was important to the ratification of the Constitution.

Bleeding Kansas   Name given to the conflict between proslavery and antislavery settlers in Kansas in the 1850s.

blockade   A formal declaration in international law in which one country denies another country access to trade from third parties (or countries).

bonds   Notes or promises to repay debts issued by governments.

bounty   A fee paid by government for a good or service they want someone to provide; for example, a fee paid to encourage the production of certain goods.

boycott   An organized refusal to buy or use a product as a means of forcing some person or party to take some action.

cabinet   A group of advisors who often head executive departments and who advise the president.

canal   An artificial body of water usually designed to link other (natural) bodies of water for improved transportation.

capital   Wealth that is used to produce more wealth; capital goods usually refers to machinery.

cash crops   Crops raised to give growers money with which they can buy other goods they cannot themselves produce. In U.S. history, cotton and tobacco are the best-known examples, but other crops were also produced in surplus to produce cash for farmers.

caucus   Meeting of party members (or like-minded people) to plan political strategy.

cede   The act of giving another party (usually country) some portion of its territory.

census   An official enumeration of a population.

charter   An official document given by a government, which grants special rights or privileges to a person or company.

chattel   Property other than real estate and the buildings put on real estate; often used in reference to slaves.

checks and balances   System of government in which the various branches are given some power to check or oversee the workings of the other branches.

civil war   War between two factions within one country.

clipper ship   Vessel of the early nineteenth century built primarily for speed.

collective biography   Biography produced by extracting the common elements from the biographies of persons from the same period in order to make generalizations about the group.

colony   A land area settled by emigrants from a country who continue their allegiance to that country; the people of a territory that is ruled by another country.

commercial revolution   The economic expansion of Europe that occurred from about 1450 to 1700 and promoted European exploration and expansion overseas.

compromise   A general agreement among all sides in a dispute or controversy, usually reached by each side giving up something it wants.

Confederate States of America.   A federation of 11 states of the South, formed after they seceded from the federal union in 1860–1861.

conquistador   Spanish explorers and conquerors of various places in the Americas.

consensus school of U.S. historians   Historians who wrote in the period after World War II, and tended to emphasize continuity and agreement on basic American values in U.S. history.

constitution A plan of government; the fundamental and supreme law of a country.

contrabands Slaves who crossed Union lines during the Civil War.

copperheads U.S. citizens who lived in the northern states during the Civil War, but who opposed the war.

cotton gin A simple machine that separated cotton fibers from the seeds; greatly stimulated cotton production in the American South because virtually anyone could make one.

Coureur de bois Early French explorers and traders in North America; French phrase literally means "runners of the woods."

Creole A person of European descent (usually French or Spanish) born in the West Indies or Spanish America; sometimes refers to settlers on the Gulf coast.

critical period The period between the end of the American Revolutionary War and the ratification of the U.S. Constitution.

crown colonies Those colonies like New York which were owned by the king rather than by individuals or companies.

customs duties Taxes placed on imported goods.

de facto In fact or in actuality; compare to the term *de jure,* which means as a matter of law.

democracy A form of government in which power is vested in the people (the electorate) and is usually exercised by them through a system of representation based on free elections.

demography The study of population, including, among many other things, birth and death rates, sickness, age, and distribution.

depression A long, usually severe, decline in economic activity; the "bust" part of the "boom and bust" business cycle characteristic of the United States in the nineteenth century.

discrimination The act of prejudging people based on such arbitrary characteristics as race, religion, or ethnic group.

due process Judicial procedures, in contrast to substantive issues of law, in civil and criminal cases.

early national period The time between approximately 1787 and 1840, the first years of the American republic.

economic history A specialized subfield of history that deals with economic activity, growth, and technological change over time.

elastic clause The portion of the Constitution that says Congress can make all laws "necessary and proper" to put its stated powers into effect.

emancipation The act of setting a person, usually a slave, free.

embargo A law or government order that prohibits trade with another nation.

enumerated powers Those powers specifically delegated to government in the Constitution.

excise tax A tax on goods usually paid by the manufacturer but passed on to the consumer.

Federalist Papers A series of essays written by John Jay, Alexander Hamilton, and James Madison to promote the ratification of the Constitution; the essays are seen as the best contribution to political philosophy ever made by Americans.

Federalists A group of people who believed that a stronger central government was necessary in the 1780s; they wrote and secured passage of the Constitution.

federal system of government A system of government in which some powers are given to a central government and some to more local governments; some powers are shared between the two.

franchise The right to vote in elections.

freedmen Former slaves, all of whom were emancipated during and after the Civil War.

free enterprise An economic system in which there is little, if any, public regulation or control of business practices.

Free Soil party A political party formed in the 1840s opposed to the idea of popular sovereignty in the territories.

French and Indian War Known in Europe as the Seven Years' War, this war was fought between the French and British (and their allies and colonies) from 1754 to 1761, essentially for domination of the world.

frontier The sparsely settled area on the edge of more densely settled regions; defined by the Bureau of the Census as an area that contains two or fewer persons per square mile.

Fugitive Slave Act   Part of the Compromise of 1850, the Fugitive Slave Act revised a 1793 law through more stringent enforcement provisions for the return of runaway slaves; many northern states enacted "personal liberty laws" to try to resist this federal law.

Gettysburg Address   President Lincoln delivered this classic expression of American political ideals at the burial site of those soldiers killed at the Battle of Gettysburg in 1863.

Great Awakening   A time of widespread religious fervor during the 1740s in colonial America; a second "great awakening" occurred in the early nineteenth century.

gross national product   GNP is a measure of the total value of goods and services produced by a nation's economy in a given year.

hard money   Gold or silver coins, also termed specie, used in commerce; "greenbacks" refers to paper money printed by the U.S. government during and after the Civil War.

Hessians   German soldiers from the state of Hesse who fought for the British during the Revolutionary War.

historiography   The history of historical writing; philosophy of history is a synonym.

hogan   A type of dwelling inhabited by Native Americans in the Southwest.

House of Burgesses   Lower houses of the Virginia and Maryland legislatures; established in 1619, Virginia's was the first representative assembly among Europeans in the New World.

House of Representatives   The lower house of the federal legislature established by the Constitution.

immigrant   A person who enters one country from another, usually with the intention of staying.

impeachment   A formal charge of wrongdoing brought against a high government official.

impressment   The British used this practice in the early 1800s to force sailors (not always English citizens) to serve in the British navy.

indentured servant   A person who worked for a specified period of time for another person, often in return for passage to the colonies.

industrial revolution   The change in the United States in the nineteenth century from home and artisan production to machine-based factory production of goods.

inflation   Rapidly increasing prices.

intellectual history   A subfield of history devoted to the study of ideas and the people who produce those ideas.

interchangeable parts   The process by which parts of a certain product are manufactured to the exact same size, shape, and weight; each part so produced may be substituted for any other.

internal improvements   The roads, canals, and harbors that were completed to facilitate commerce in the period after 1820.

Intolerable Acts   The name the British colonists gave to the series of acts passed by Parliament in 1774 to punish the colonists for the Boston Tea Party.

joint-stock company   A venture aimed at outfitting colonial enterprises in the seventeenth century; a company whose investors own shares of its stock.

judicial review   The right of the courts to review laws and test their legality under the Constitution.

Kentucky and Virginia Resolutions   Written by Jefferson and Madison in 1798, these resolutions questioned the power of the federal government over states' rights.

Know-Nothing party   The name often applied to the Native American party during the 1850s; sworn to secrecy, the members of this party, when asked about their activities, are said to have replied, "I know nothing."

laissez faire   The doctrine that government should not meddle in the affairs of business; "that government is best which governs least."

loose constructionist   A person who believes that the powers of the federal government may be expanded beyond the powers explicitly stated in the Constitution.

Lowell system   A method first used in 1813 in Massachusetts to produce cheap textiles by recruiting a local labor force, often of young, unmarried females, who operated the power looms.

Loyalist   Also called a **Tory**; a person who remained loyal to the British government during the American Revolution.

manifest destiny   The idea, prevalent in the 1840s and 1850s, that it was the destiny of the United States to occupy the entire North American continent, without regard for the rights of other inhabitants of the area.

manumit   The act of an individual owner freeing his (or her) slaves.

Mason-Dixon line   The boundary between Pennsylvania and Maryland; also the traditional dividing line between North and South.

Mayflower Compact   A document written by the Pilgrims in 1620 that provided the legal basis of self-government.

mercantilism   The ideas that gold and silver make a nation (and by extension, an empire) powerful, that a nation should export more than it imports from other nations, and that colonies are essentially for the benefit of the mother country.

mestizo   A person of mixed Spanish and Indian blood; Spanish word for "mixed."

middle passage   The voyage of black slaves from Africa to the Western Hemisphere, so-called because it was the middle leg of a triangular voyage.

militia   The citizens who were capable of bearing arms in the defense of their communities; they would gather several times a year to drill and target practice.

minutemen   Civilians who were trained to fight in the Revolutionary War on short notice.

Missouri Compromise   The result, in 1820, of the concern with the relative balance of political power in the federal government between slave and free states (Maine was admitted to the Union as a free state, Missouri as a slave state).

monograph   A term used for historical writing, especially as it relates to books and articles about richly researched, but somewhat limited, questions.

nationalism Patriotic feelings for one's own country.

nativist A person who feels so fervently for their own country that he/she belives that everyone else is unworthy of being a part of it.

natural aristocracy The notion that there was a group of persons who were the most able, best educated, and most industrious, and who should run the society/government.

naturalization Granting full citizenship to a person born in a foreign country.

naval stores Such products as pine tar, pitch, turpentine, wood for masts, and other commodities essential for a navy of wooden vessels.

neutrality A policy of not taking sides in a dispute between two other nations.

nullification The doctrine that a state could declare null and void an act of the federal government.

parliament The legislative body of the British Empire.

Patriots Those persons who favored American independence during the Revolutionary War.

patronage The distribution of government jobs to political supporters; also known as the "spoils system."

peculiar institution Term for slavery in the antebellum South.

Pilgrims A community of English people who broke with the Church of England over religious practices and who traveled to North America to practice their religion as they desired.

plantation Early usage referred to the initial colonies planted by English colonists; later the term referred to the large farms of the American South.

popular sovereignty The idea that the persons who live in an area or region should decide for themselves the questions that concern them; in the mid-nineteenth century the term referred more specifically to the question of whether or not slavery would be allowed in a territory.

progressive historians People who saw the past as the conflict between the good guys and the bad guys; writing during a period of reform, they were optimistic that the good guys would win in the end.

protective tariffs   High taxes (or customs duties) on imported goods levied with the express intent to protect some product from foreign competition; compare with **revenue tariffs.**

Puritans   People who wanted to purify the practices of the Church of England; they traveled to North America to practice their religion as they saw fit.

Quakers   A radical religious group whose major beliefs include religious toleration and pacificism (opposition to war).

ranchos   Very large estates owned by Mexican citizens, usually given over to cattle grazing.

ratify   To give formal approval to something.

ratifying conventions   The formal meetings in 1787 and 1788 held to ratify (or not) the newly written U.S. Consitution.

representative government   A form of government in which the people are represented by persons elected in free elections.

republic   A form of government in which power is exercised by representatives elected by the people they represent.

Republican party   Originally Thomas Jefferson's and James Madison's party in the early days of the Republic; a second Republican party was formed in the 1850s to oppose the spread of slavery in the territories.

reservations   Geographical areas set aside by the U.S. government for Native American tribes.

revenue tariffs   Taxes or customs duties on imported goods levied to produce revenue.

revolution   The sudden, often violent overthrow of an existing government.

salutary neglect   The way England governed its North American colonies during the late 1600s and early 1700s; refers specifically to the nonenforcement of the Acts of Trade and Navigation.

secede   To formally withdraw from a group; in 1860 and 1861, eleven southern states attempted to secede from the Federal Union and to establish their own confederated government.

secondary source A source written by a historian who usually used primary sources—those contemporary to the events described.

sectionalism Loyalty (similar to patriotism) to a region of the country such as the South, the North, or the West.

sedition The act of inciting rebellion against the existing government.

segregation The separation of people according to some arbitrary criterion—usually race—in housing, schools, and public accommodations.

Senate The upper body of the U.S. Congress, to which each state elects two members for terms of six years each.

Seneca Falls Convention The meeting in 1848 of a group of women's rights advocates in New York; using the Declaration of Independence as a model, they declared they should be given the same rights and privileges as men.

separation of powers The constitutional principle that gives the powers of making (legislative), enforcing (executive), and interpreting (judicial) the laws to different branches of government.

slave codes A series of laws enacted in Southern states to regulate the lives and treatment of slaves (for example, prohibiting teaching slaves to read and write).

social history A subfield of history concerned with the history of the family, women and children, and racial and ethnic groups, among other topics.

sovereignty The locus of ultimate authority in a governmental system; the U.S. Constitution located that authority with "the people," rather than with the states.

staple crop The primary agricultural crop grown in a specific region.

states' rights The constitutional principle that has sought to limit the power of the federal government because only certain limited powers were given to the federal government.

status quo The ways things are at any particular time.

stock Shares of ownership in a joint-stock company or other corporation.

strict construction A constitutional interpretation that holds that only those powers explicitly given the government are legitimate powers.

subsistence farming Farming in which the product is almost entirely for the farmer's own consumption.

suffrage The right to vote.

tariff A duty or tax placed on imported goods, the intent of which is either to produce revenue or to protect domestic businesses.

temperance movement The movement to prohibit the consumption of alcoholic beverages.

Three-fifths compromise An agreement made among the writers of the U.S. Constitution to include three-fifths of slaves in apportioning taxes and Congressional representatives.

trail of tears The forced movement of Native American tribes from the Southeastern United States to the Indian territory (now Oklahoma) in the 1830s.

triangular trade A trading pattern among the Northern colonies, the West Indies, and England.

underground railroad The organized process by which slaves escaped from bondage in the South to Northern states and Canada.

vaqueros Spanish cattle herders who invented virtually all the tools of the cowhand's trade.

veto The power given the President to reject bills enacted by Congress.

virtual representation The idea that representatives represent everyone in a region, whether or not the people of that region actually vote for the representative.

Whigs Political party formed in the late 1820s to oppose Andrew Jackson's Democratic party.

Index

319